IMAGES of America

LAWRENCE COUNTY INDIANA

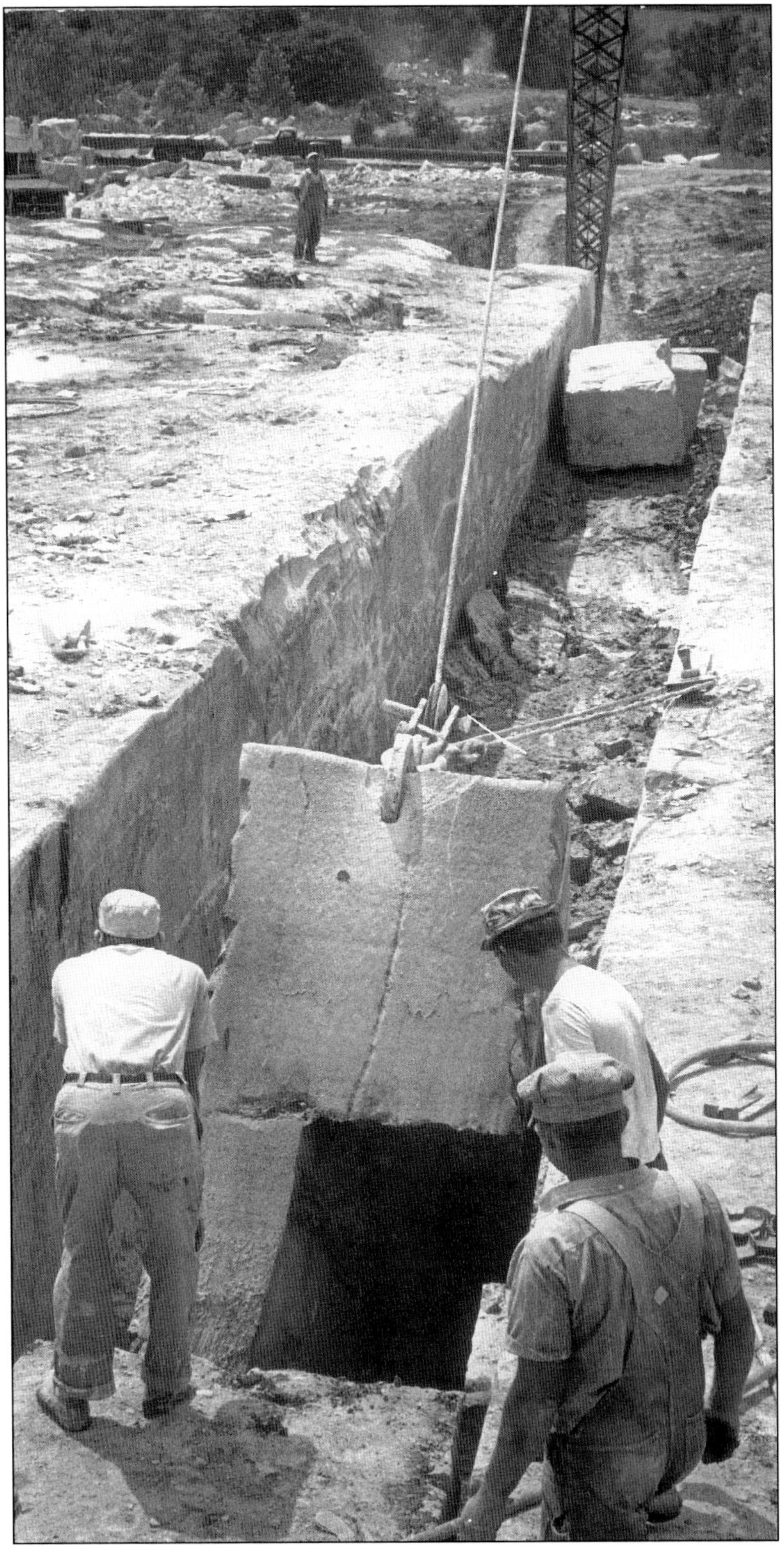

Pictured here is a group of quarry workers lifting a cut of stone by way of derrick, c. 1920. The limestone industry was at its peak in the early quarter of the 20th century and was Bedford's biggest employer.

IMAGES
of America

LAWRENCE COUNTY INDIANA

Maxine Kruse

ARCADIA
PUBLISHING

Copyright © 2001 by Maxine Kruse
ISBN 978-0-7385-0806-1

Published by Arcadia Publishing
Charleston, South Carolina

Printed in the United States of America

Library of Congress Catalog Card Number: 2001086667

For all general information contact Arcadia Publishing at:
Telephone 843-853-2070
Fax 843-853-0044
E-Mail sales@arcadiapublishing.com
For customer service and orders:
Toll-Free 1-888-313-2665

Visit us on the Internet at www.arcadiapublishing.com

CONTENTS

Acknowledgments

Thanks must be given to the early writers of the history of Lawrence County. Special thanks must be given to the following: Helen Burchard, curator at the Lawrence County Museum; John Bridges, photo collection; Lawrence County Historical and Genealogical Society, photo collection; Mary Margaret Stipp, photos, research, and editing.

INTRODUCTION

Lawrence County was purchased from the Native American tribes in a series of three treaties, the last called the Harrison Purchase in 1809. The Piankeshaws, Delawares, Shawnees, and Pottawattomies, all who held claim to the land, signed the treaty. By a legislative act on January 7, 1818, the county was formed. The first county seat was Palestine, located on the east fork of White River. On March 30, 1825, the county seat was moved to Bedford because the water supply was bad, and several deaths occurred from malaria.

The first permanent settlement was probably Leesville in Flinn Township. The Guthries and Flinns came from Lee County, Virginia, to develop a settlement. Another early settlement was Fort Ritner, a booming town when the B&O Railroad was being built during the mid 1800s.

Other settlements in the county were Mitchell, birthplace of Virgil "Gus" Grissom, and famous train robber, Sam Bass. Oolitic was settled by Italians who came to the area to work in the stone mills. Williams is noted for its covered bridge, the longest bridge span still in use. Heltonville is the home of basketball fame, Damon Bailey. Famous actor Claude Akins was from Bedford.

The central region of the county, north of White River, is hilly, and the western and southwestern is rough and broken. Most of the county is under laid with St. Louis limestone, comprising a broad belt. Salem or Bedford stone lies underneath. This is the fine building stone that makes us "The Limestone Capital of the World." Throughout the county there are about 300 caves, the most famous being the Bluespring Caverns, located in the southwest portion of the county.

One

Cities and Small Towns

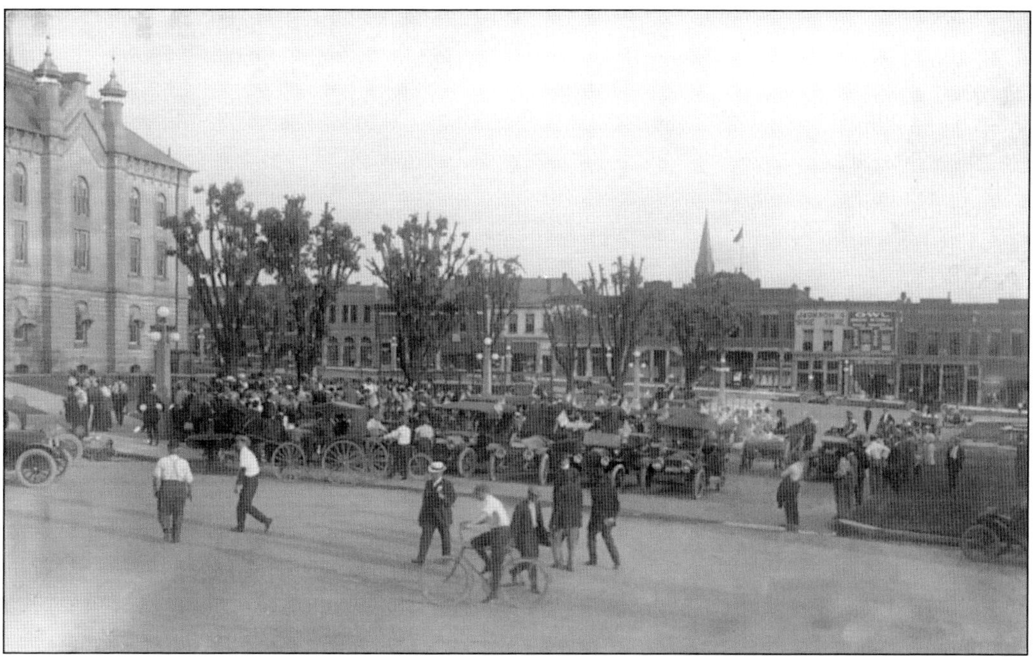

This photo captures a scene of the Bedford Square during the early 1920s, before the addition to the courthouse. The buildings in the background are the south side of the square. Notice the stone light posts, and steeple of the St. Vincent Catholic Church in the distance. It is not known the occasion that has brought this group of people to the downtown square.

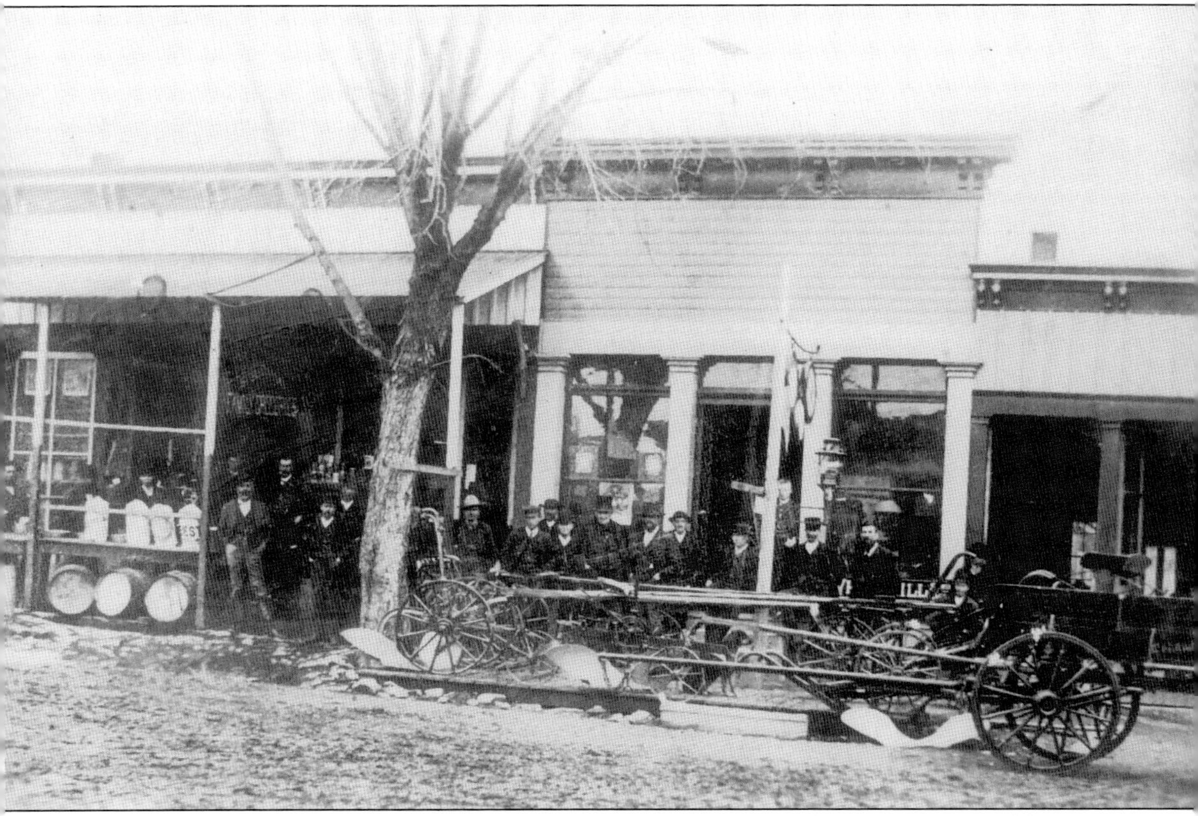

The south side of the Bedford Square in the 1870s had one of the square's four oil lamps. It is not known why so many men were present for this photo. During the rainy season the street could be very muddy. On March 13, 1889, this side of the square was destroyed by fire and had to be rebuilt.

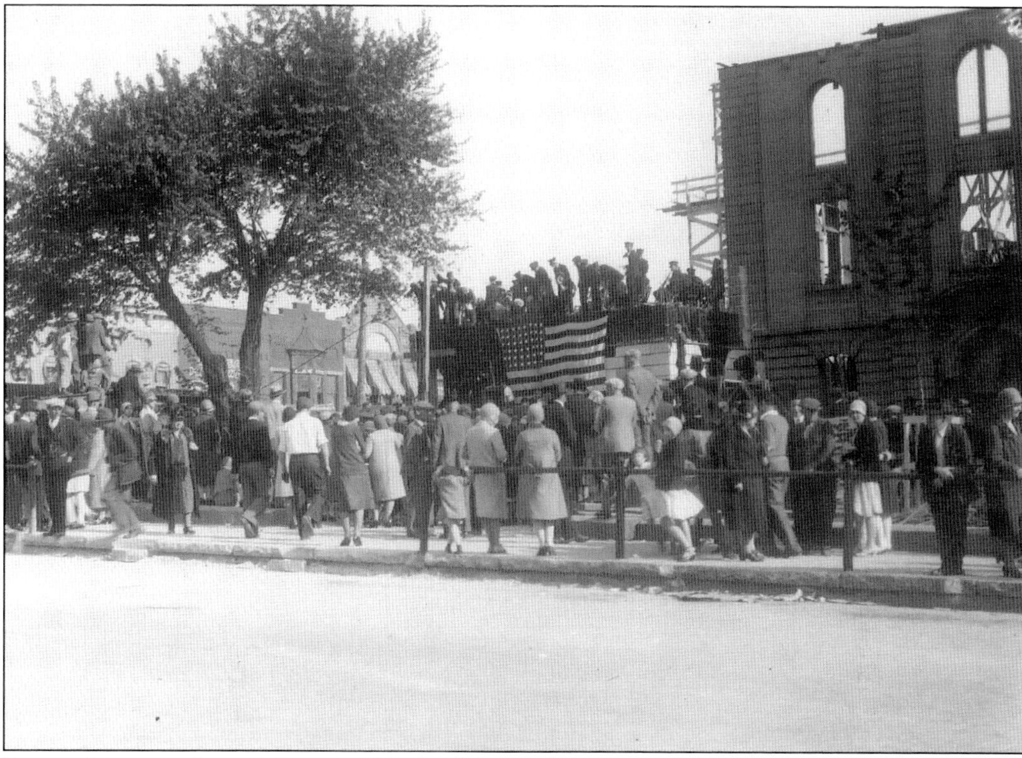

Pictured here is the celebration for the laying of the cornerstone at the new courthouse in Bedford in the early 1930s. Notice the hitching rack along the sidewalk.

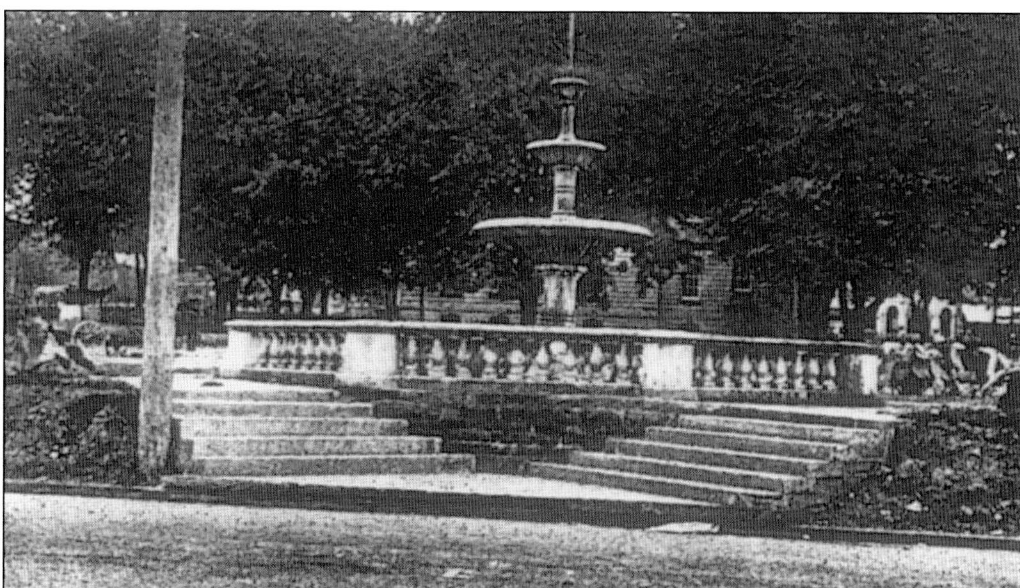

Lawrence Park was located on the west side of the Bedford courthouse. It was a beautiful park with a stone fountain. It became a popular meeting place to discuss the events of the day when families came to town to do business.

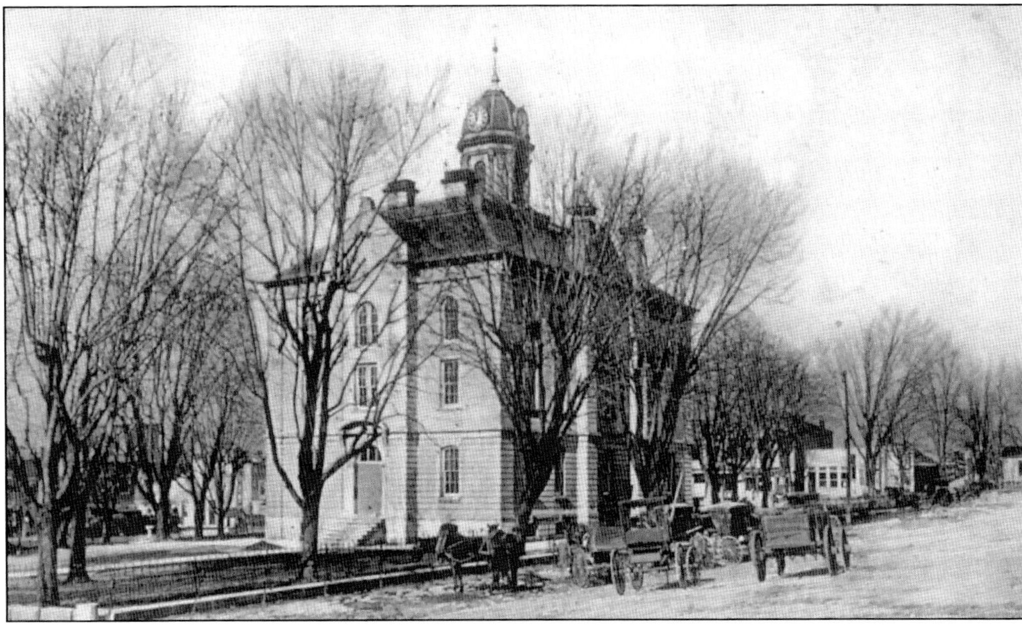

In 1910, the courthouse in the middle of the square in Bedford looked as pictured. The wrought iron fence served as a hitching post. This part is now the center section of the present courthouse.

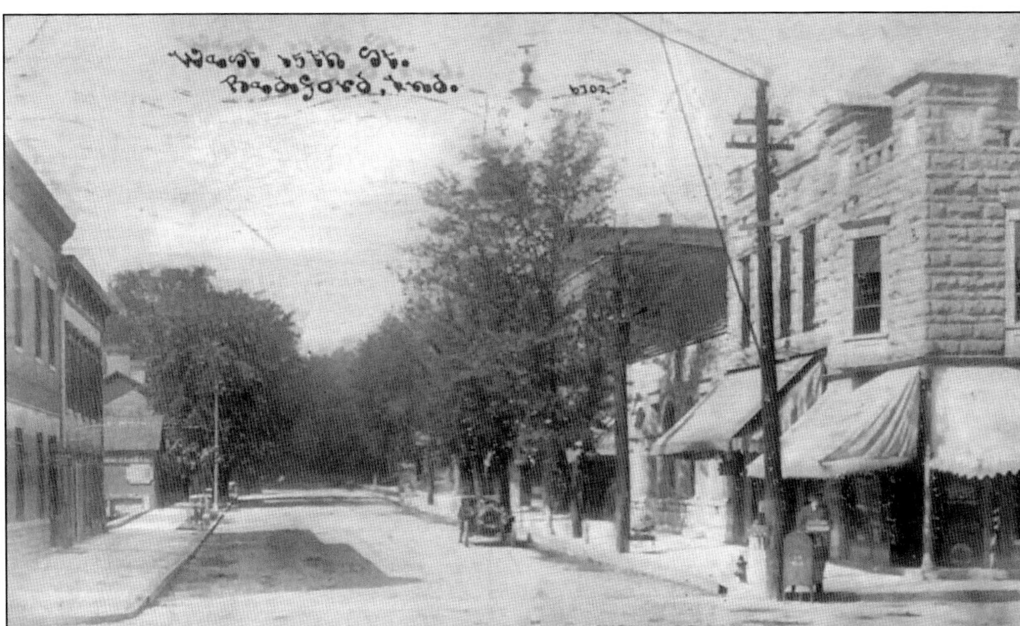

Pictured here is West 15th Street in Bedford. This postcard is dated 1912. Many of the business facilities around the square were built of stone. The city of Bedford was called "Stone City."

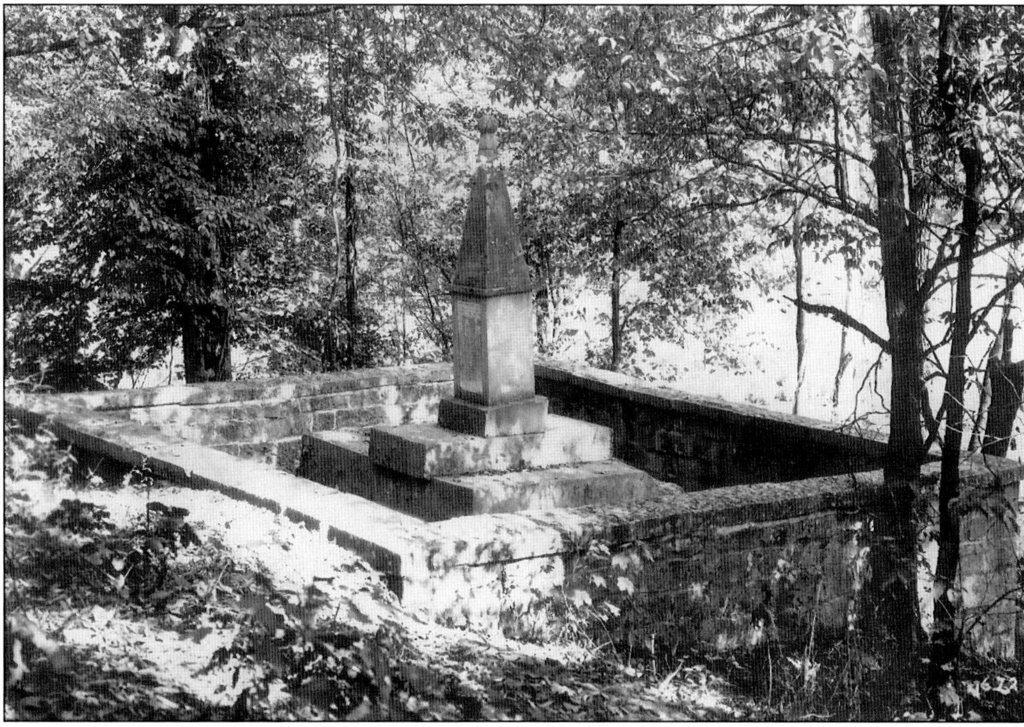

Foote's Tomb is located on the east side of Bedford. Dr. Winthrop Foote is the father of Bedford limestone. His tomb is carved from a huge boulder that was quarried from the Blue Hole Quarry, which he owned.

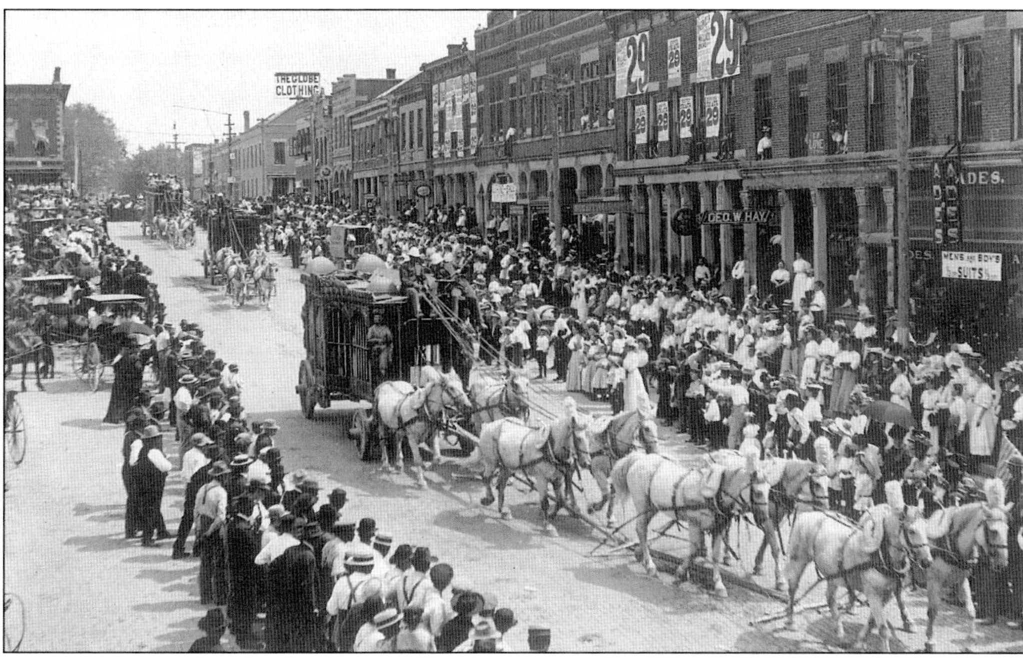

Barnum and Bailey Circus came to Bedford in 1908, and paraded around the public square. It was an event that drew many people.

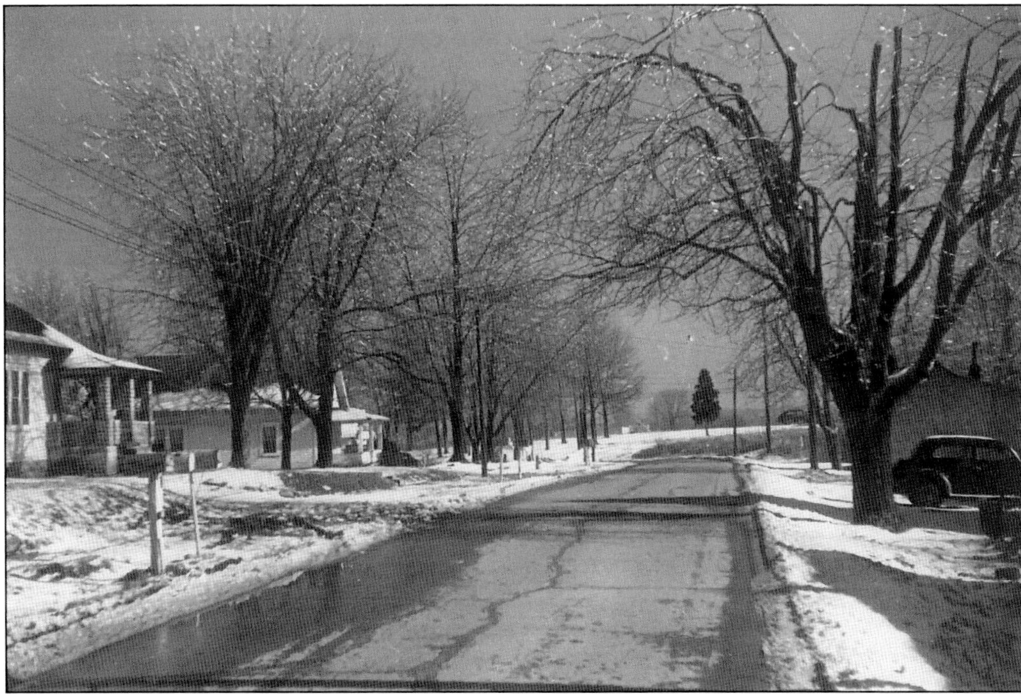

This is a winter scene in Bedford *c.* 1948, looking east on Sixth Street. The Bedford WBIW Radio Station is located at the end of the street on the right hand side. This street was also SR 58, a road that went to Heltonville.

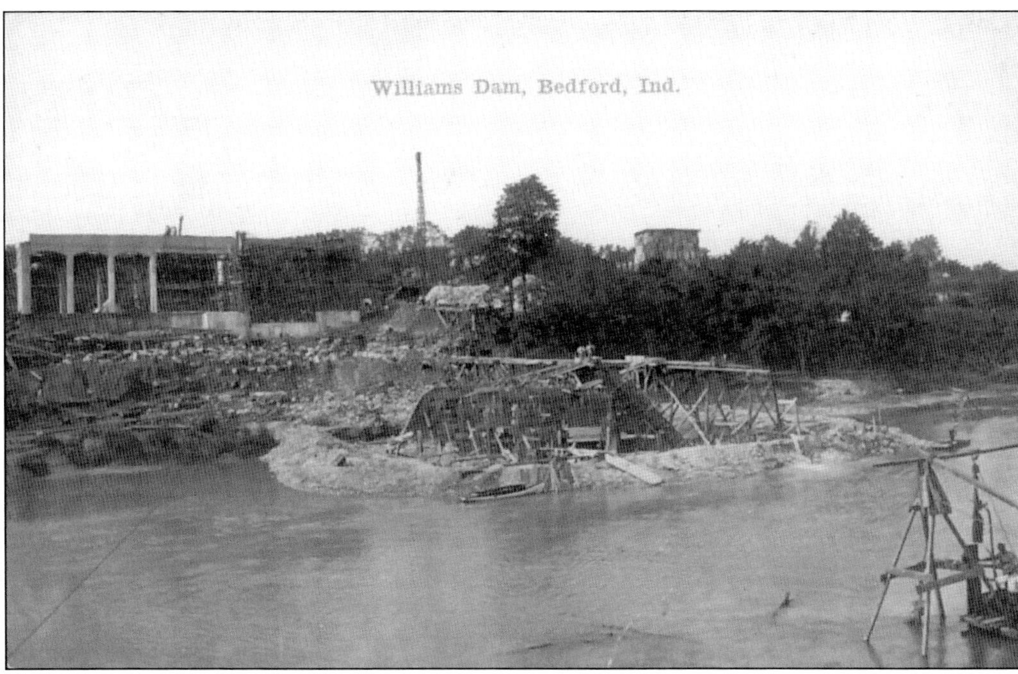

In the early 1930s, the Williams Dam was in the process of being built. It is located southwest of Bedford, and still a favorite fishing spot.

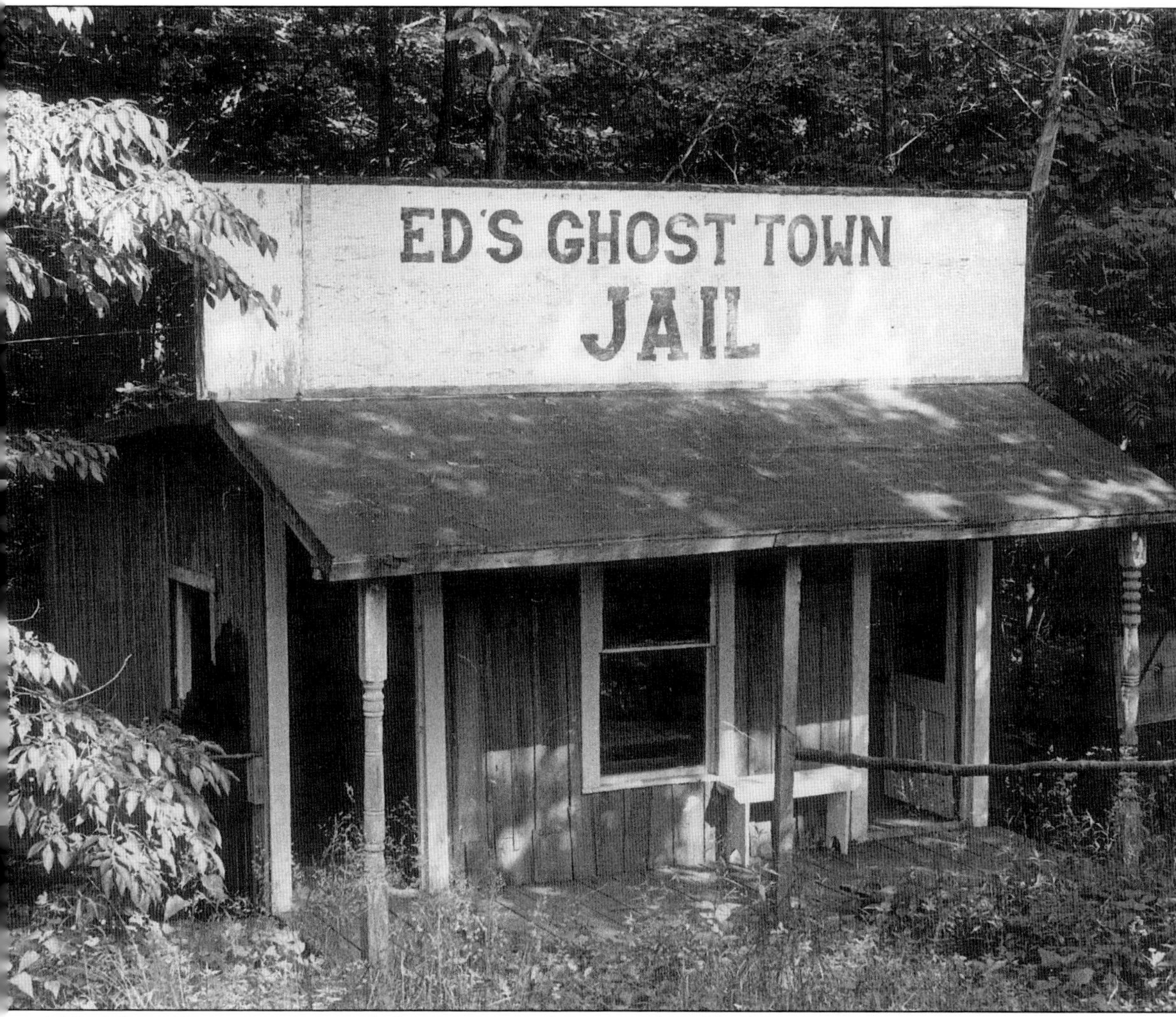

Ed's Ghost Town was situated about seven miles west of Bedford on US 50, and attracted kids in the 1960s. The buildings in the make-believe town were purchased by Ed Hirsch and brought to Lawrence County from out west. For a small fee, you could tour the little town that included a jail. The iron cells from inside were once used in the jail in Lyons, Indiana. A shop nearby was filled with souvenirs and gift items.

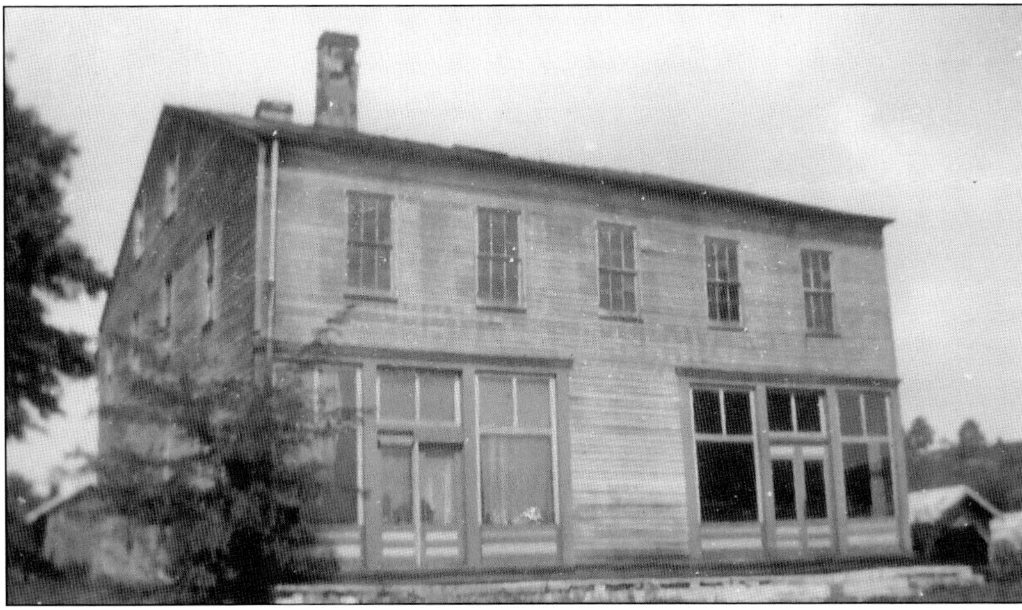

In 1928, this old building was still standing in the small town of Fort Ritner. It had once been a general store owned by Mr. Holland. During the days of the building of the B&O Railroad, Fort Ritner was a thriving town.

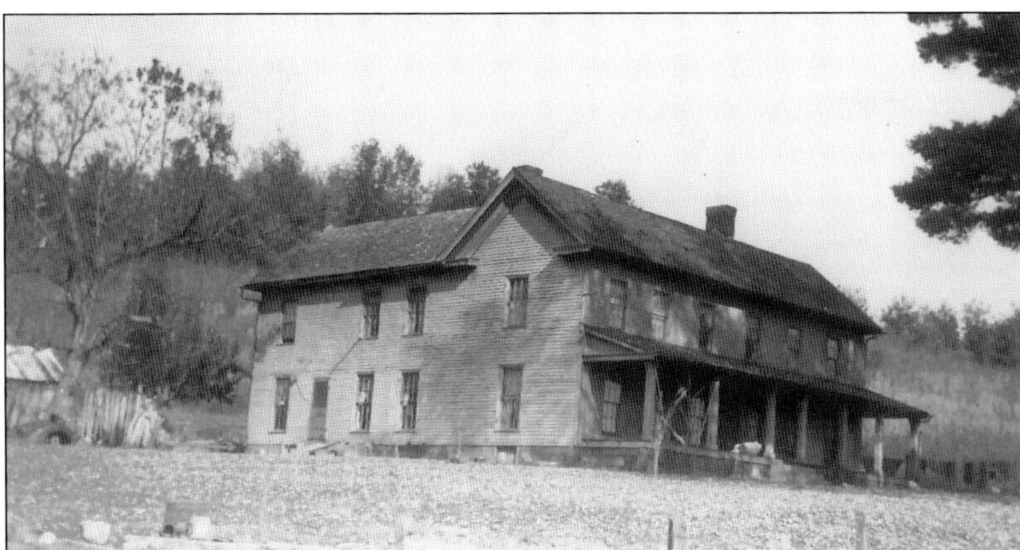

The Quigley House is pictured here in 1948. It was located near the town of Fort Ritner, and was used as a boarding house during the building of the B&O Railroad in the mid 1850s.

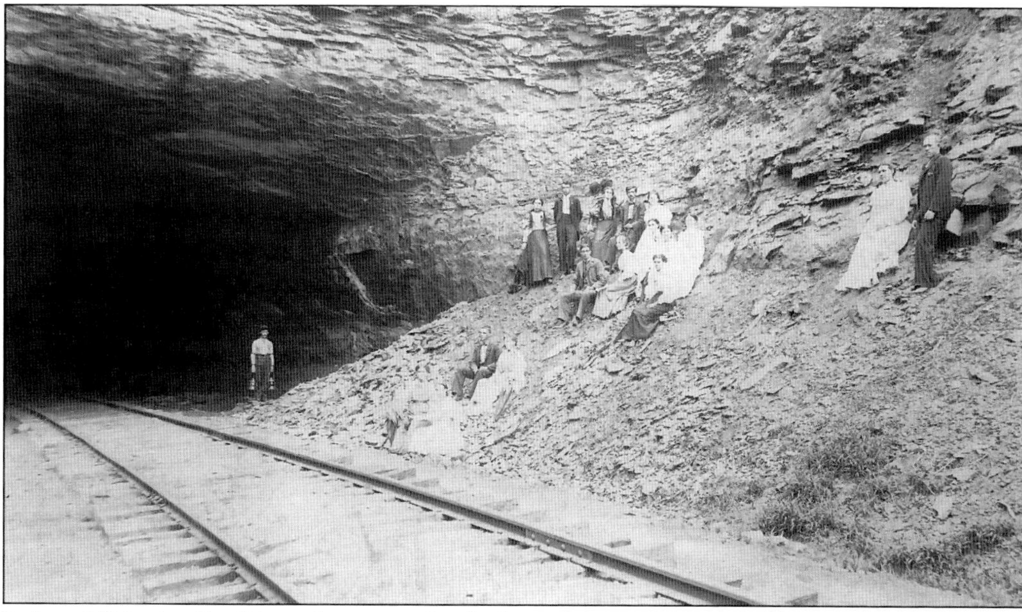

Before 1898, the Big Tunnel was not bricked on the inside. Pictured here is the Fort Ritner end of the tunnel, east of Tunnelton. The length of the tunnel was one mile long, causing many accidents.

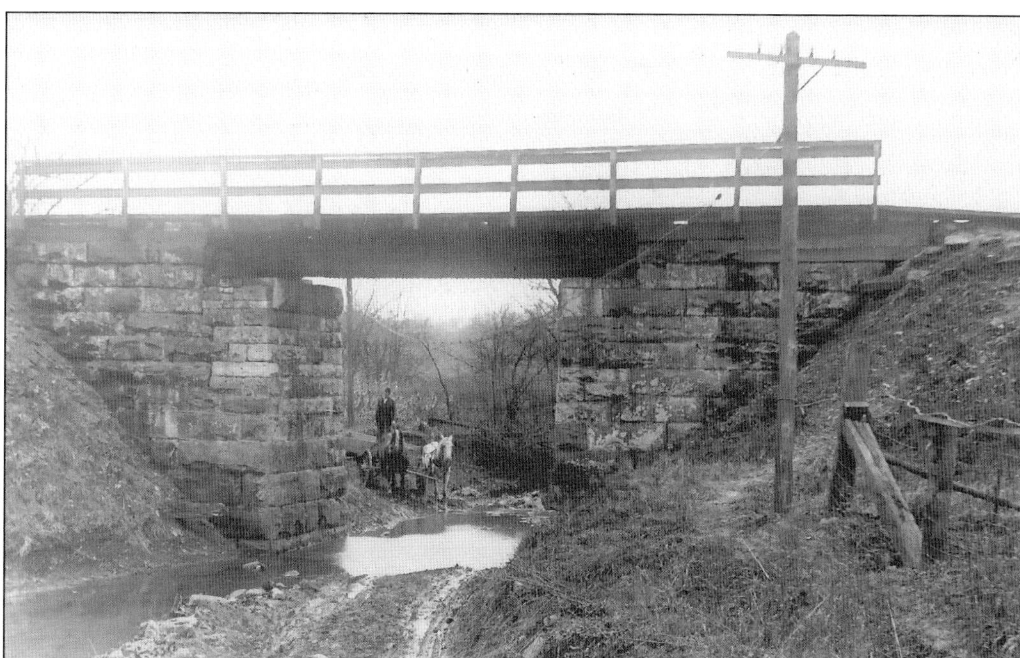

Pictured here in the late 1890s is the railroad bridge at Fort Ritner, Indiana. The road was a mud road and could get difficult at times. The present day road follows the same path but is now blacktop. The man in the wagon is not known.

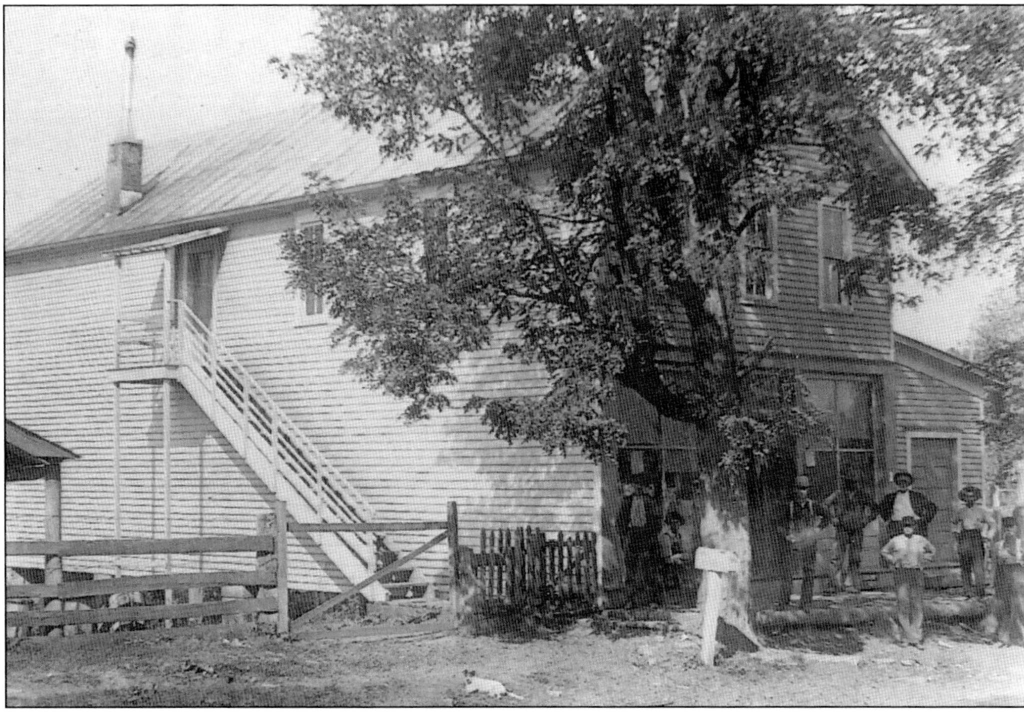

This is a picture of Frank Holland's Store in Leesville. Those pictured from left to right are: Pat Clark, Lige Brock, Timmy Wilson, Newt Hughes, Henry Woolery, Ed Bennett, Jacob Brock, and Tom Wilson.

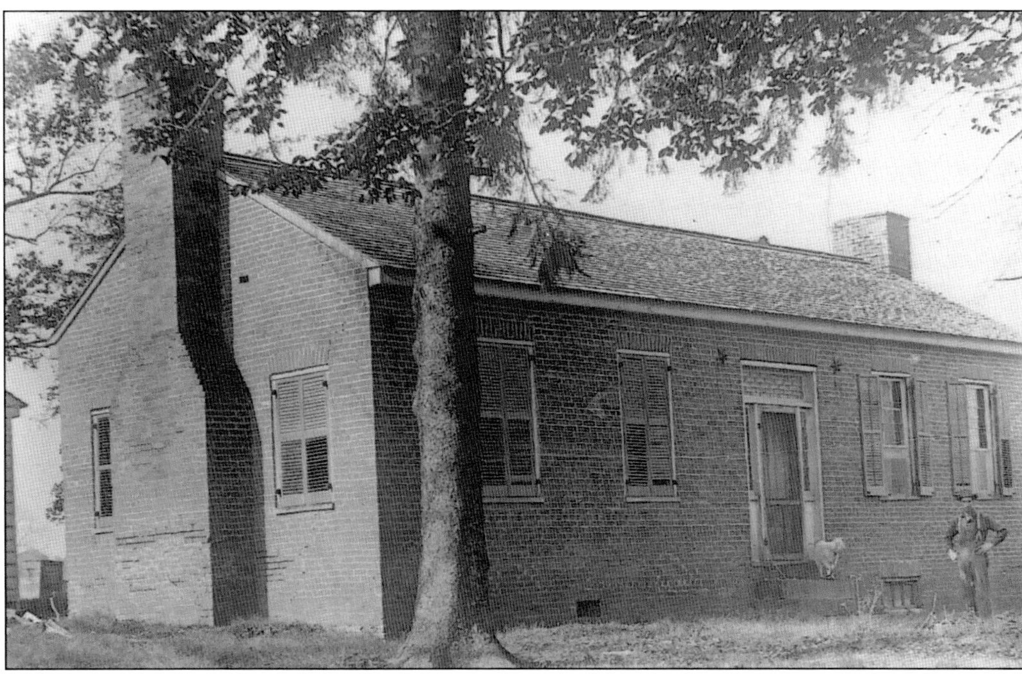

In the 1930s, this house stood in the little town of Leesville. It has since been torn down. It is not known the identity of the gentleman in the yard, or the name of his dog.

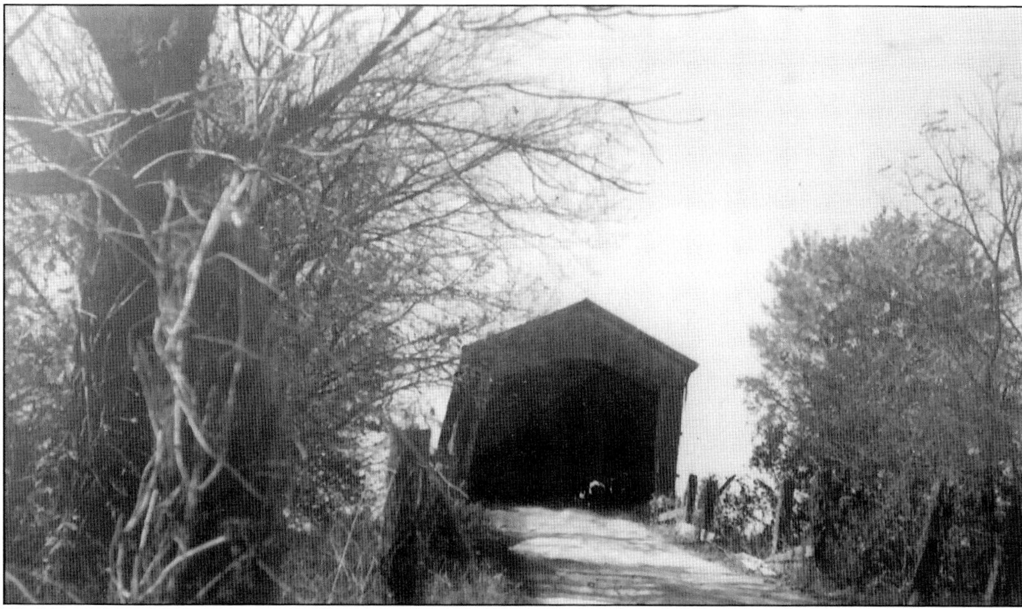

In 1939, this photo was taken of the Tunnelton Covered Bridge, one of five in the county. Presently there is only one. This is the east end of the bridge, going over White River. It was replaced *c.* 1960.

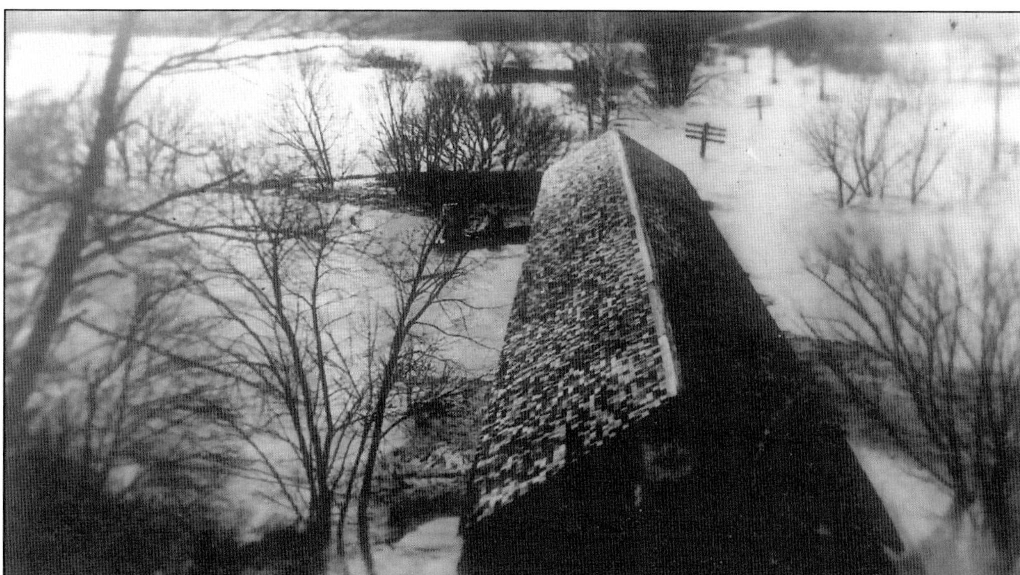

Salt Creek Covered Bridge as seen during the 1913 flood. This bridge was located between Oolitic and Bedford and no longer exists.

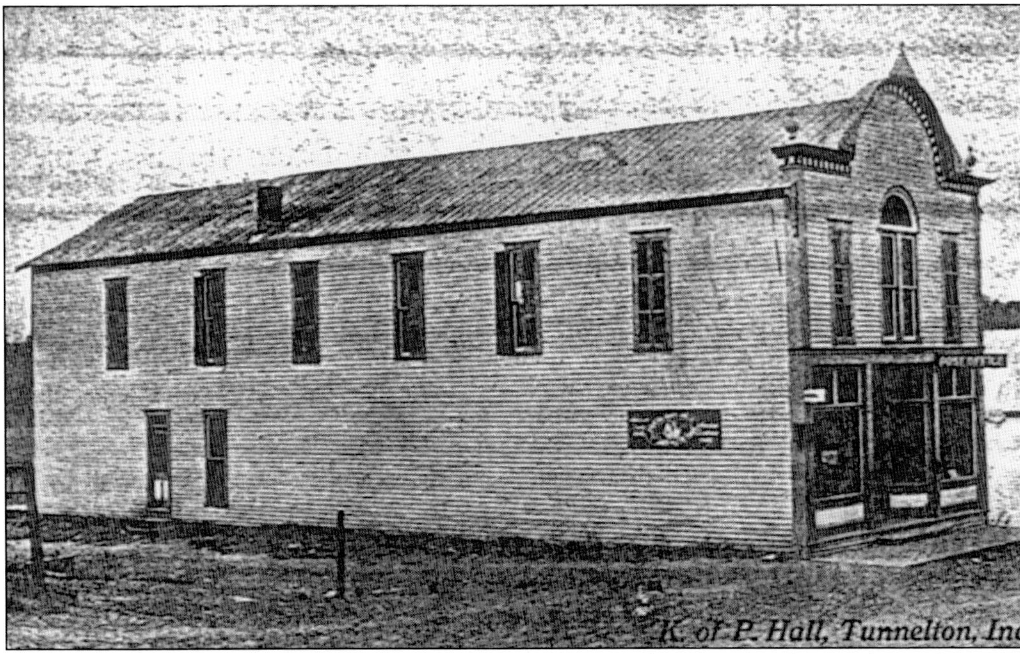

The old Knights of Pythias Hall in Tunnelton was once full of activity during the early 1900s. The main floor was a general store and post office. The upstairs was the meeting room.

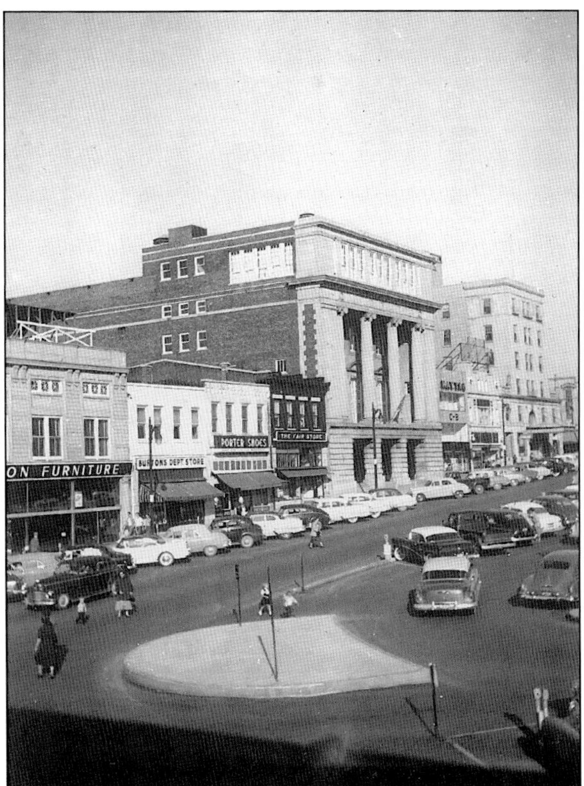

In 1955, the north side of the Bedford Square looked like this with the beautiful Masonic Temple and its stone pillars. Buck Lemon Furniture, Burton's Department Store, Porter Shoes, and The Fair Store are also seen.

Two

PEOPLE

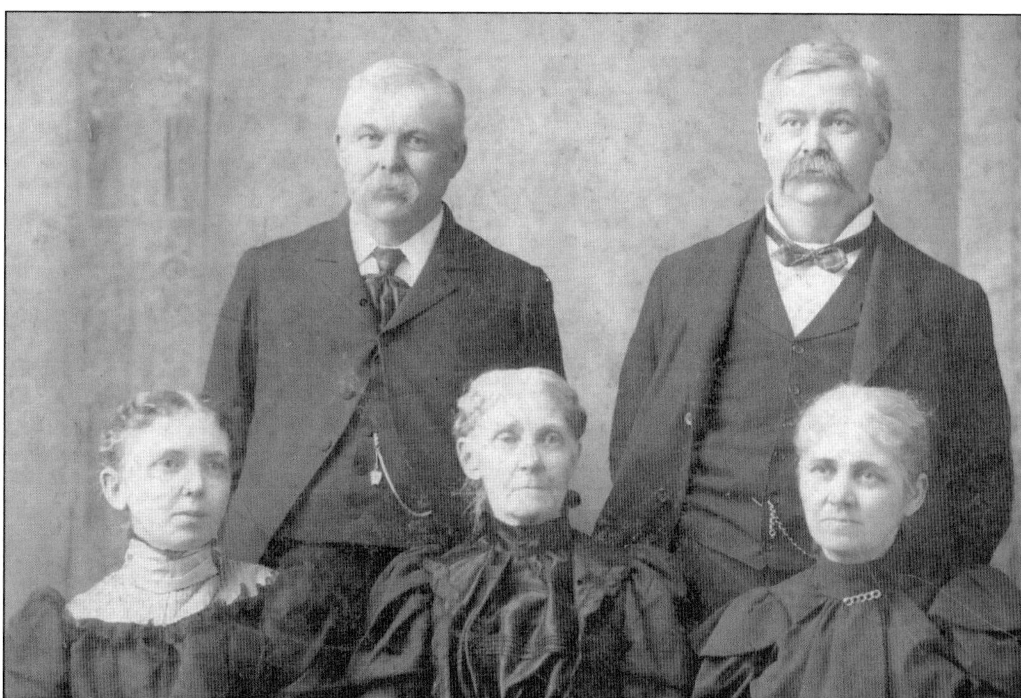

The Houston family is pictured here when they lived on M Street in 1890. The photographer, Mr. Walters, had a studio in Bedford during this period.

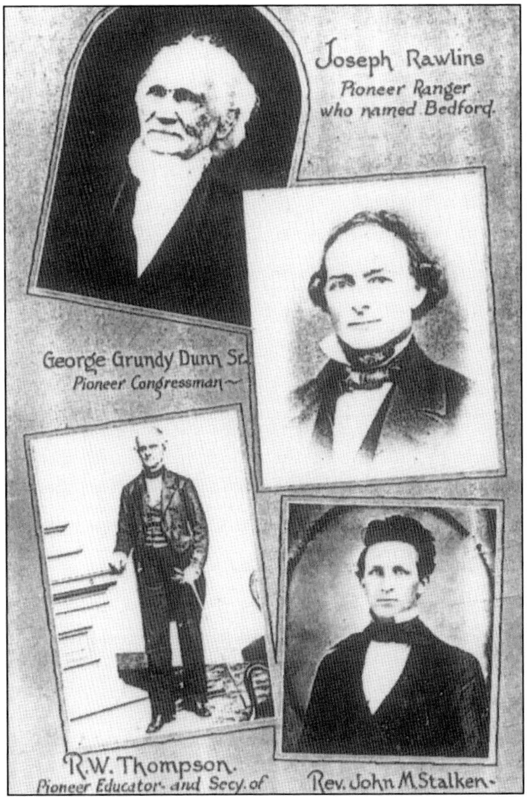

This is a picture of some very prominent men of early Bedford, from the top: Joseph Rawlings, pioneer ranger; George Grundy Dunn, pioneer congressman; R.W. Thompson, educator and Secretary of State; and Rev. John M. Stalker, educator and minister.

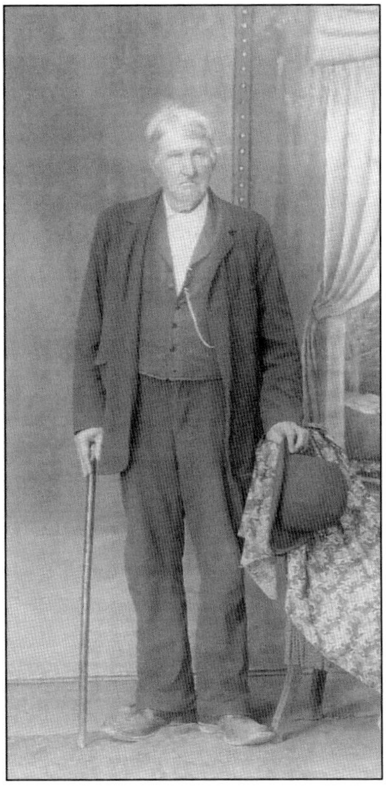

John D. Thommason, one of Bedford's oldest businessmen, was born in Henry County, Virginia. In 1889, he was the first elected mayor of the city of Bedford, and held office only three months until he resigned.

Mary Jane Robertson was married to John D. Thommason on April 20, 1834. She is pictured here, c. 1890.

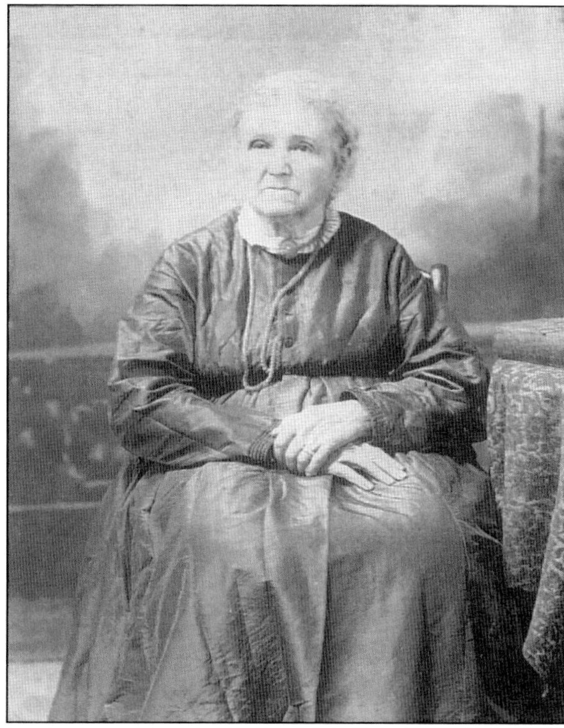

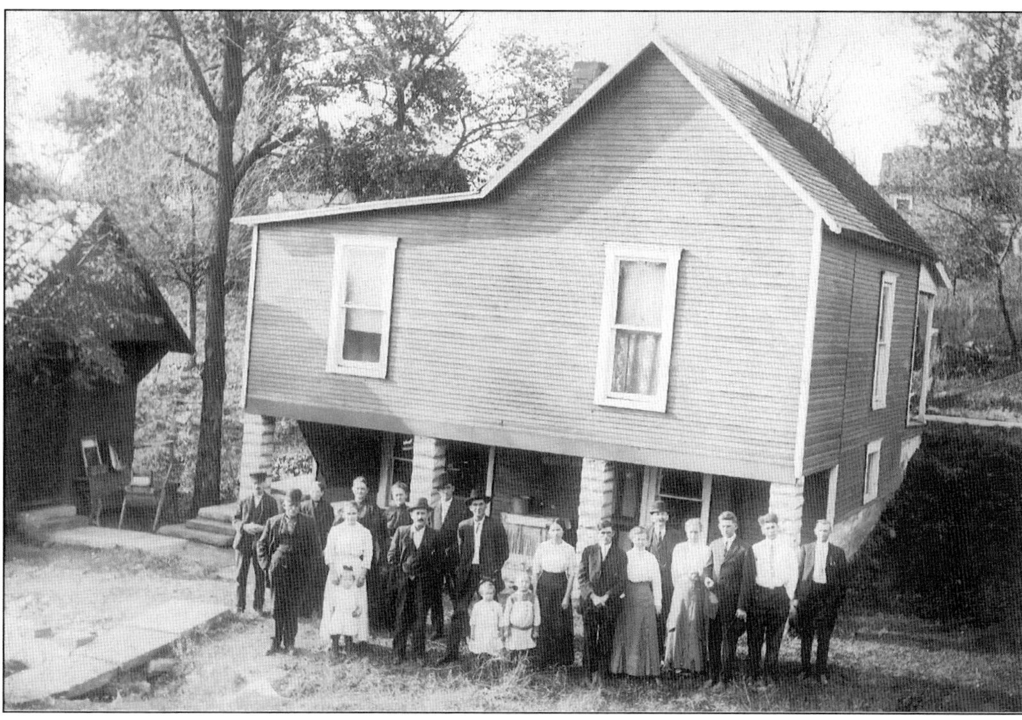

The Francis Richardson home was located on 16th Street, near their grocery business. This is a picture of their home with members of the family out in the yard. The photo was taken c. 1910.

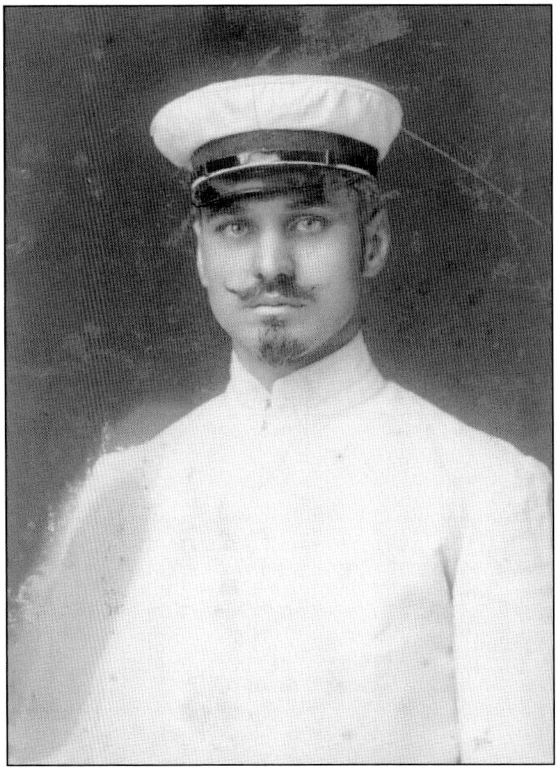

Charles Morton Dodd served in the Spanish-American War, and is seen here in 1898 while he was in Panama. After the war he returned home and became a master stone carver. Much of his work can be seen today.

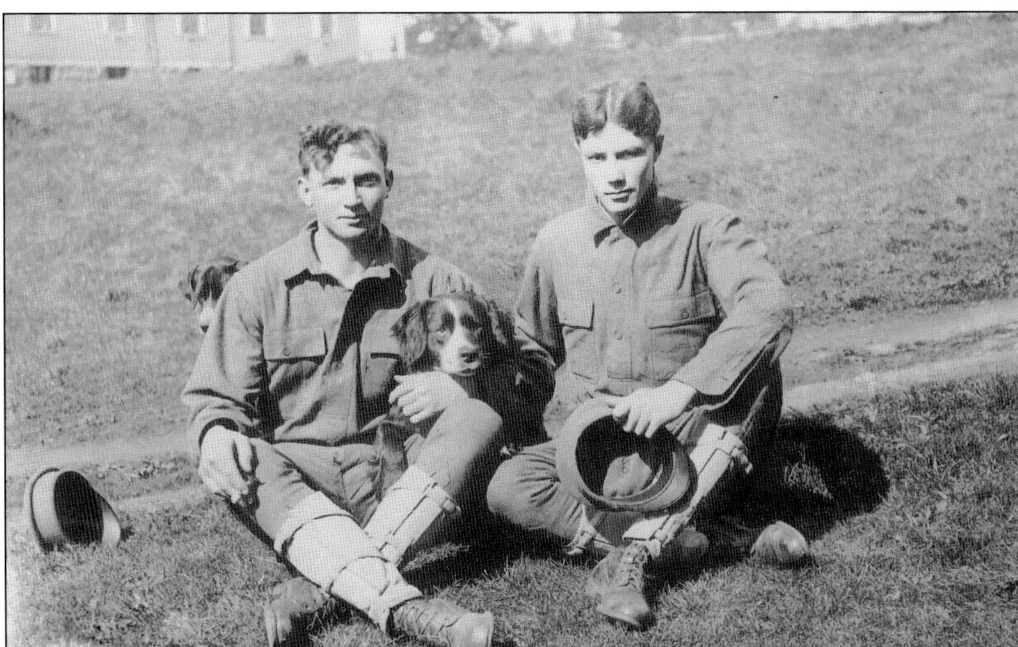

This picture was taken in the Philippines during the Spanish-American War c. 1889. Randal Evans of Needmore, Indiana, is seen on the right. He joined the army at the age of 17. The other soldier is not identified.

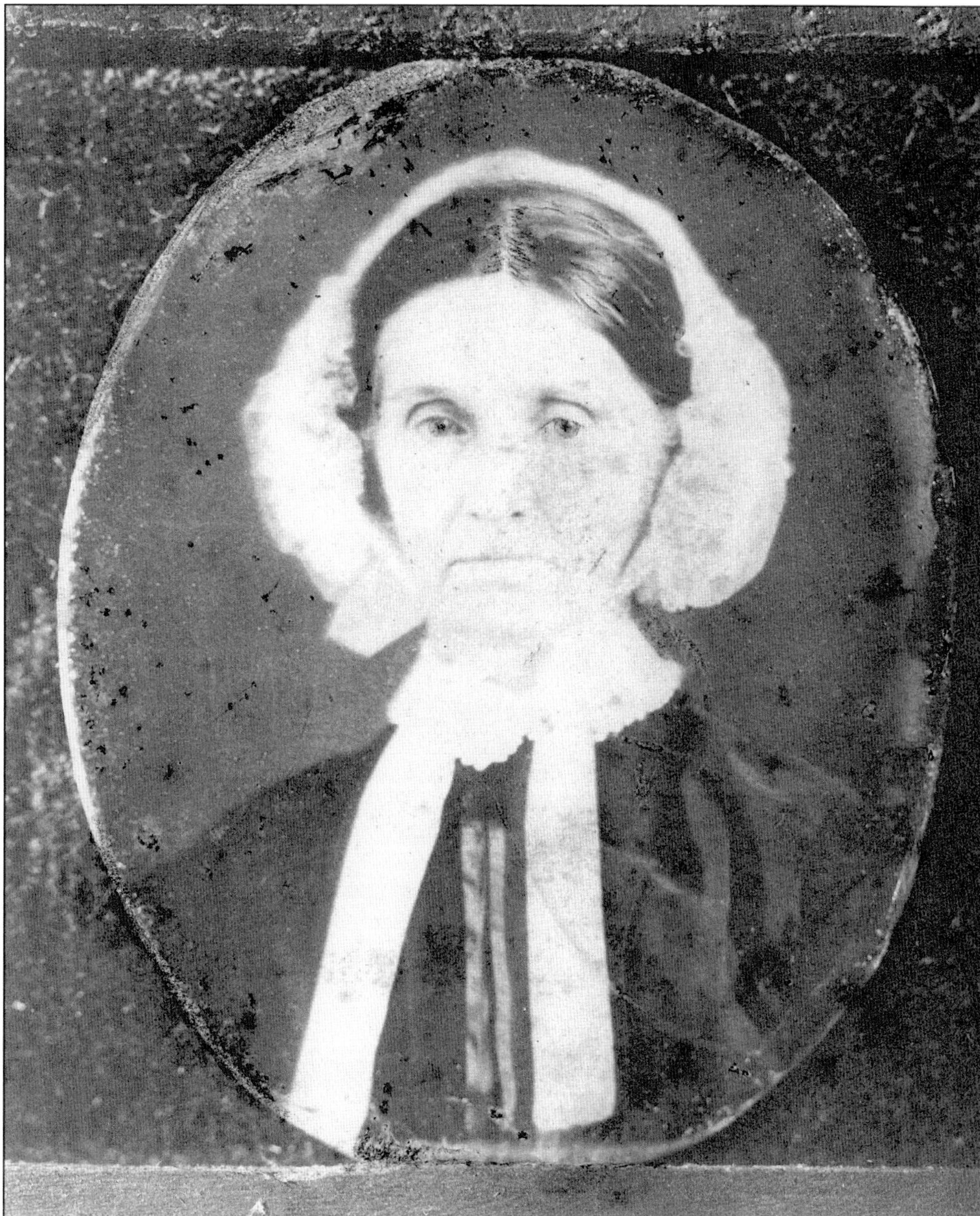

Sarah McMannus came from Kentucky to Lawrence County before 1817. She married Joseph Rawlings on Jan. 5, 1817, and lived at the site of the present Planter Union Bank in Bedford. This picture was taken *c.* 1855 before her death.

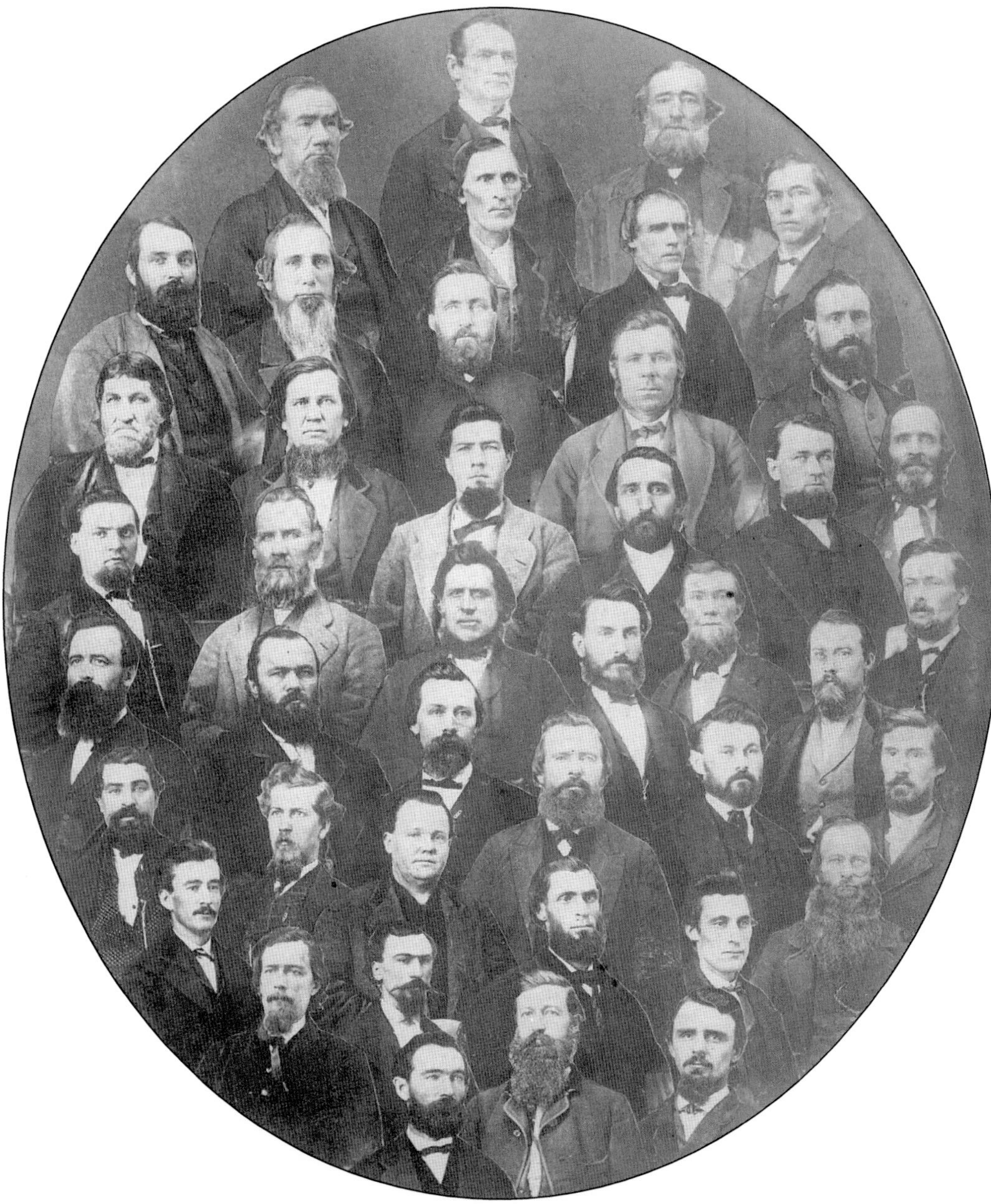

The Shawswick Lodge, No. 177, I.O.O.F. (International Order of the Odd Fellows) met every Monday night in the upstairs of the city hall building. Known members in 1866 are: Michael A. Malott, John P. Francis, Joe Hendricks, Joseph Basley, Will (Bill) Malott, James Northcraft, Tom Adams, Dr. Joseph Gardner, Mr. Simmons, Mart Burton, Mr. Blake, Joe Johnson, Ed Howel, J.D. Thommason, Col. Henry Davis, Tom Whitted, John Glover, Tom Malott, Frank Whitted, Lycurgus Dalton, Bill Carter, Alonzo Malott, Cyrus Davis, Levi Dale, Stephen Bowers, M.H. Pearson, Calvin Aley, Mr. Peak, Frank Bracston, John Acoams, and Wes Cosner.

Captain William J. Cook was a volunteer for the 120th Regiment in the spring of 1864, for a term of three years. Serving under Col. F. Barter, he fought at Resaca, Kennesaw Mountain, and the Battle of Atlanta. This picture was taken c. 1890.

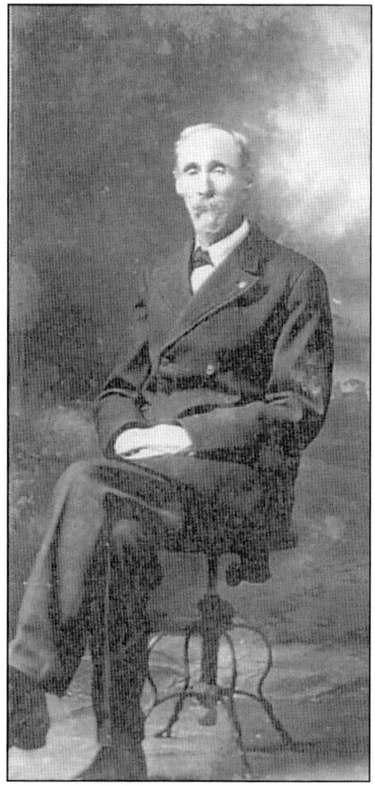

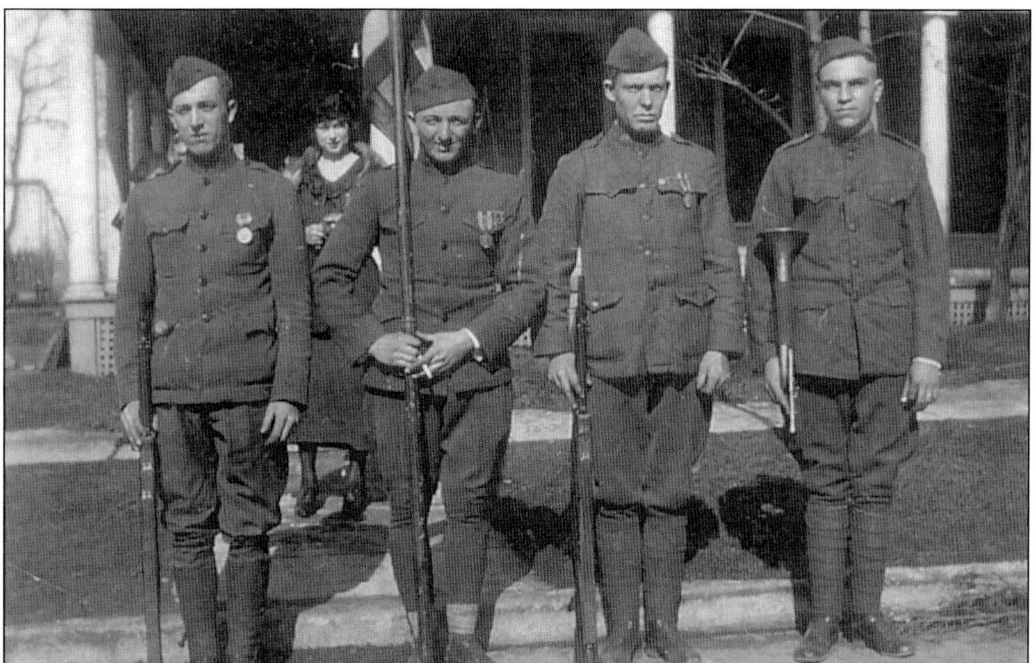

This photo is a group of World War I soldiers, possibly a color guard. It is not known the identity of these Lawrence County men.

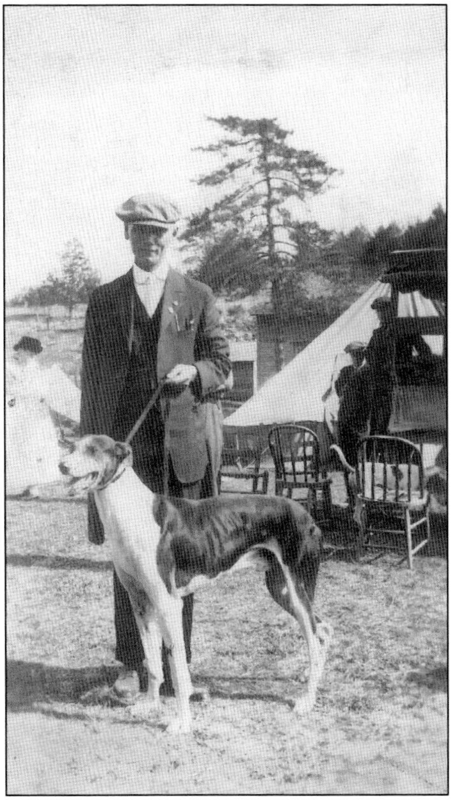

During the 1920s, there was a Fox Hunter's Association near Springville, Indiana. Pictured here is Mr. Blackburn with his hunting dog.

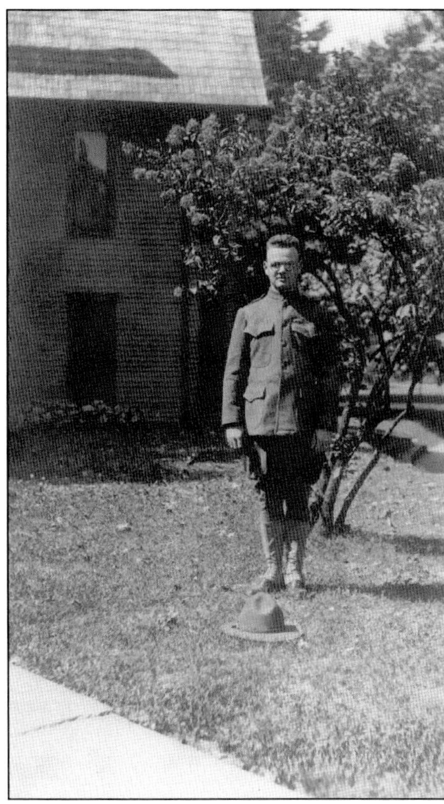

Tunnelton resident Pvt. Theran H. Huddleston, Company B, Second Platoon R.O.T.C., is pictured here in 1919.

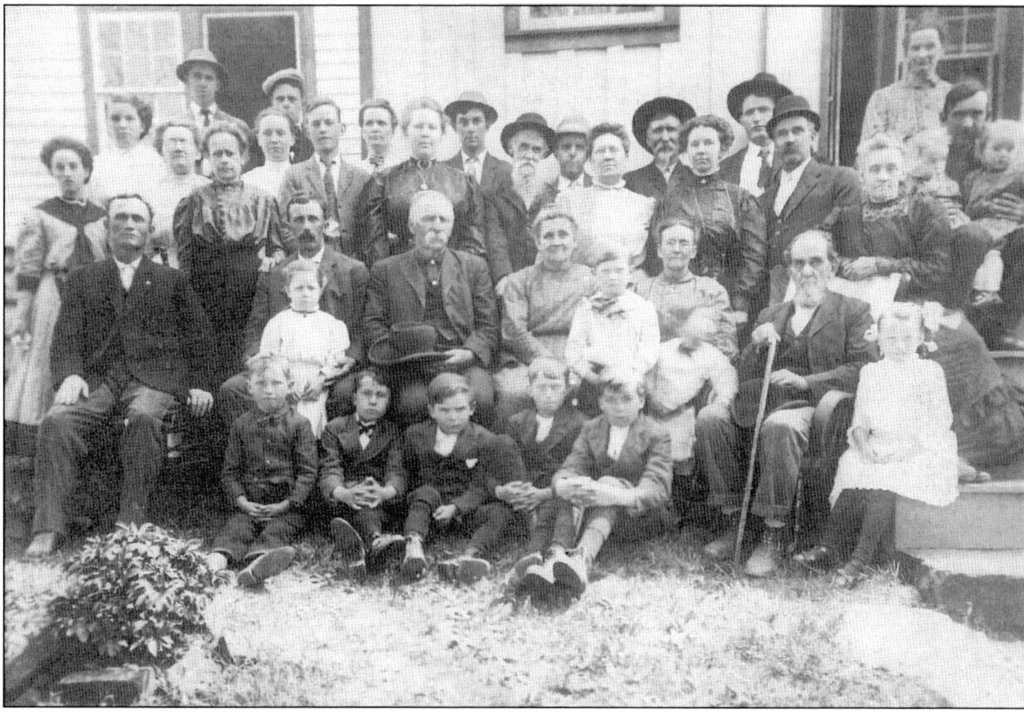

In 1910, this photo was taken at the Smith Reunion at an unidentified home in Lawrence County. Some of the family names in the picture are: Smith, Sterling, Hotz, Crane, and McCullough.

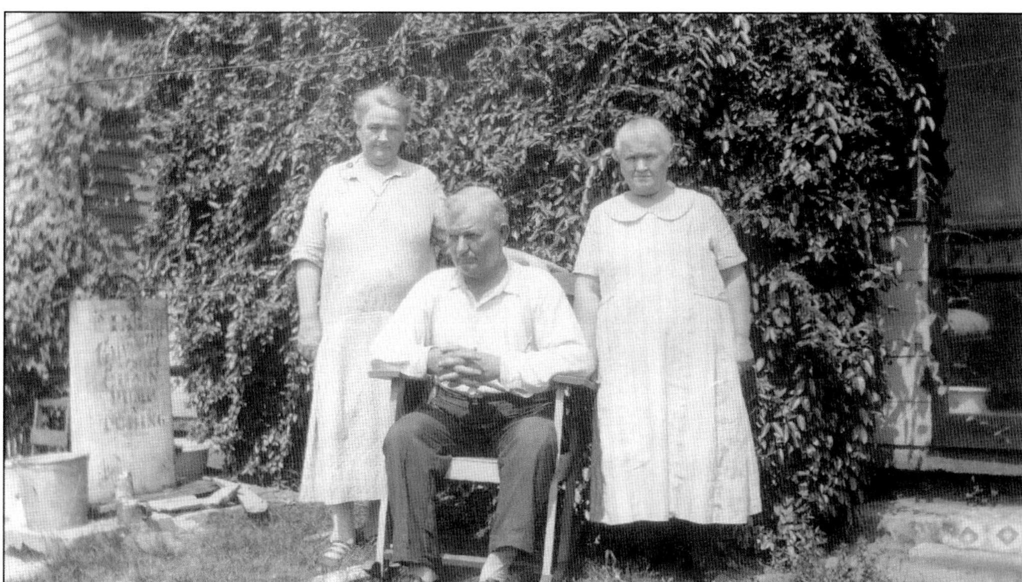

Photographed here is Harve Reed, his wife, and her sister. It was taken around 1930 at their home in Tunnelton

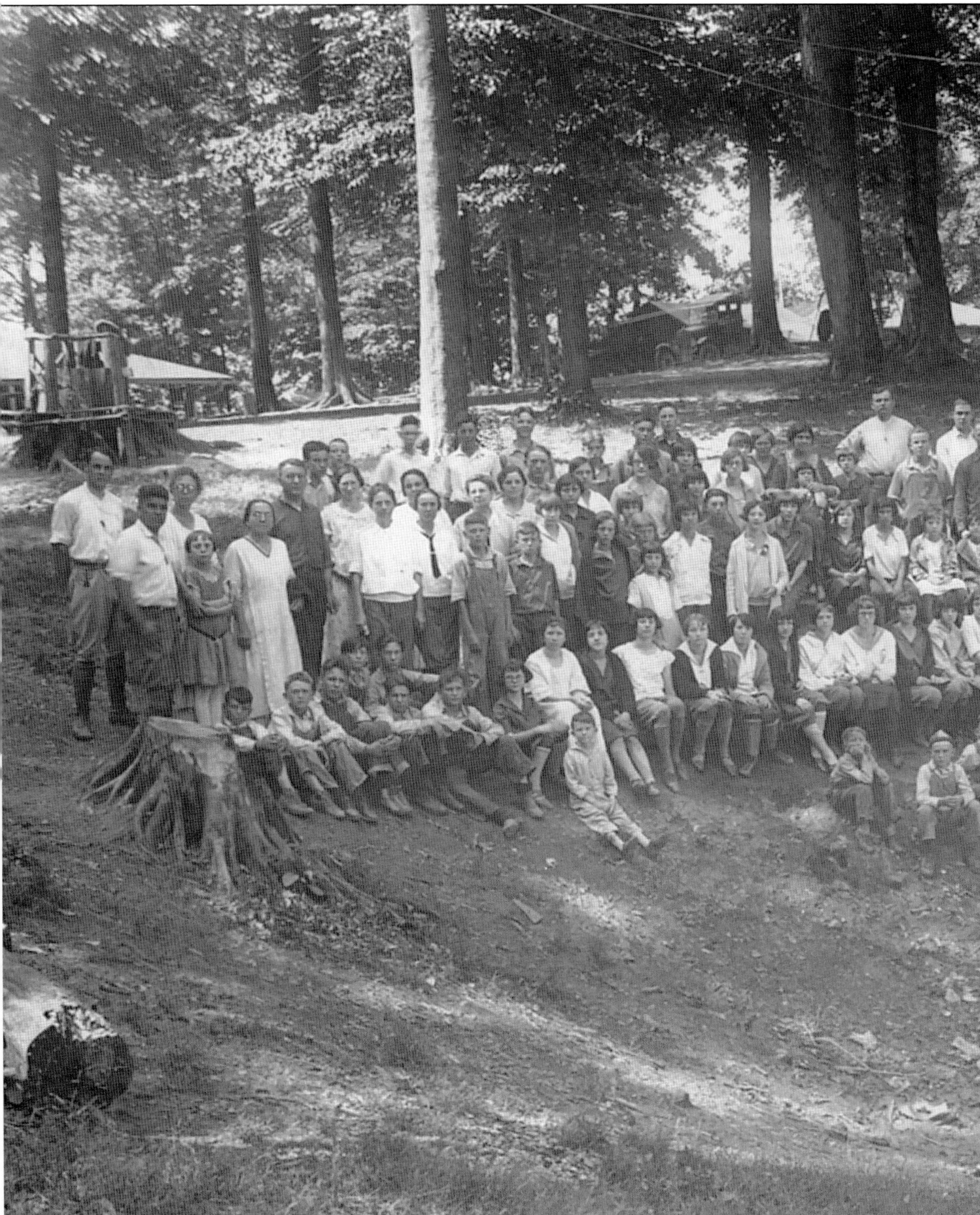

Pictured here is a gathering at Camp Bedford in 1925. The camp is located on South I Street near White River and is still in existence. It is owned by the Christian Church, and is now

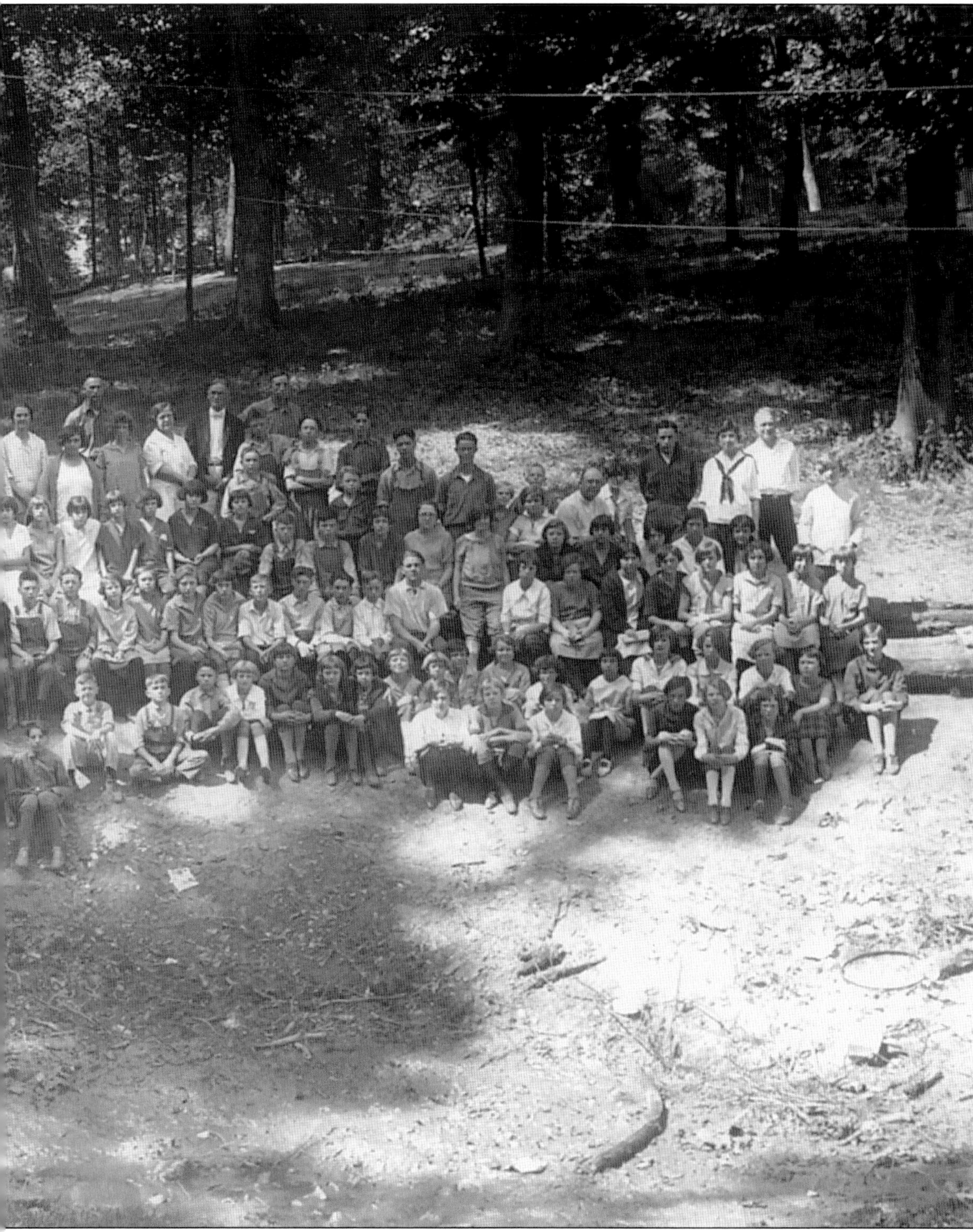

called Christian Church Camp.

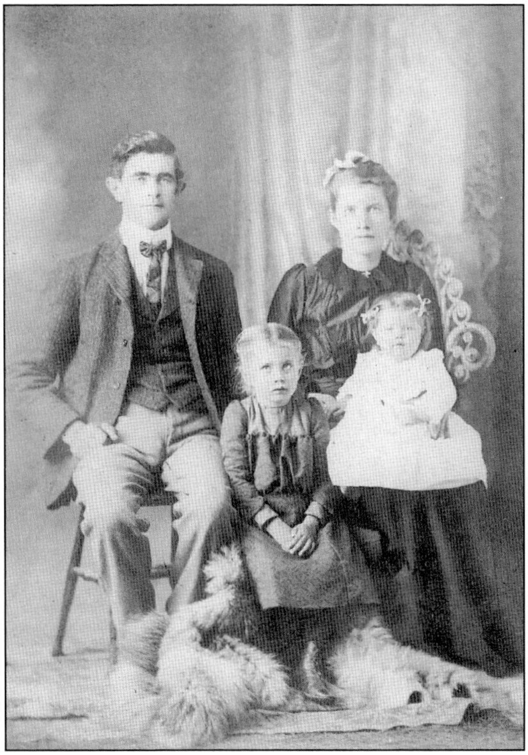

Luther and Mandy White pose for this picture with two of their children *c.* 1890. The White family lived in Lawrence County.

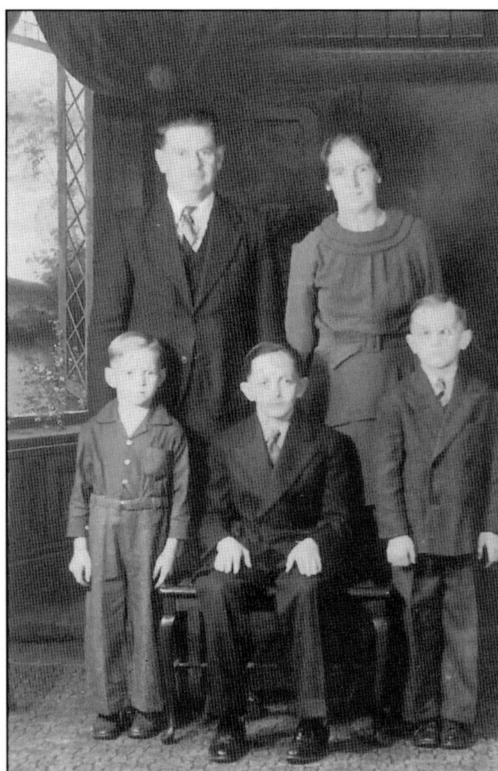

This is a picture of the Virgil Lively family, taken *c.* 1930. The early ancestor, Andrew Lively, came to Lawrence County in 1840. He was a farmer and raised stock.

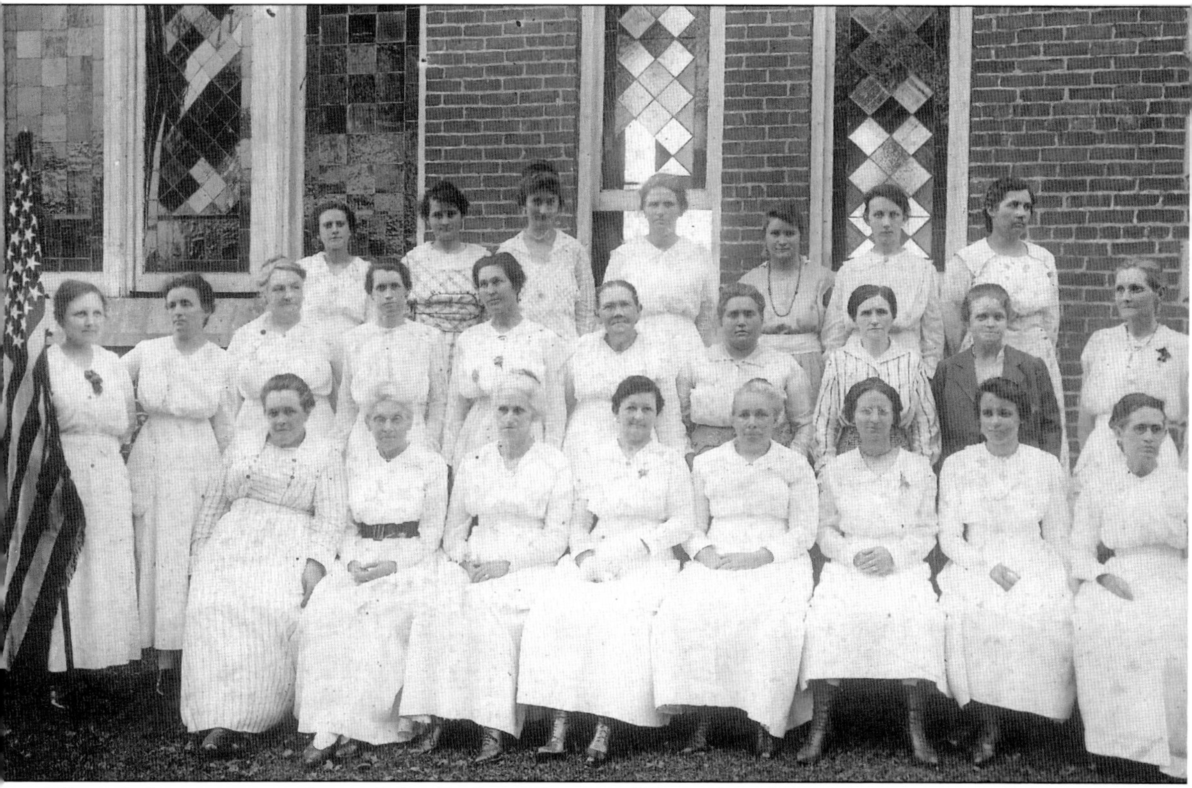

These ladies were members of the Pythian Sisters of Tunnelton No. 401. Front row, left to right are: Laura Sallee Thomas, Frances Brooking Brown, Ida Thomas Crawford, Jennie Baufle Guthrie, Mary Hoopingarner Root, Hattie Bailey Guthrie, Minnie Brooking Allen, and Mary McLaughlin Guthrie. Second row: Fleta Allen Mathis, Mary Malott, Ella Clark Reed, Rubie Guthrie Nichols, Florence Guthrie Batman, Mrs. Butler, Gertrude Ingle Brooking, Ella Wilcox Matlock, Molly Davis Huddleston, and Lena Clark. Back row: Clemma Crawford Allen, Ella Wright, Annis Crawford, Lottie Crawford Bever, Marie Hoopingarner, Marie Hill Thomas, and Cora Ingle Stipp.

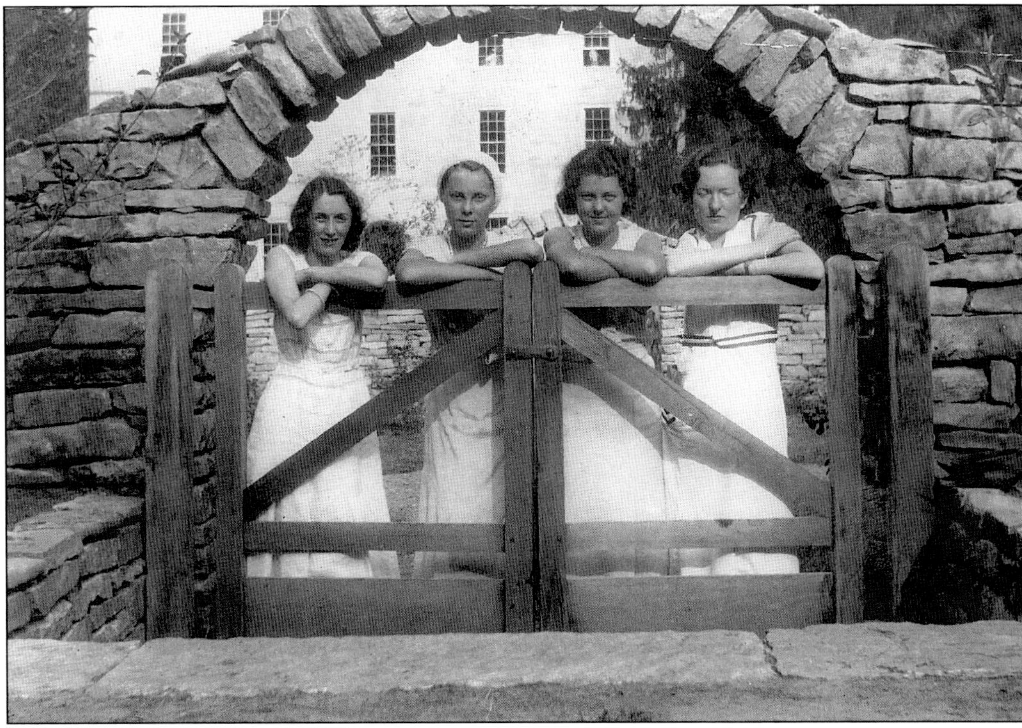

Four young girls from Tunnelton, Indiana enjoy an afternoon at Spring Mill State Park c. 1935. The gristmill can be seen in the background. The two girls on the right are Mary Lemon and Annis Crawford.

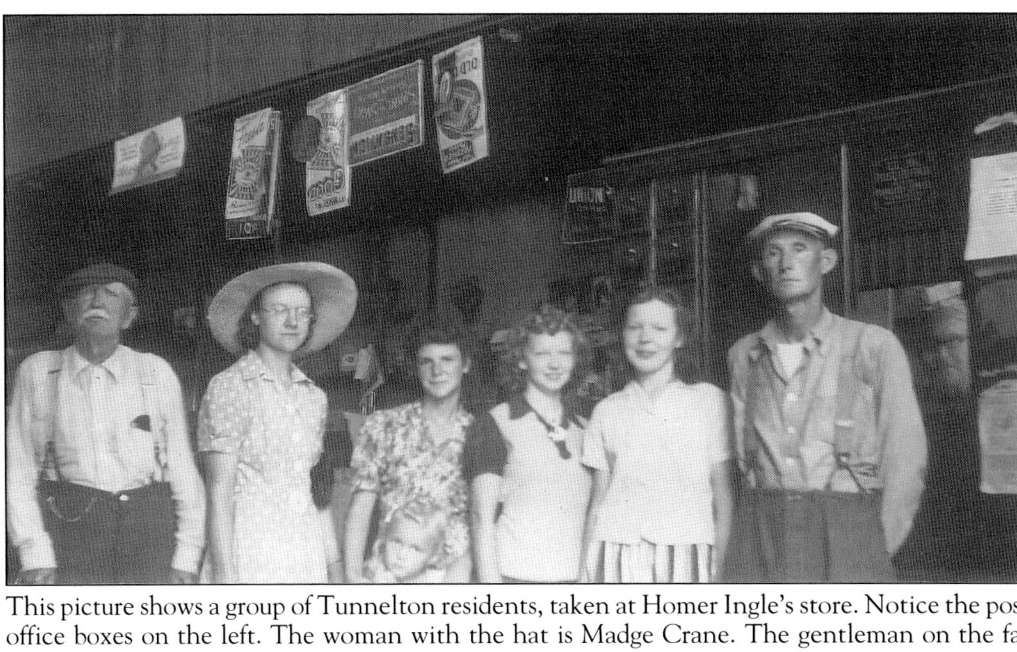

This picture shows a group of Tunnelton residents, taken at Homer Ingle's store. Notice the post office boxes on the left. The woman with the hat is Madge Crane. The gentleman on the far right is believed to be Perry Mullis.

In the 1920s, Jackson's Studio took many photos of Lawrence County people. This picture is Bertha Baker, taken *c.* 1928.

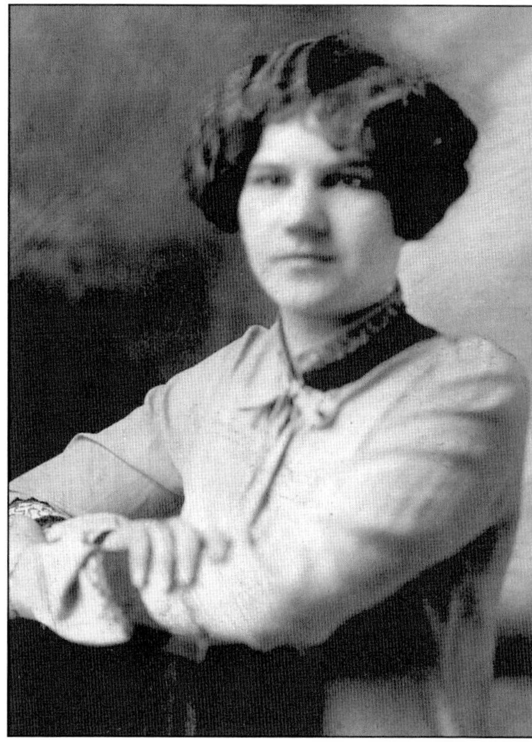

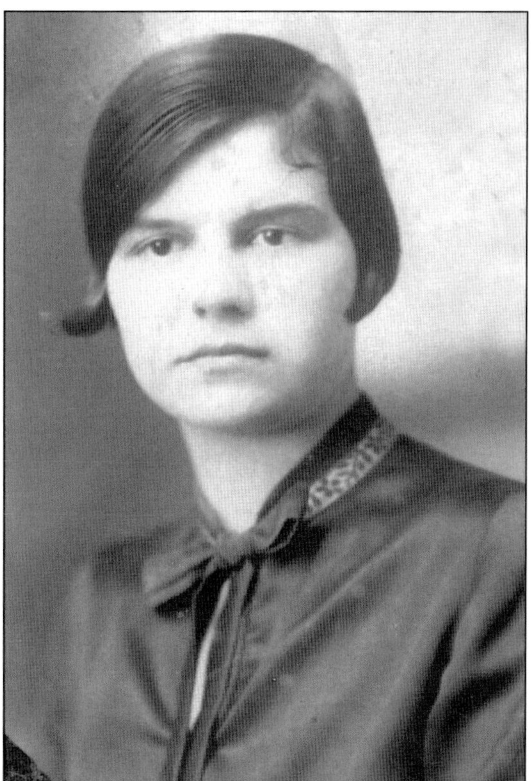

Mable Martin is shown in this picture, taken *c.* 1928. She was a first cousin to Bertha Baker, whose picture is above. Mable married Sollie Guthrie and later moved to Indianapolis.

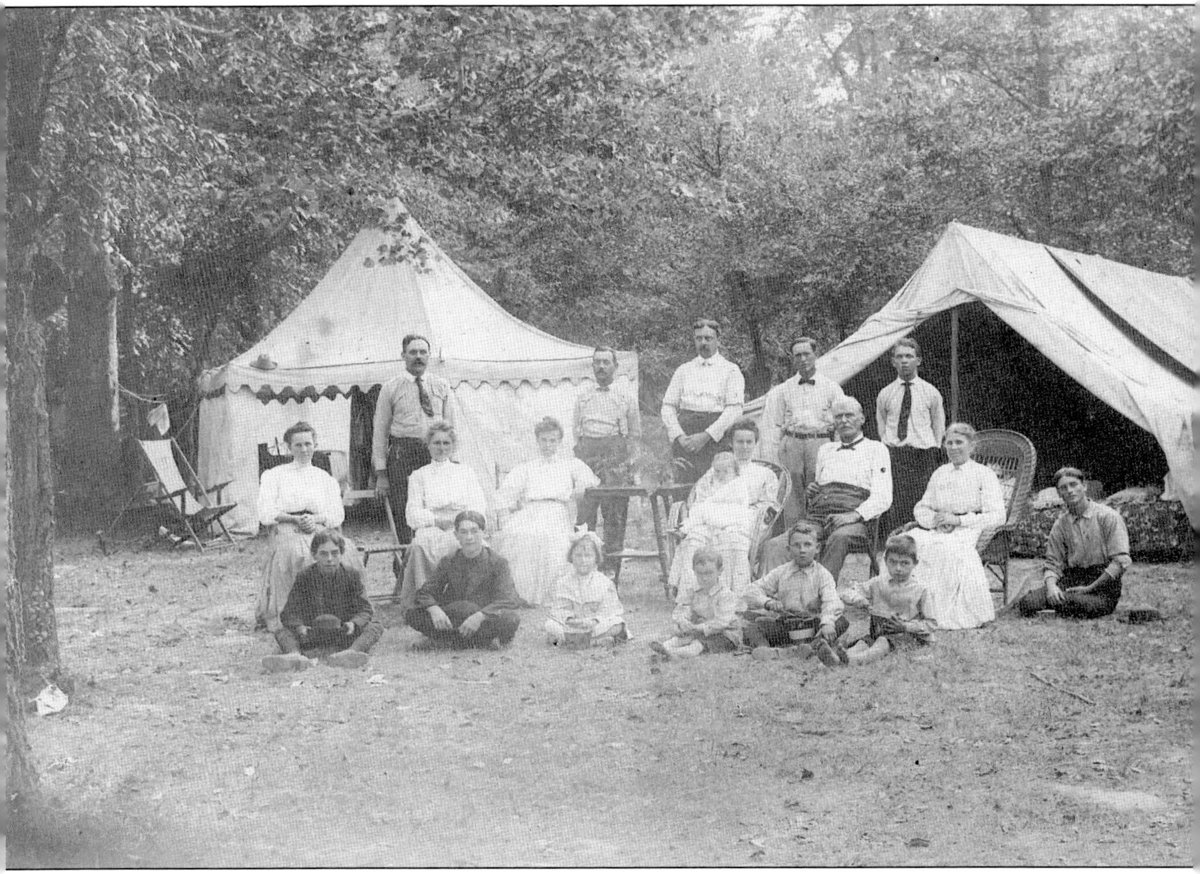

This picture is a camping party at Trinity Springs, Indiana. In the party is Mr. and Mrs. Pete Fillion of Bedford, and Mr. and Mrs. Hubert Ferguson of Williams, Indiana. This photo was taken *c.* 1900. Mr. Fillion was an early mayor of Bedford.

Lottie Hitchcock is seen *c.* 1885. She was married to Mancel Hitchcock. Their son, Ben Hitchcock, was a businessman and farmer in Bedford in the early 1900s.

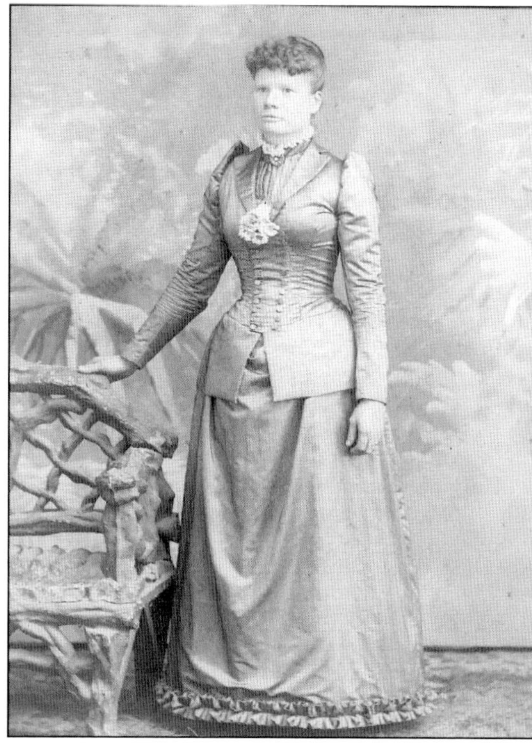

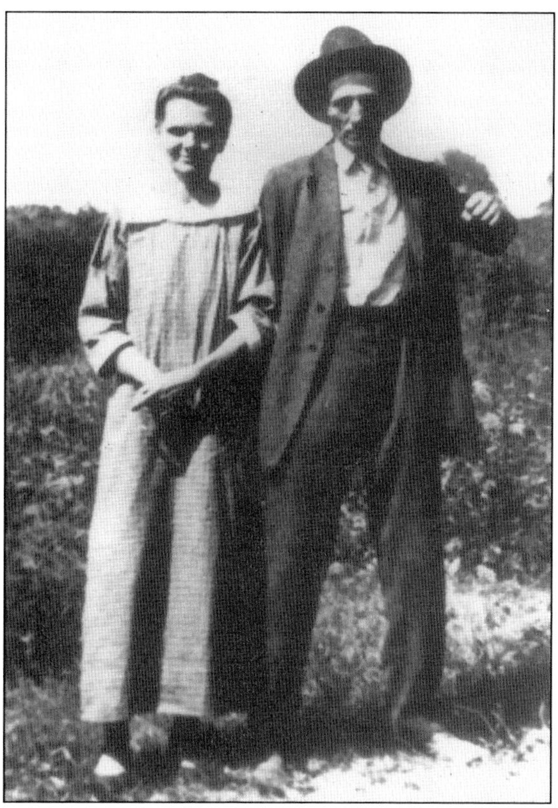

Daniel and Minnie Kinworthy Baker are pictured here *c.* 1917. Daniel worked for Miles Standish, and raised mules to sell to the army and the coal mines. He would drive the mules to Seymour, Dugger, and Bloomfield for shipment.

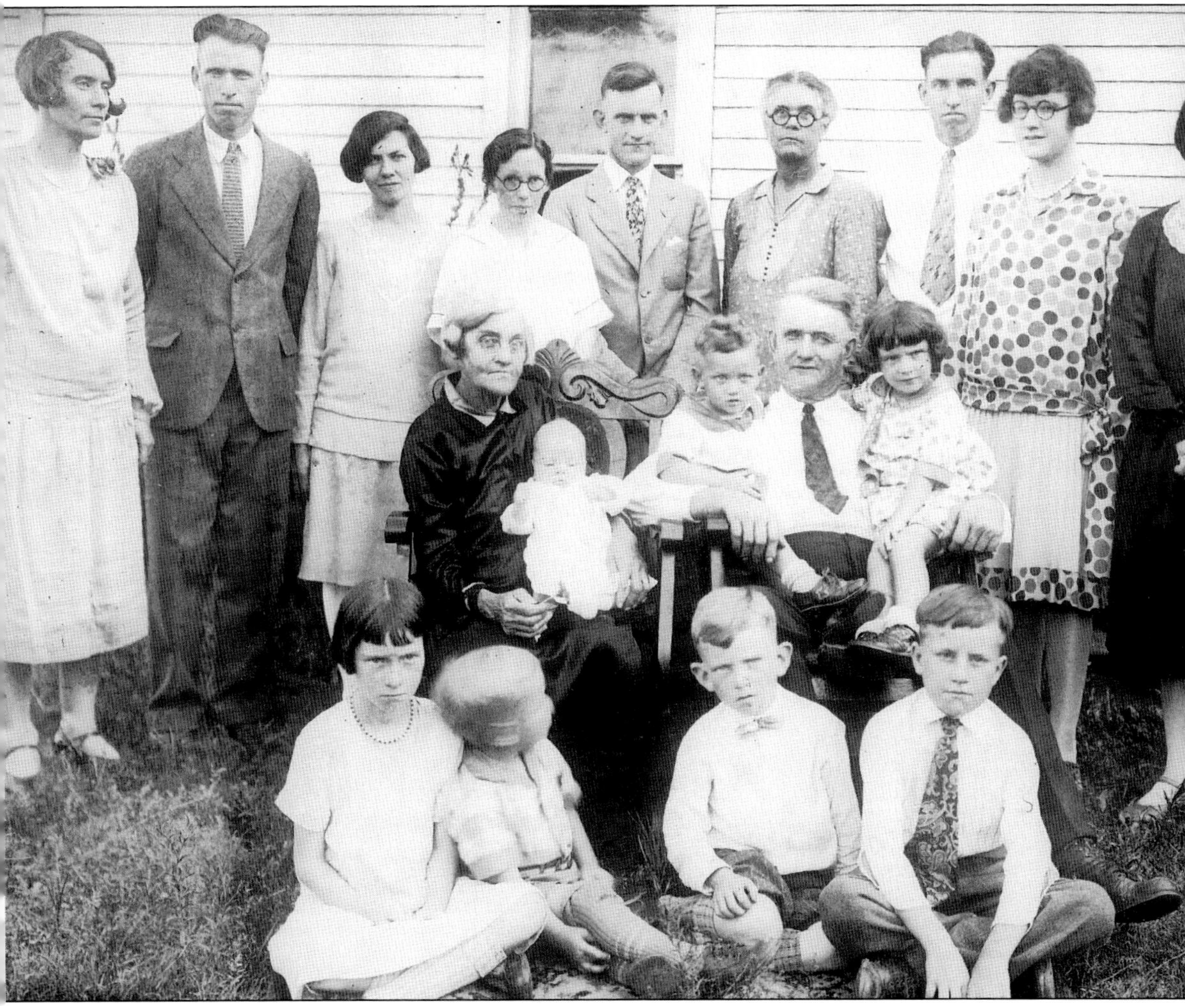

.In 1928, the Hester and Frank Crane family had this family portrait taken. This picture includes all their children and some of their grandchildren. It was taken beside their home in Tunnelton, Indiana.

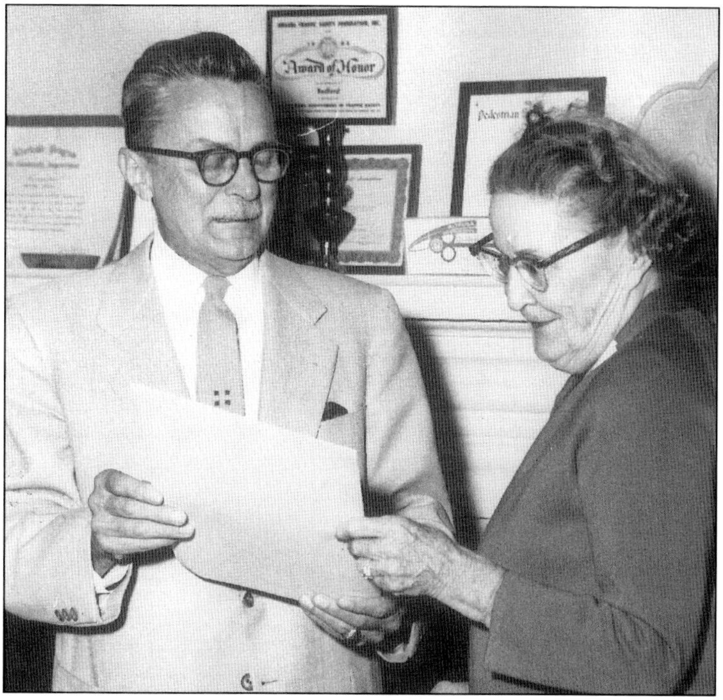

This picture was taken in 1969, and the gentleman is retired Gen. C.J. Hauck, who later became mayor of Bedford. He is issuing a proclamation to the local John Wallace Chapter of the NSDAR. The woman remains unknown.

William Murphy was an avid collector of Native American artifacts. In this picture he is showing members of the John Wallace NSDAR some of his prize pieces. Mr. Murphy lived on a farm south of White River near Mitchell, Indiana.

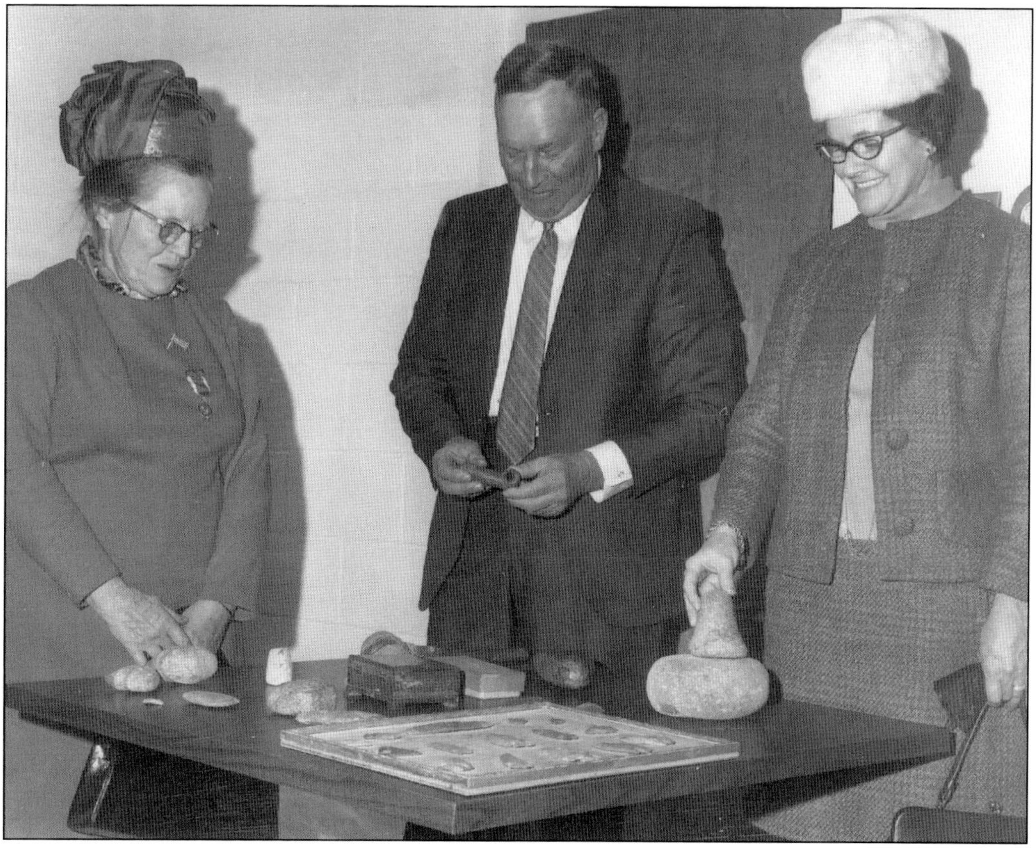

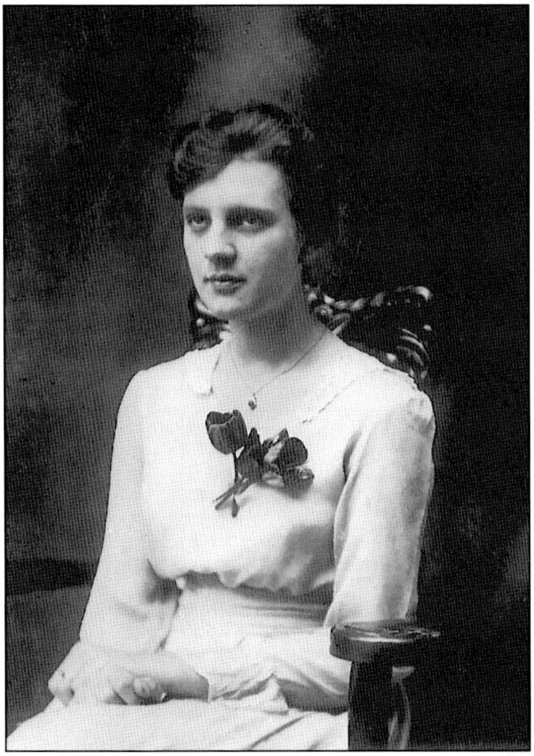

This is a photo of Lena Short of Fayetteville, taken *c.* 1928. It is not known the occasion for the roses pinned to the dress.

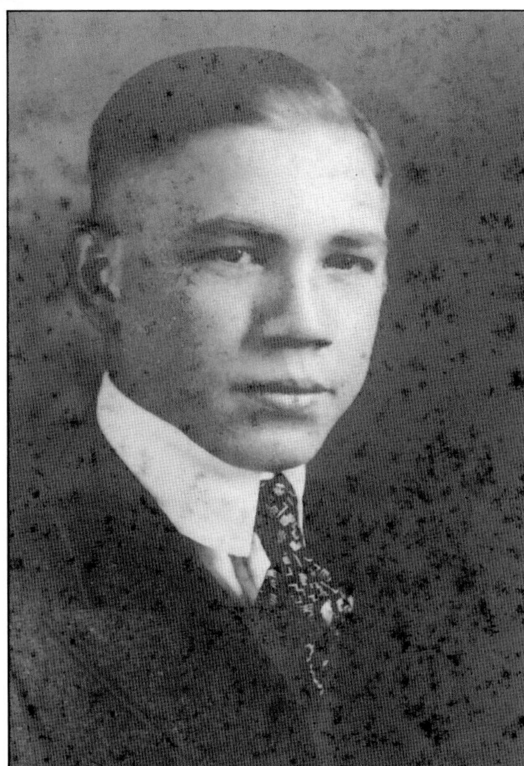

Pictured here is young Sam Hitchcock of Bedford, taken *c.* 1930.

This picture of Hobson and Inez Rosenbaum Crane was taken in 1925. The baby is their son, just a few months old.

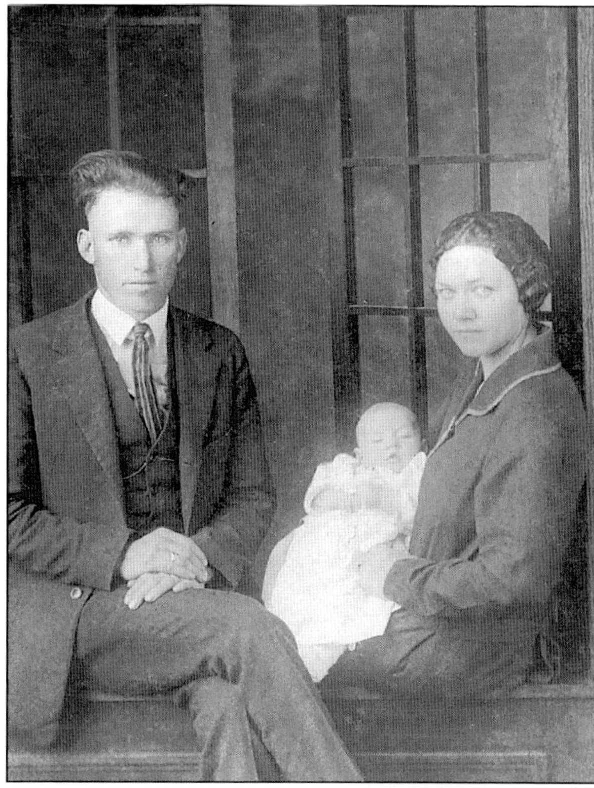

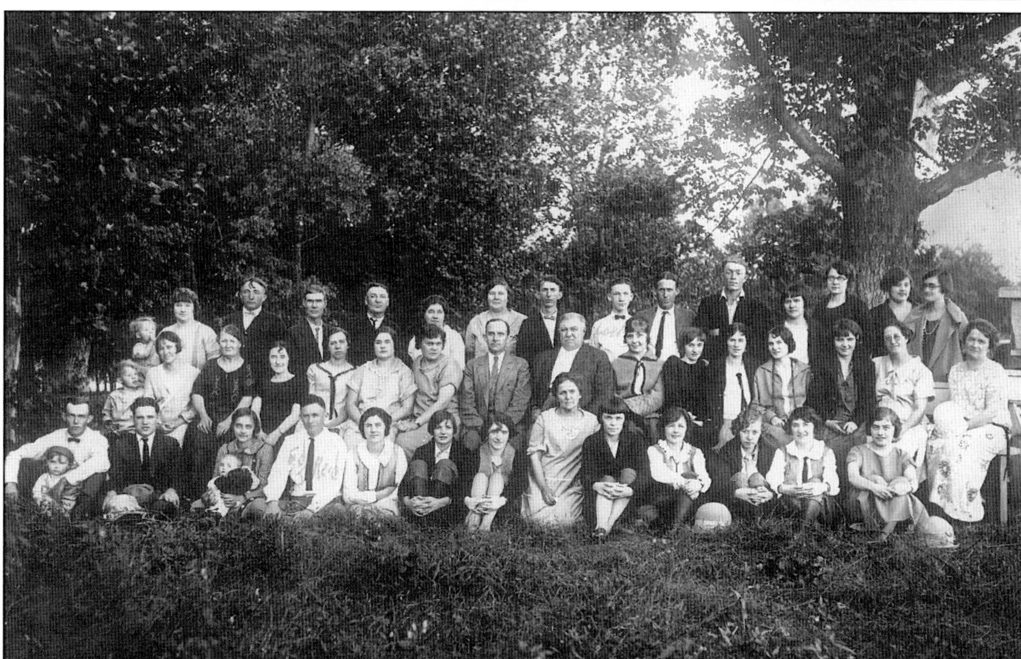

This picture was taken at a picnic for the Bell Telephone Company employees and their families. It was taken in the 1940s.

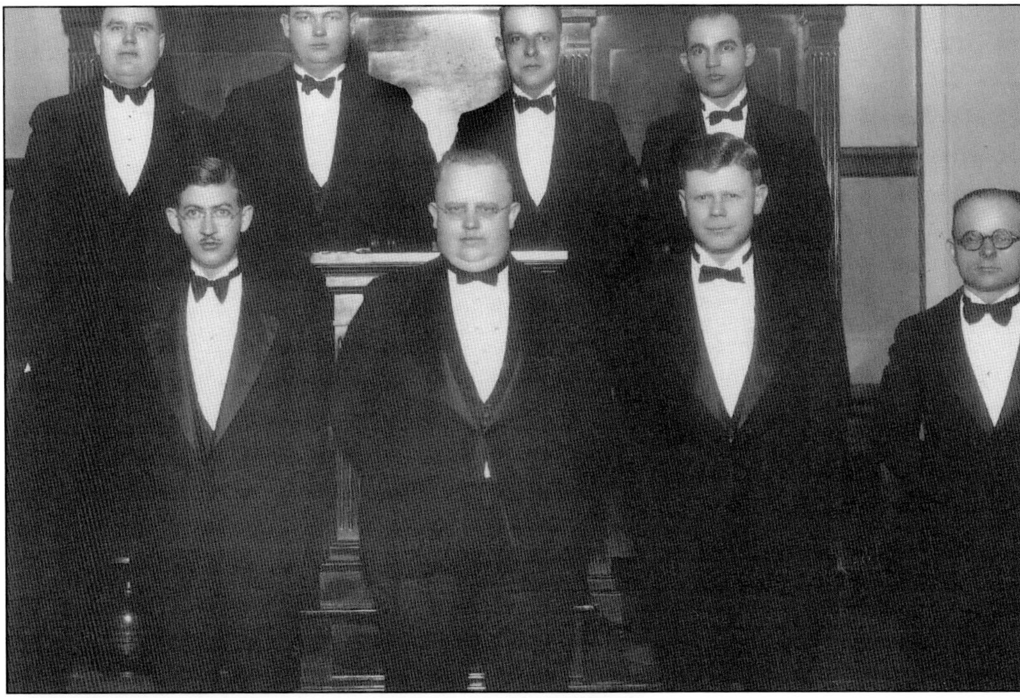

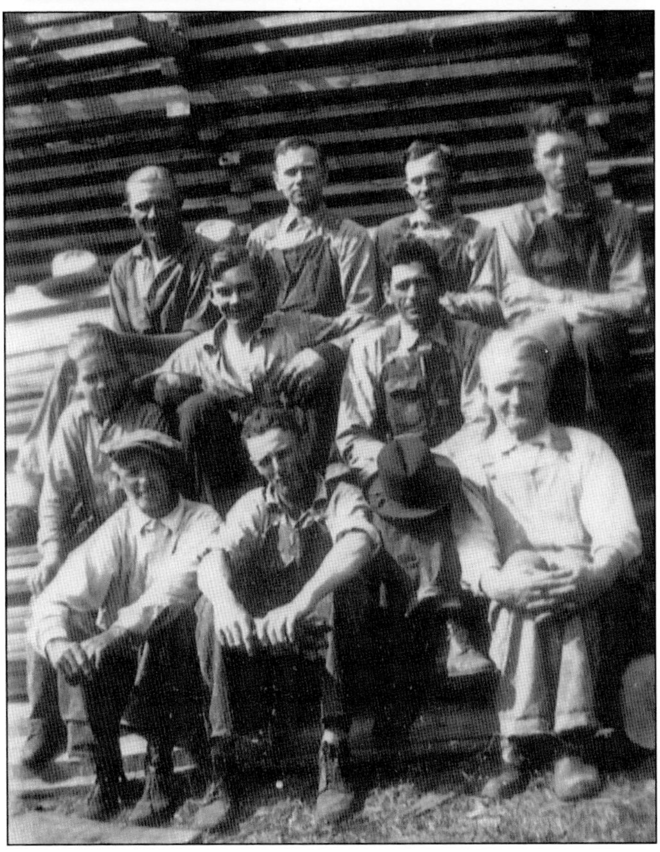

Shown here is an early Elks Lodge Degree Team. Front row, left to right, are: Rhea Houston, Bright Hanner, Eddie Johnson, George Bair, and Rudy Deering. Back row: Walter J. Long, John Donovan, Chic Wood, and George Wallner.

A group of Tunnelton residents stop their work for a moment to have their pictures taken during the late 1920s.

Ezra Allen was an early superintendent of the schools in the early half of the 1900s.

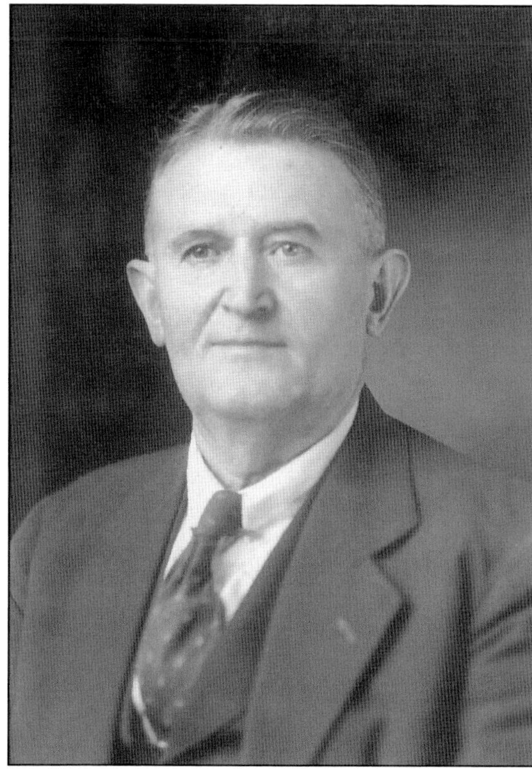

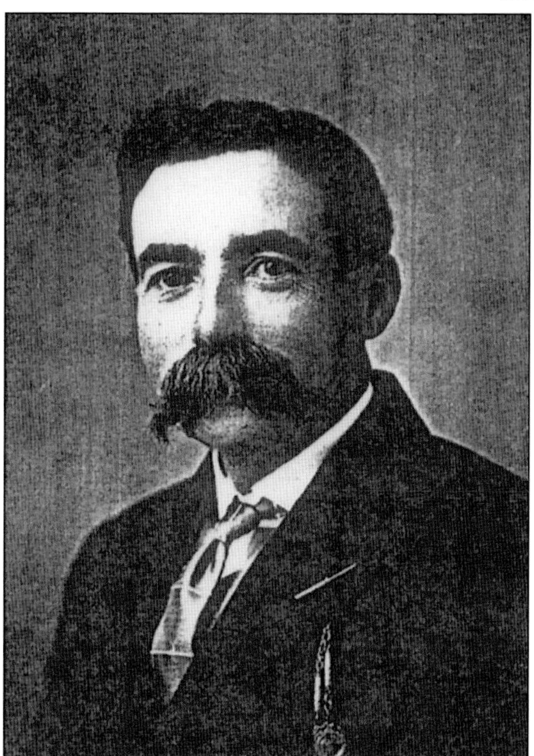

Grant Wright was a photographer in Tunnelton and had his studio in the Victorian style home, which had once belonged to Asher Wilcox. He took photos in the 1930s.

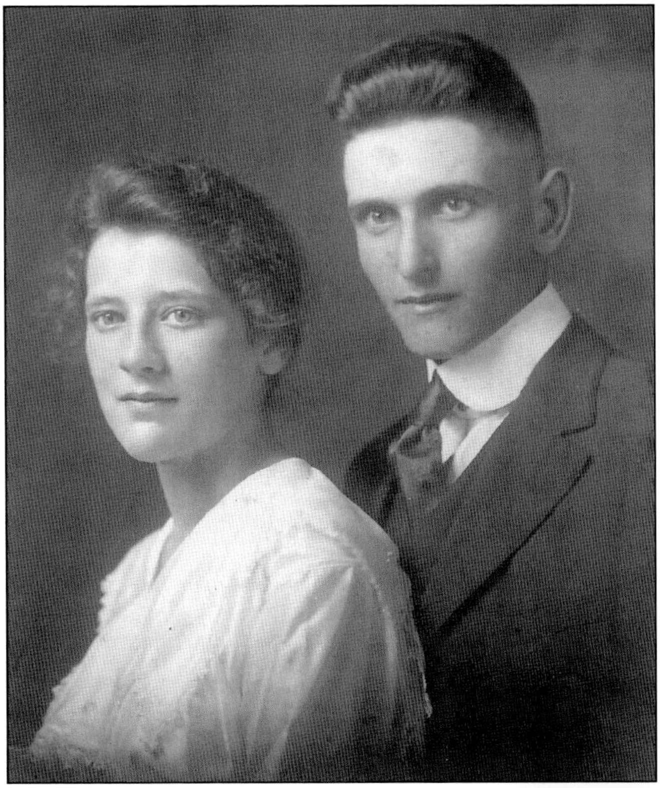

Gilbert and Ruth McPike lived in rural Lawrence County. This photo was taken about 1928.

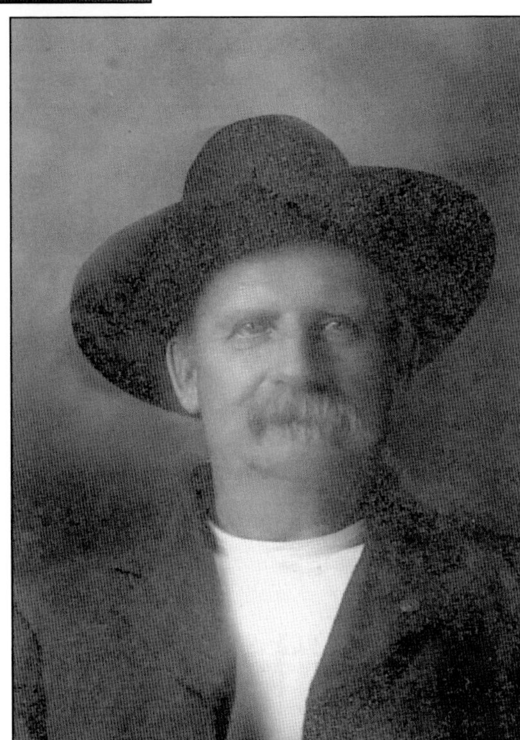

This is a picture of Jacob L. Faubion. He was a descendant of one of Lawrence County's pioneer families who came to Indiana in 1828.

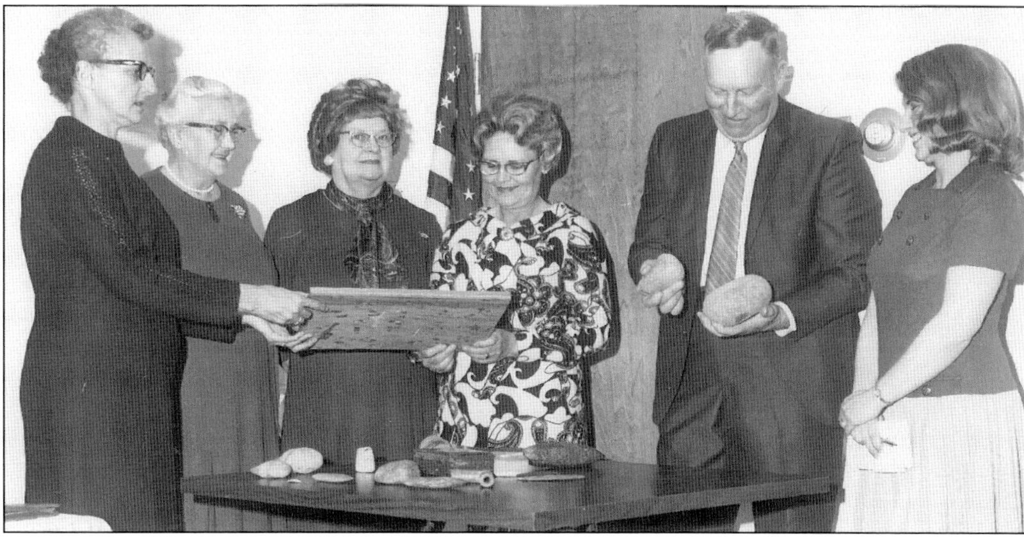

Bill Murphy of Mitchell is seen here telling the John Wallace Chapter NSDAR about the various Native-American artifacts that he found on his farm south of White River.

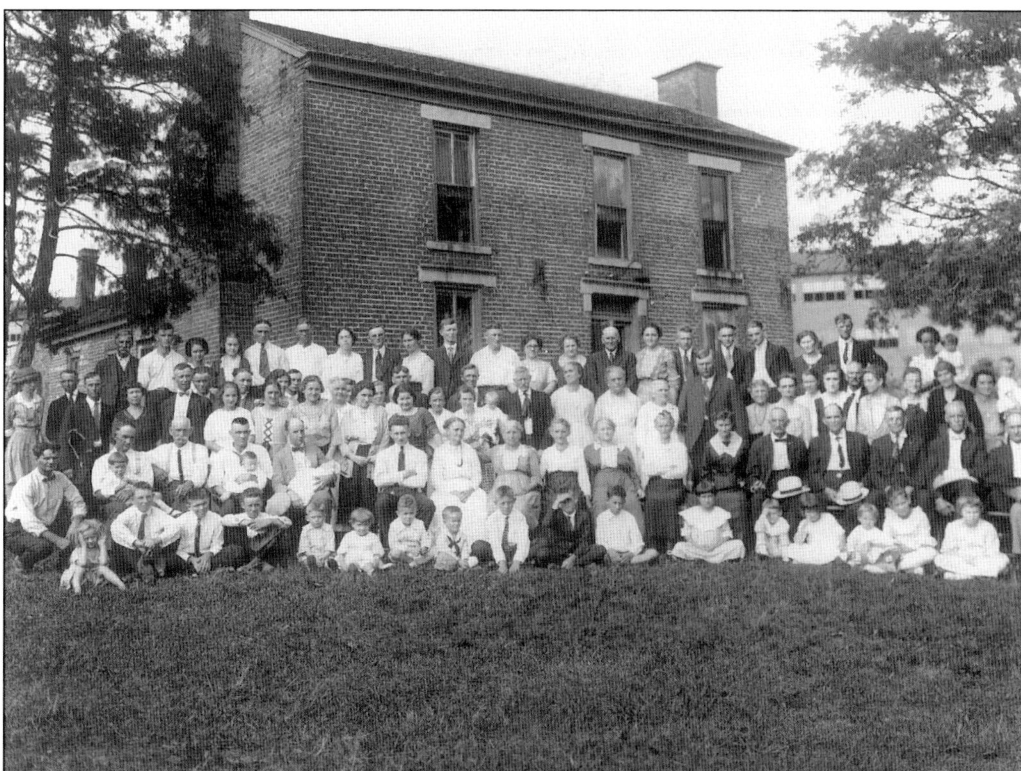

This group attended the George Hays Reunion in Oolitic, Indiana, in 1921. Notice the huge brick house in the background; it is no longer standing.

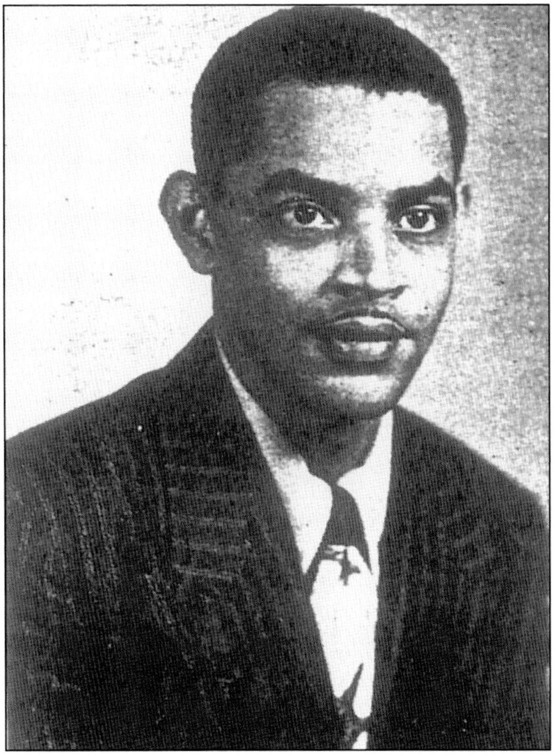

"Bobby" Brooks, as he was commonly known, traveled with Earl "Father" Hines' dance band playing theaters, ballrooms, and nightclubs. He later joined the Louis Armstrong band and traveled in 42 states.

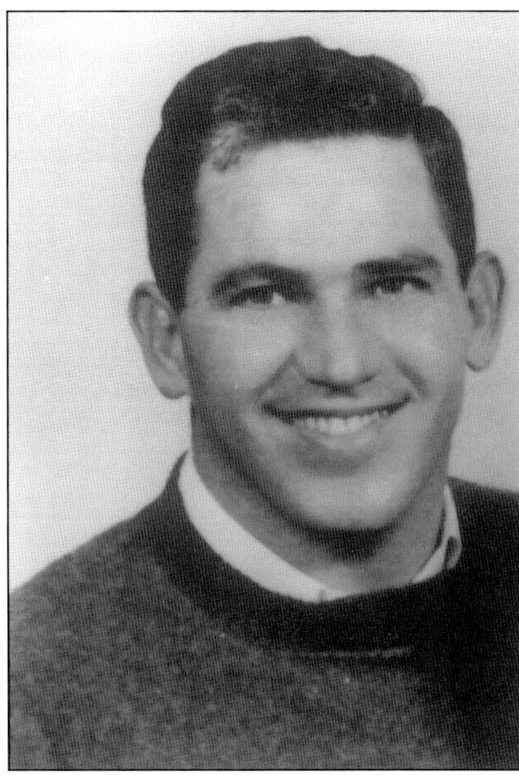

This is a photo of William "Bill" Franklin Crane who lived in the town of Avoca. He met an untimely death in an automobile accident in 1961, at the age of 29.

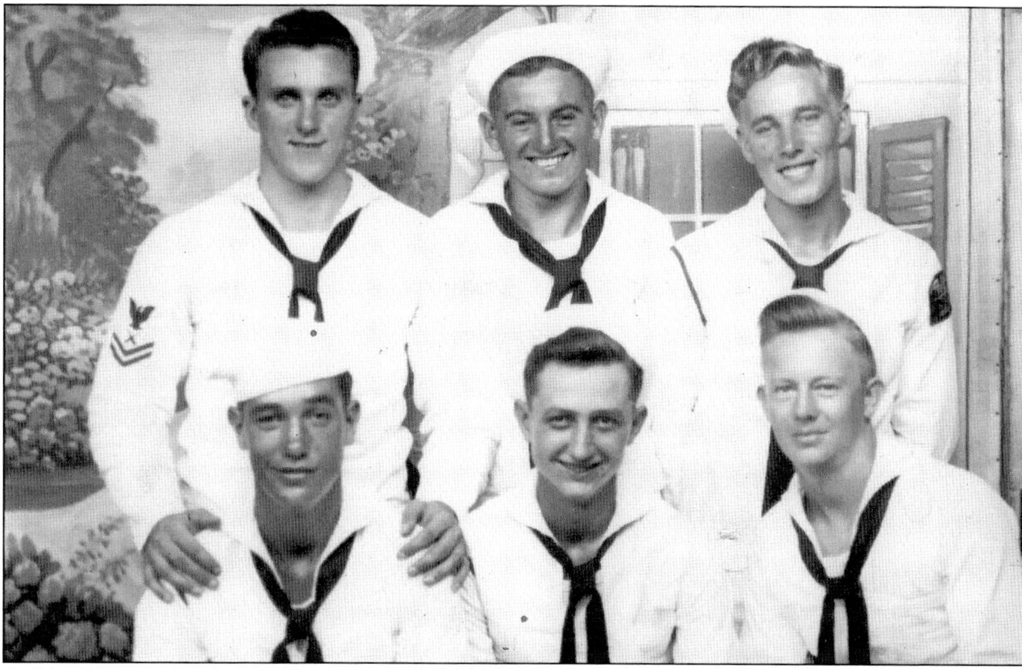

Bedford native Paul Terrell is pictured in the back row, far right. He served in the navy during World War II, and shown here with some of his buddies.

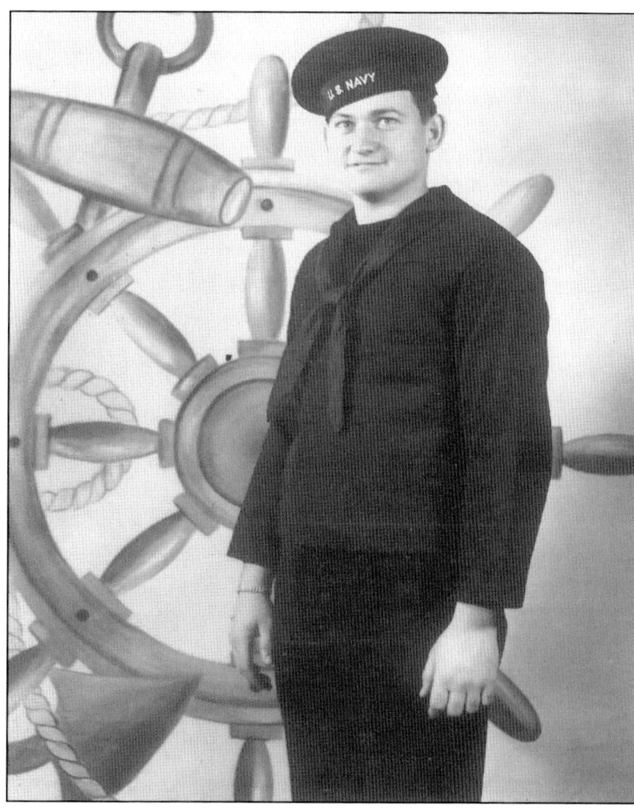

This is James Marvin Crane, a short time after joining the navy in 1943. James lived in Tunnelton, but later moved to Indianapolis.

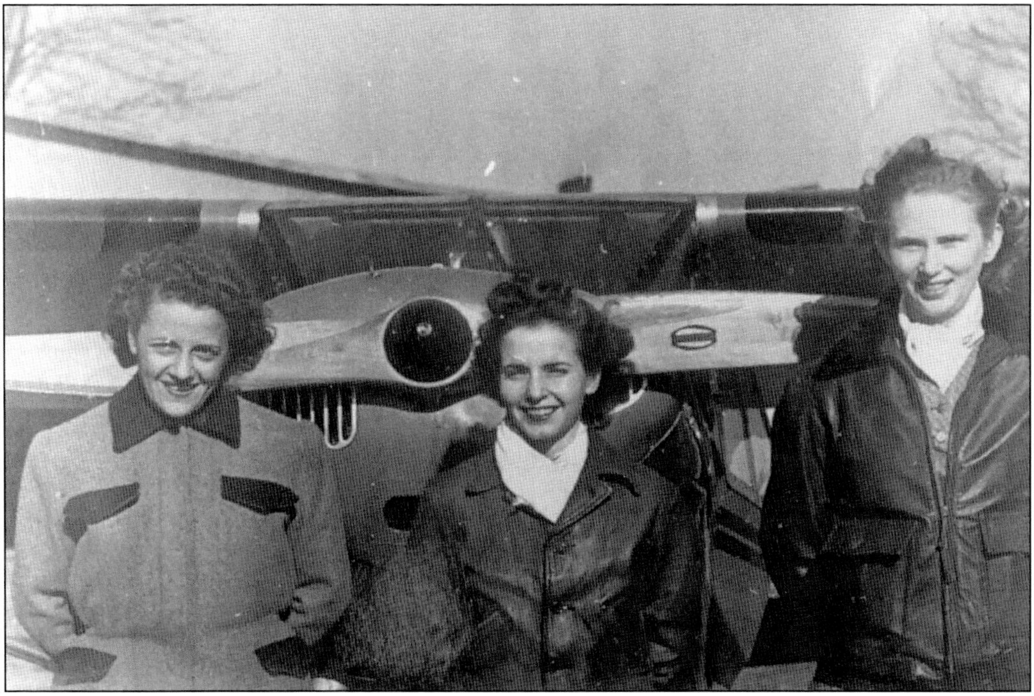

Pictured here, left to right, are Eva O'Brien, Jane Edwards Bieze, and Carrie Walls during World War II.

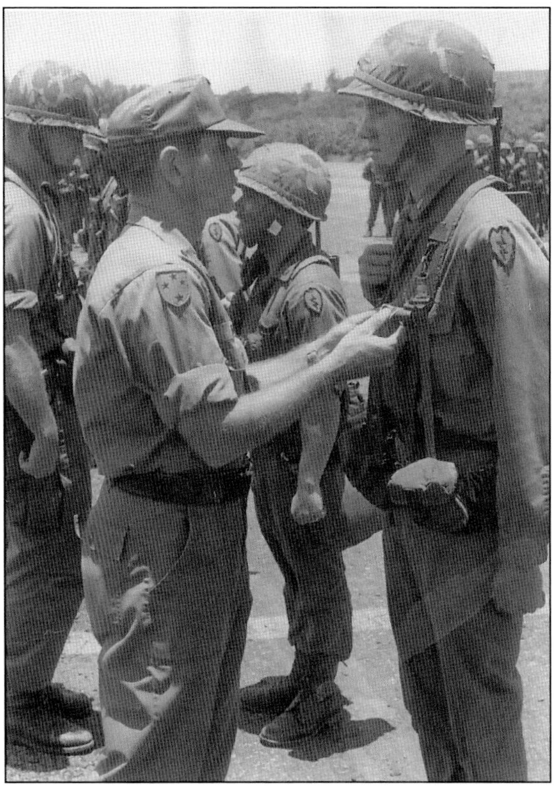

In 1980, SP4 Jan Kruse is shown here during an award ceremony. This photo was taken at Schofield Barracks, Hawaii. Kruse is a Lawrence County native.

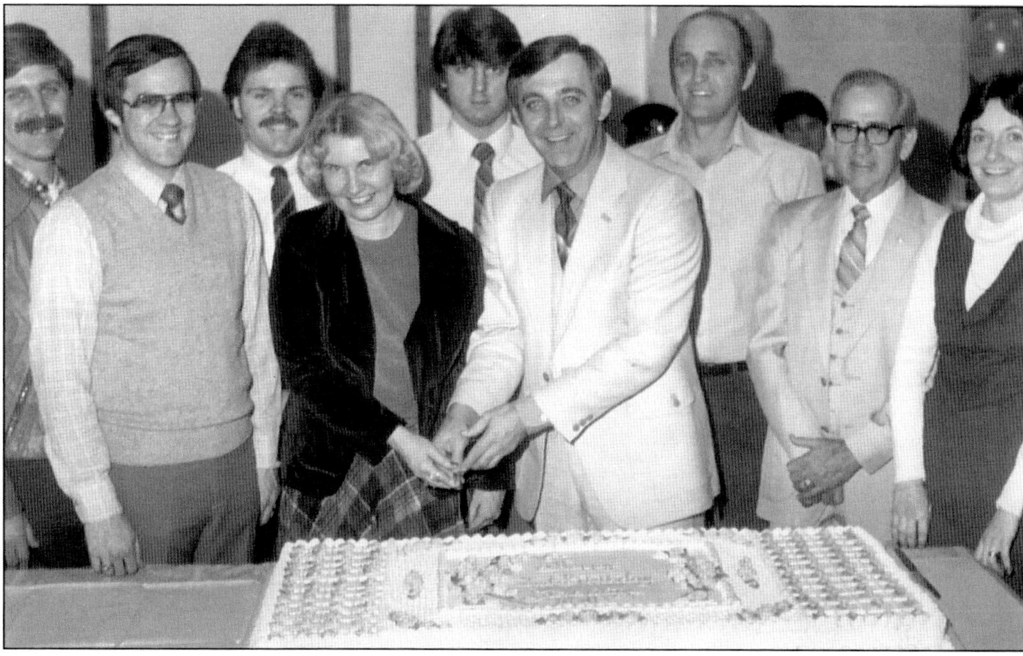

In 1980, the Stone City Mall celebrated a first anniversary. Shown here are managers of the various stores. John Williams, mayor of Bedford, is getting ready to cut the cake.

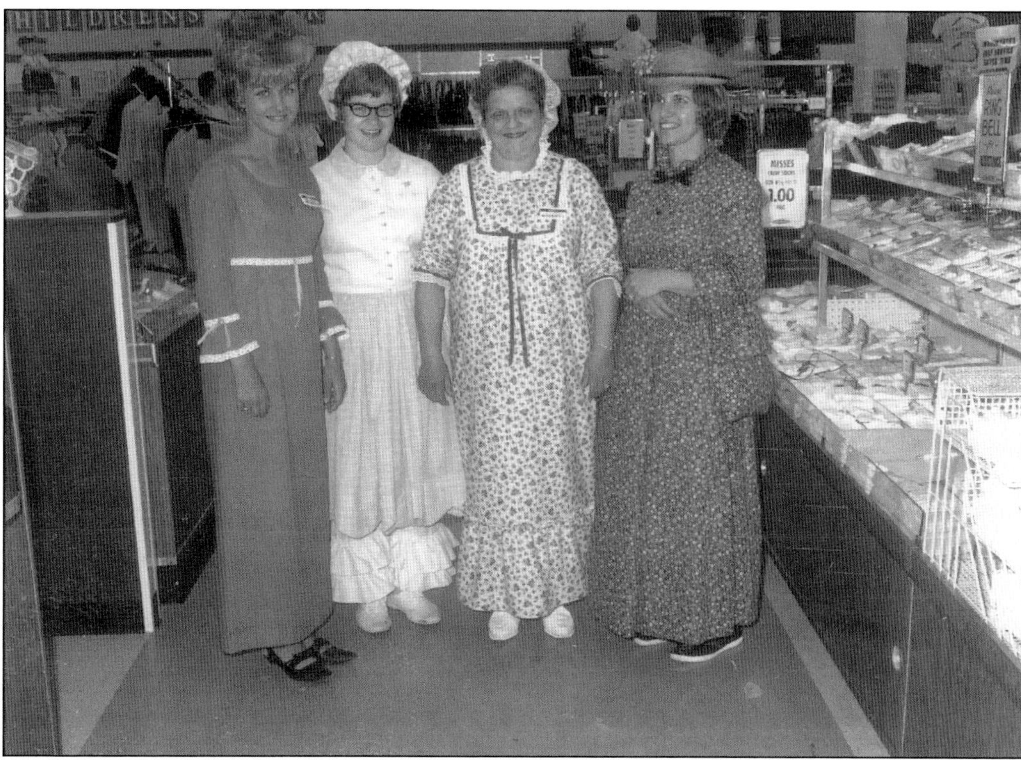

This group of girls worked at the local Woolworth Store. They are dressed for "Old Fashion Days" in July of 1966.

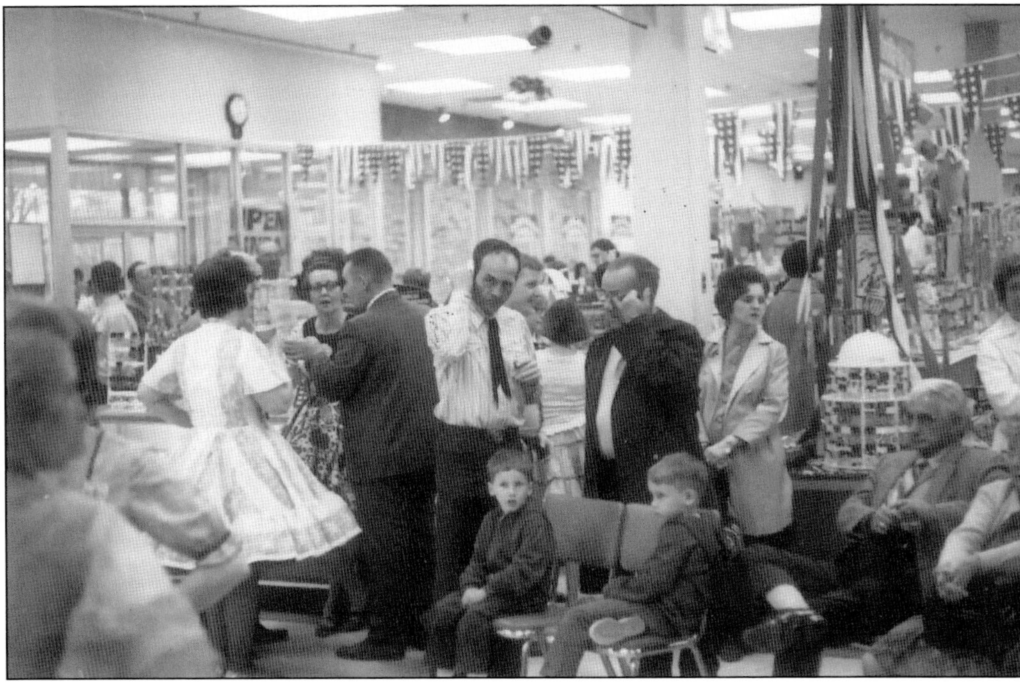

In 1972, W.T. Grant had a square dance inside the store. The local square dance club sponsored the event which brought several people to the retail store.

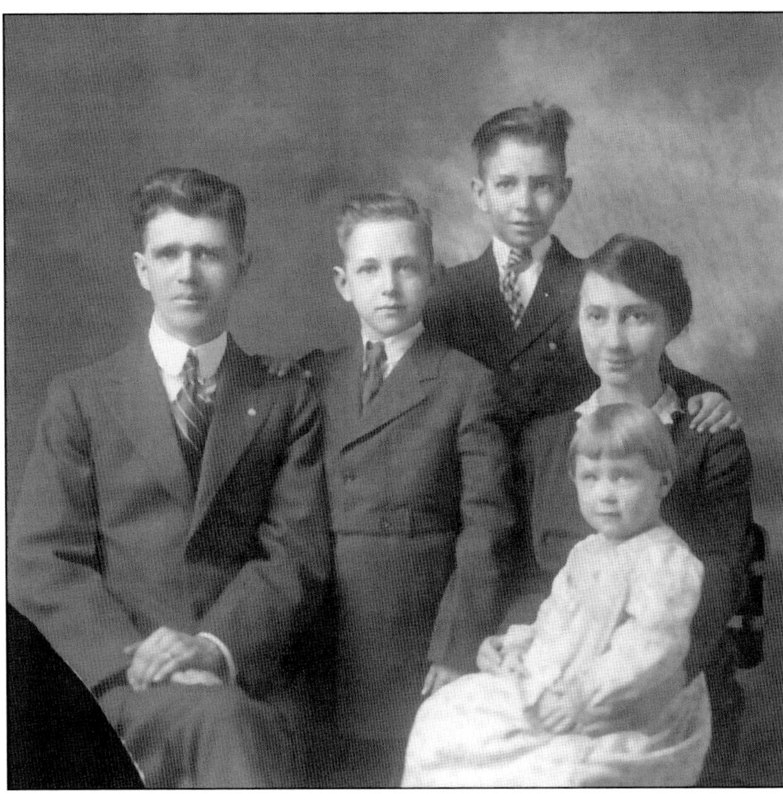

This is a picture of the Nelson Chambers family of Bedford. Mr. Chambers was the wire chief for the Central Union, an early telephone line company.

This is the graduation picture of Bonnie Rollins, daughter of Homer and Colleta Turner Rollins of Avoca. It was taken in 1952.

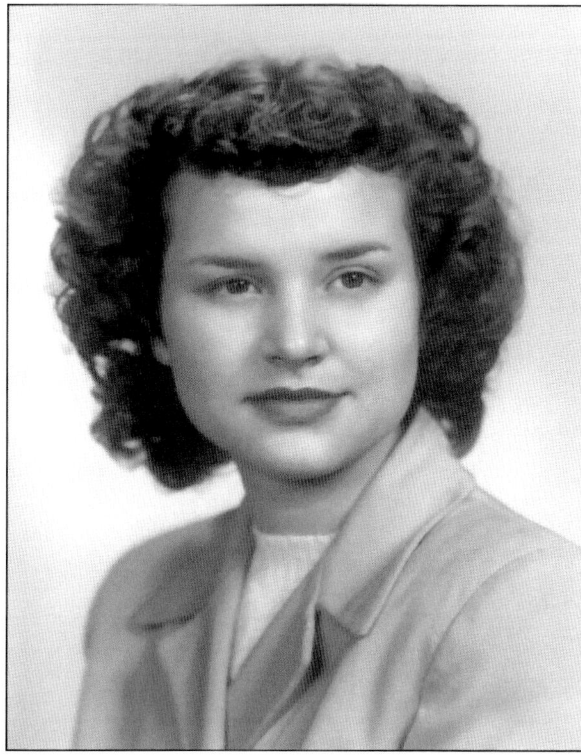

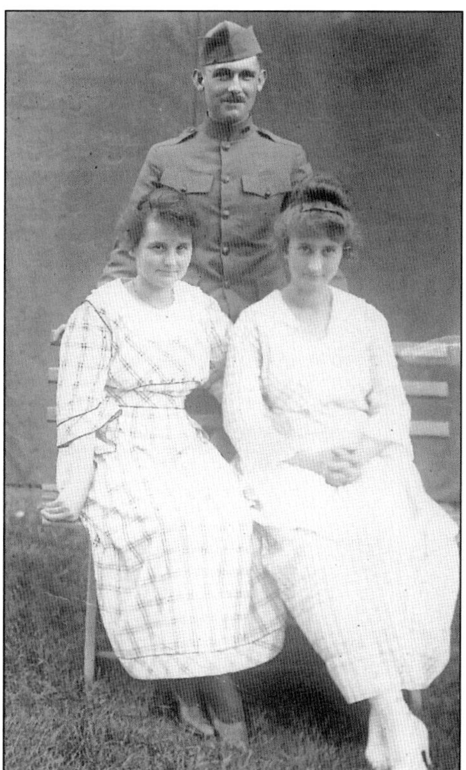

This is a picture of Ella Wright, the girlfriend of a World War I soldier who is not identified. Ella's brother, Grant Wright of Tunnelton, probably took this picture.

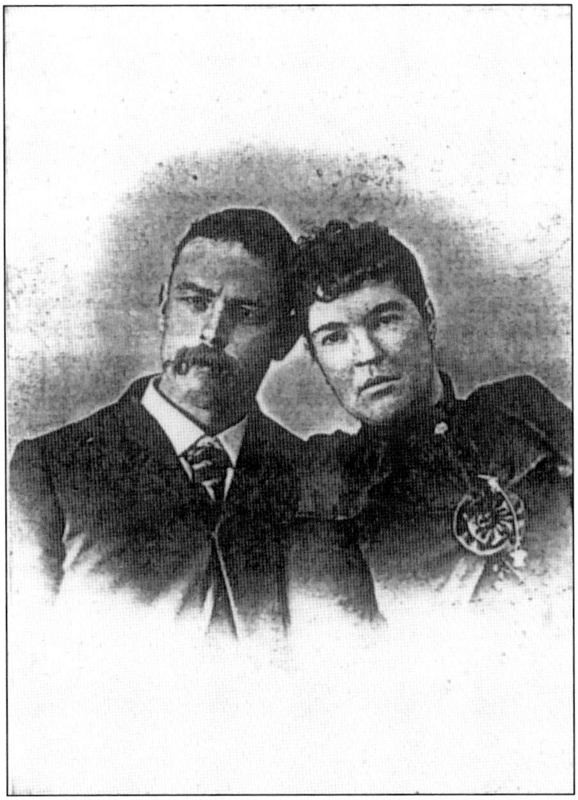

Elmer and Sarah Farris are seen here in this early photo taken at the turn of the century.

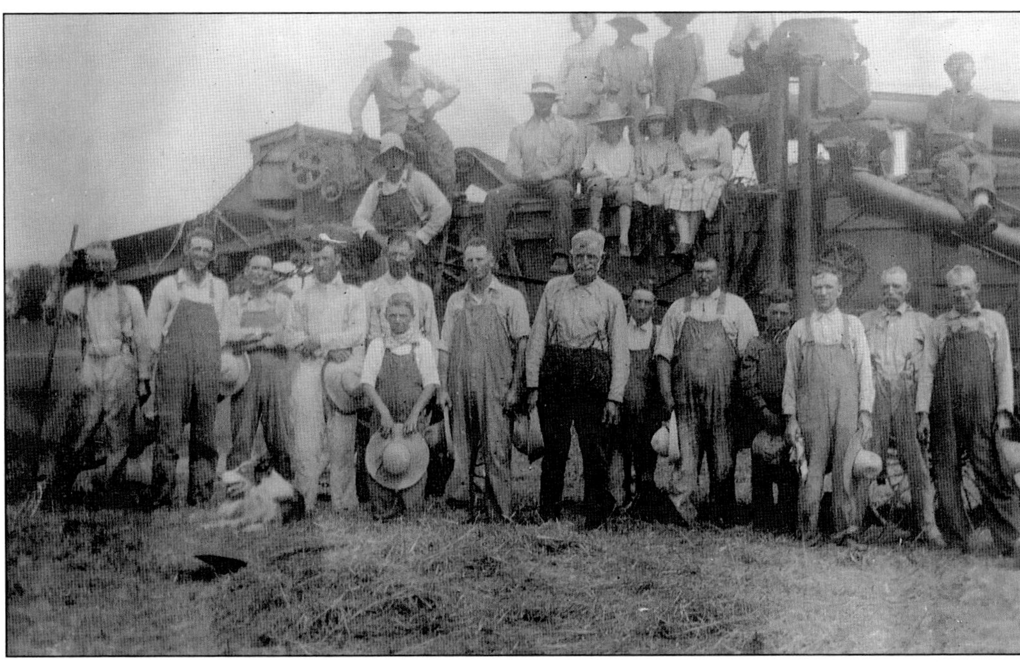

Here is a threshing crew posing to have a picture taken after the work is done. This photo was taken in the 1920s.

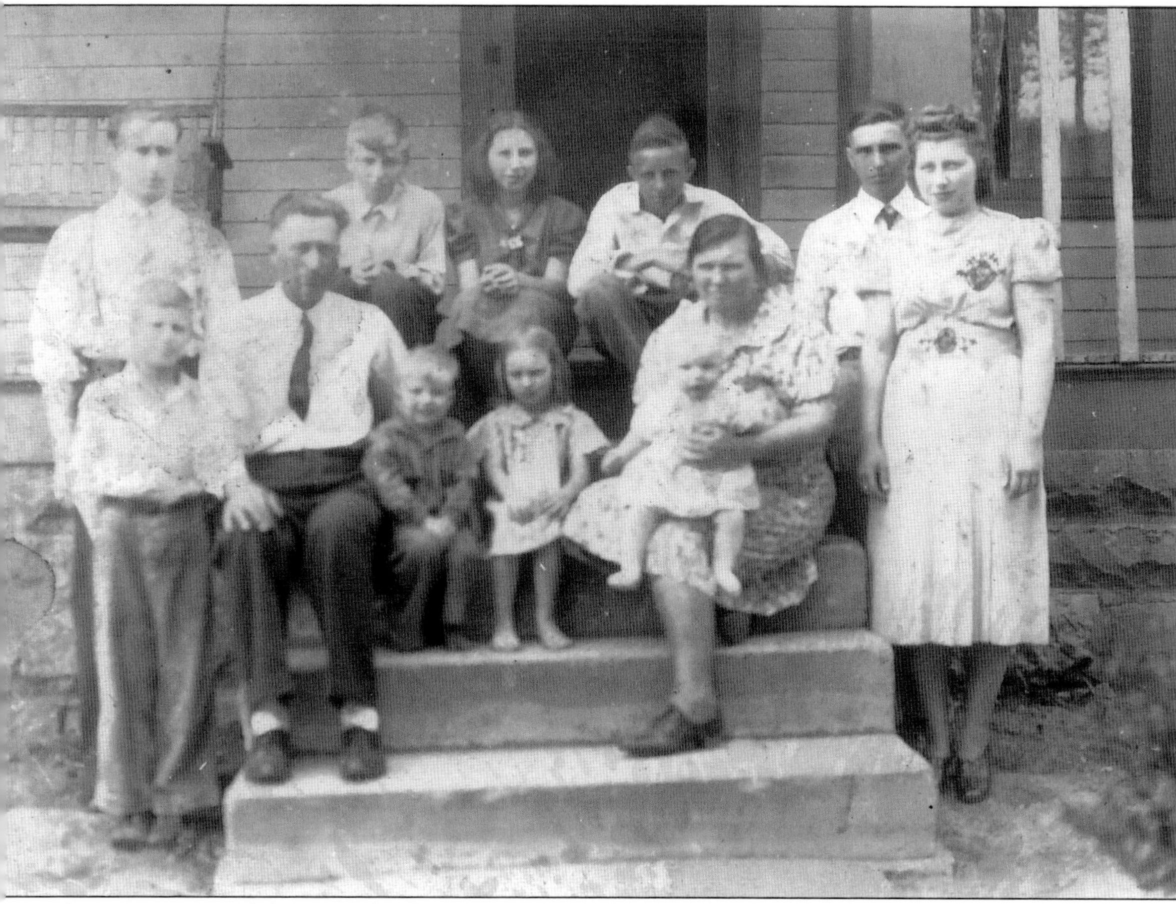

This is a picture of the Kern family in front of their home in Bedford. The earliest ancestor of the Kern family came to Lawrence County in the mid 1800s.

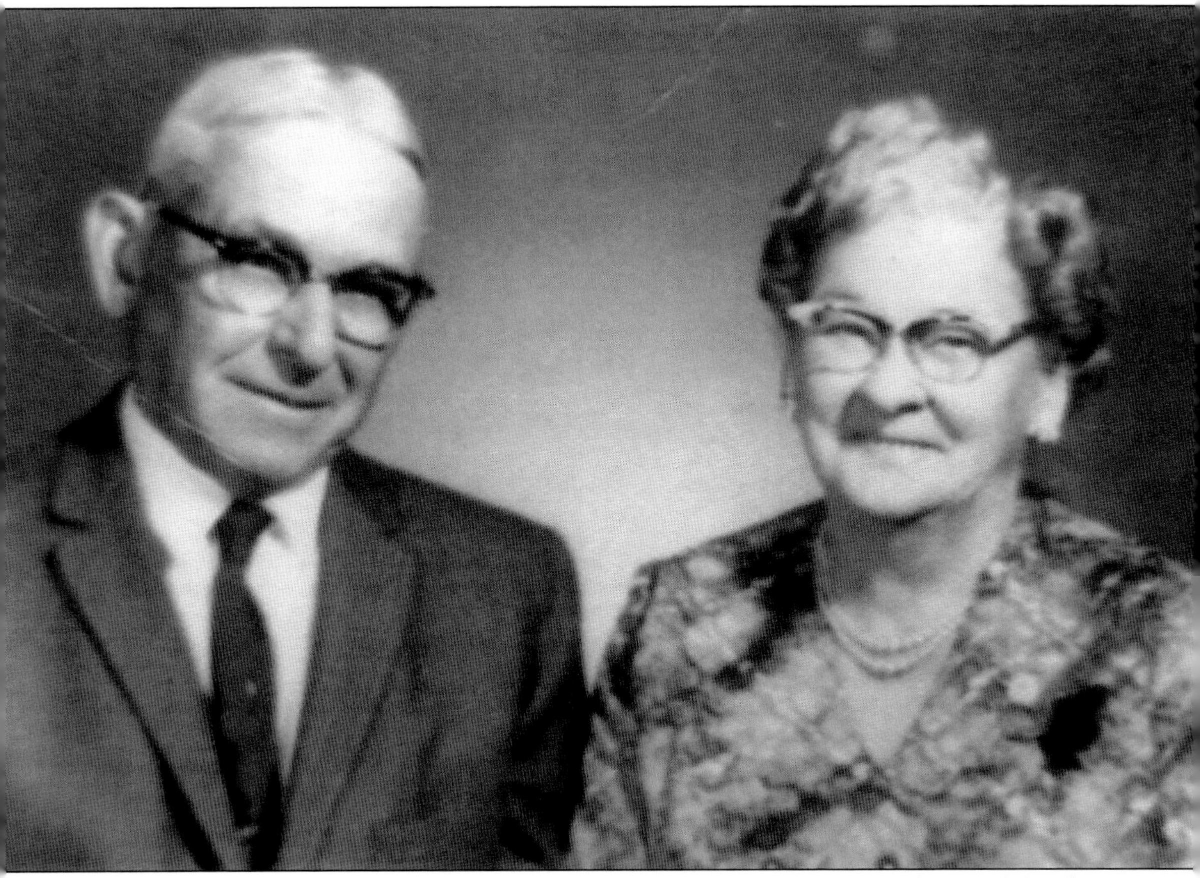

Maudie and Virgil Cecil are shown in this photograph taken in 1940. The Cecil family were members of the Methodist Church in Tunnelton.

Three

LIMESTONE INDUSTRIES AND BUSINESS

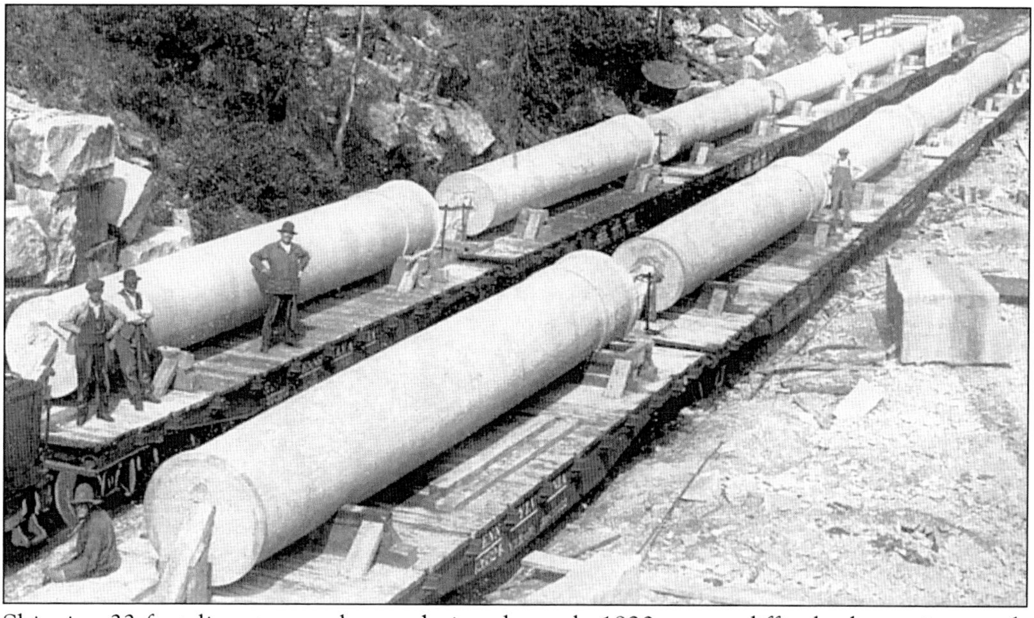

Shipping 33-foot limestone columns during the early 1920s was a difficult chore, since each column required one car. At that time, the market was in the east. The limestone industry was very healthy after the railroads came offering a means of shipping the stone.

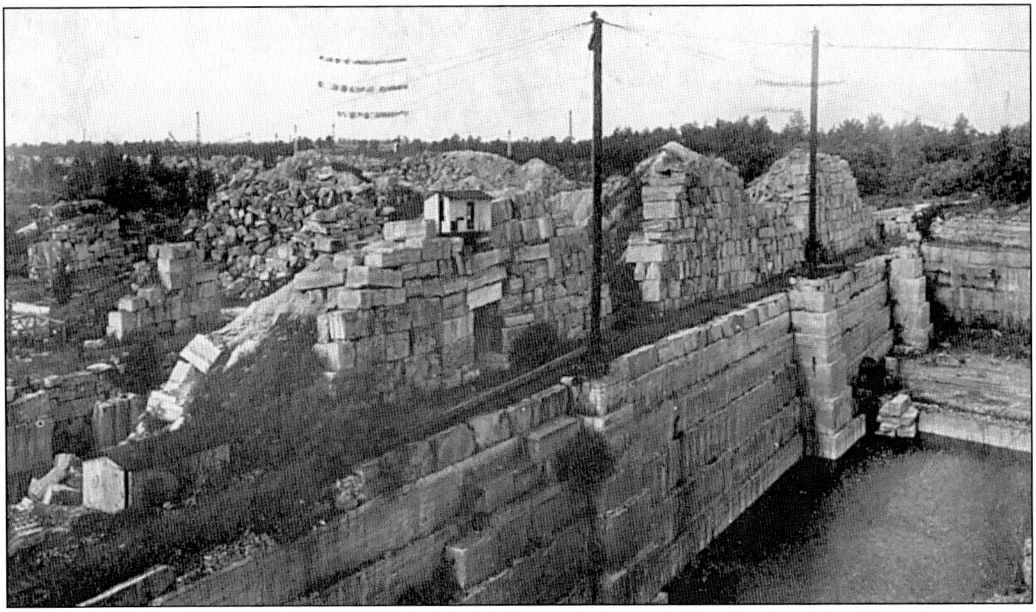

Quarries such as this are numerous throughout the "Heart of the Limestone Belt." This picture was taken during the 1920s

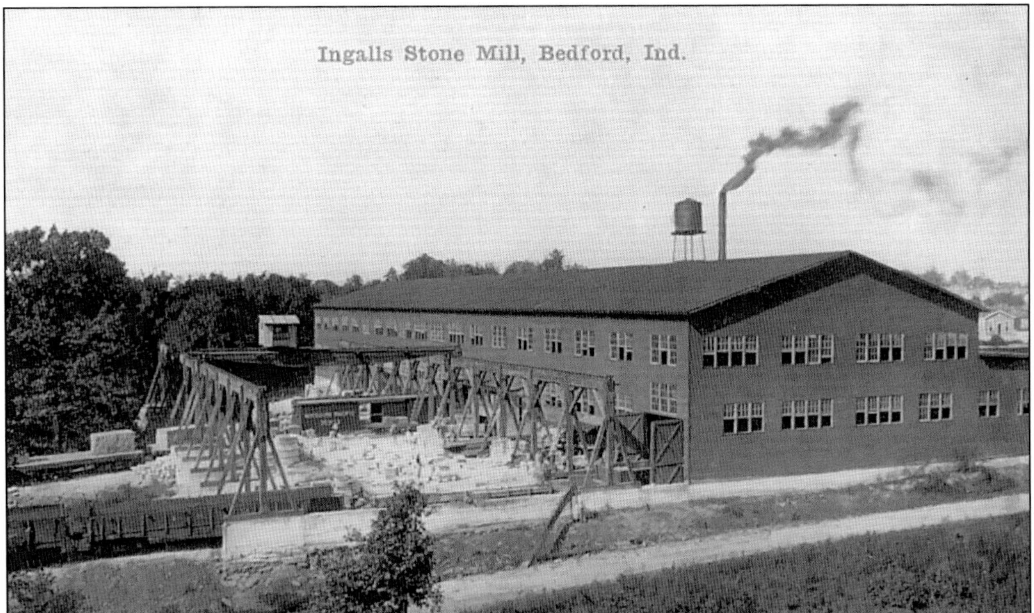

Pictured here is Ingalls Stone Mill as it looked during the 1920s.

These two photos show stone workers getting ready to turn a cut. First, they drill holes in the stone, fill the holes with black powder, and blast the cut. This quarry worker is driving spikes into the stone, getting ready to turn a cut. Black powder will be poured into the holes to break the bed of stone.

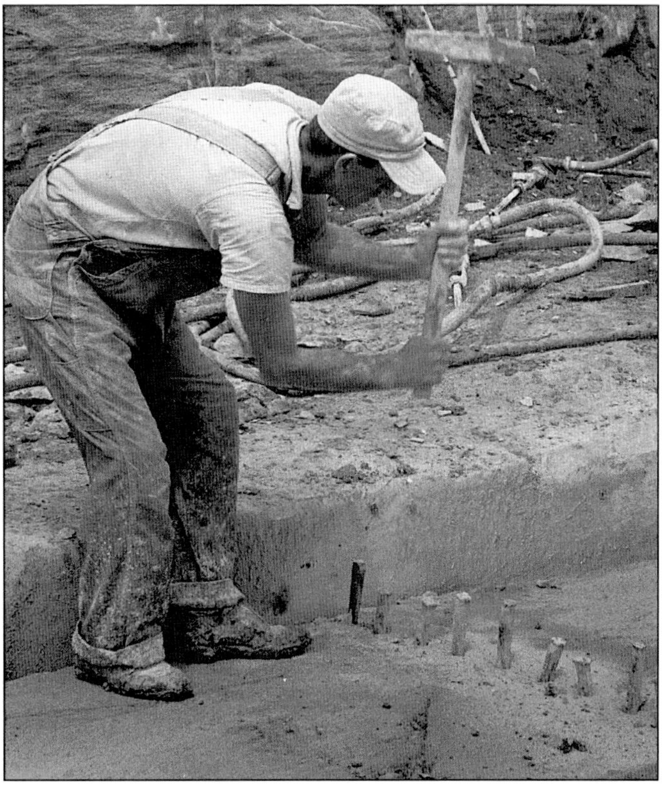

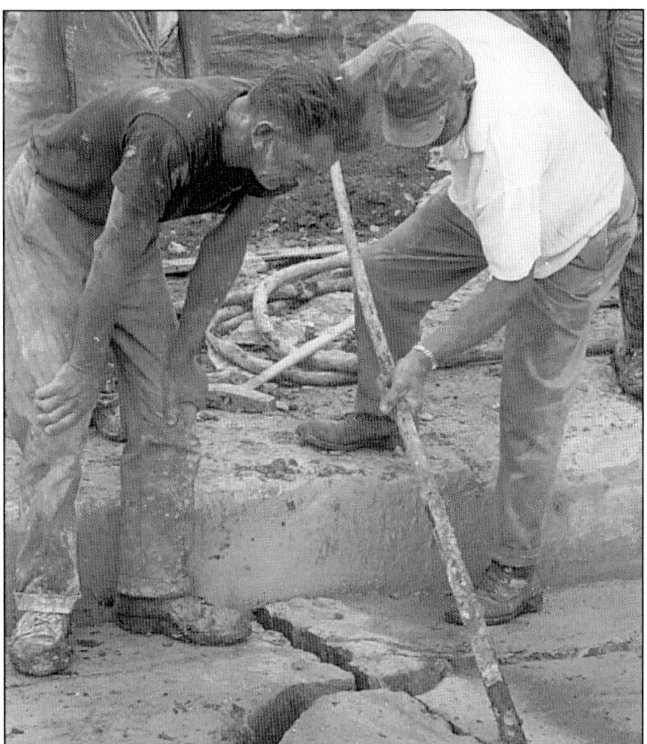

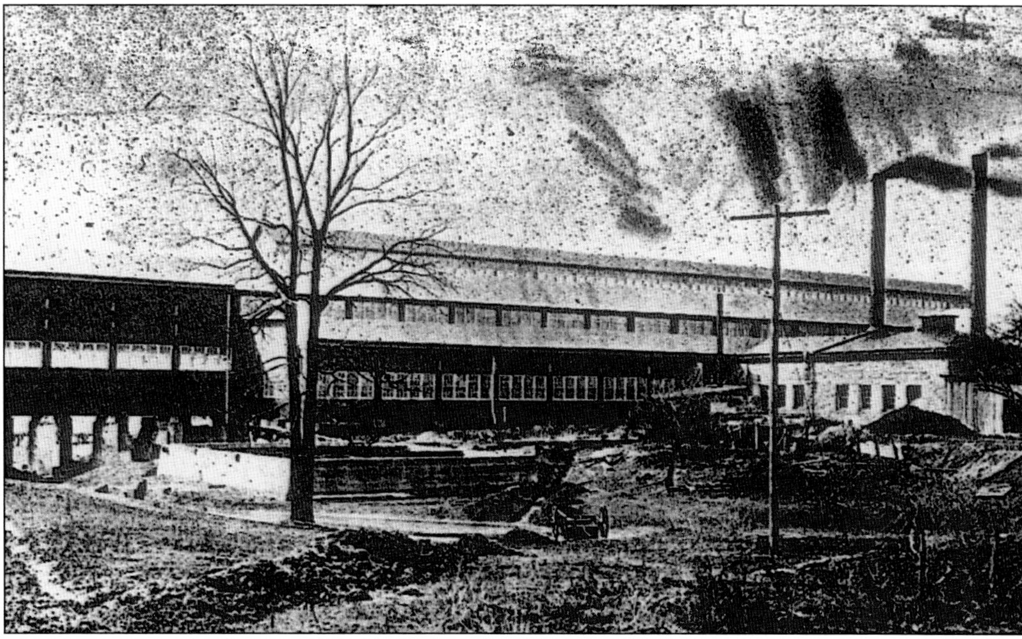

This is the Furst-Kerber Cut Stone Works of Bedford.

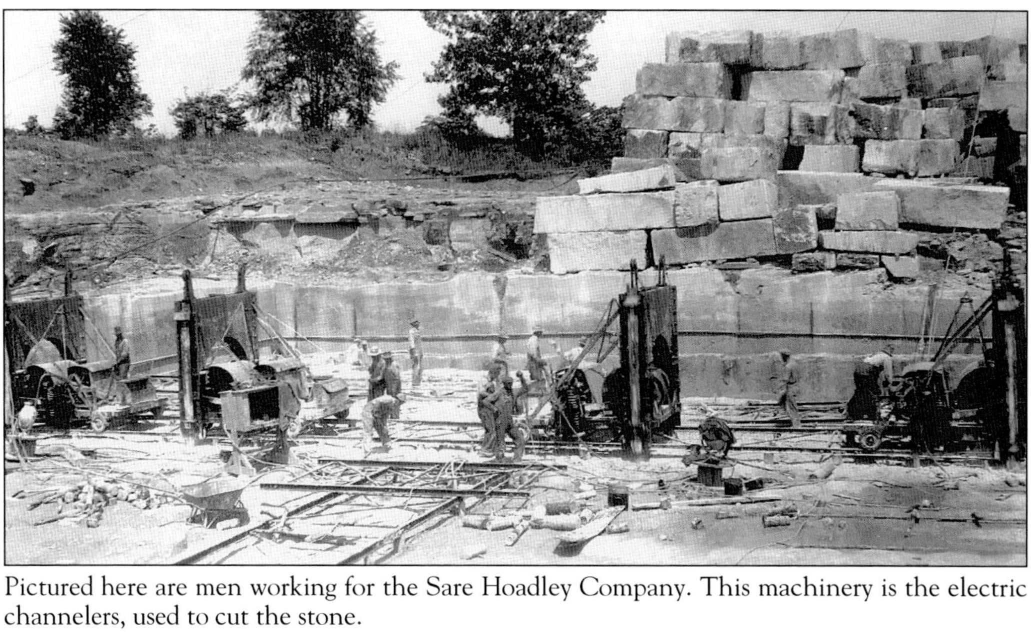

Pictured here are men working for the Sare Hoadley Company. This machinery is the electric channelers, used to cut the stone.

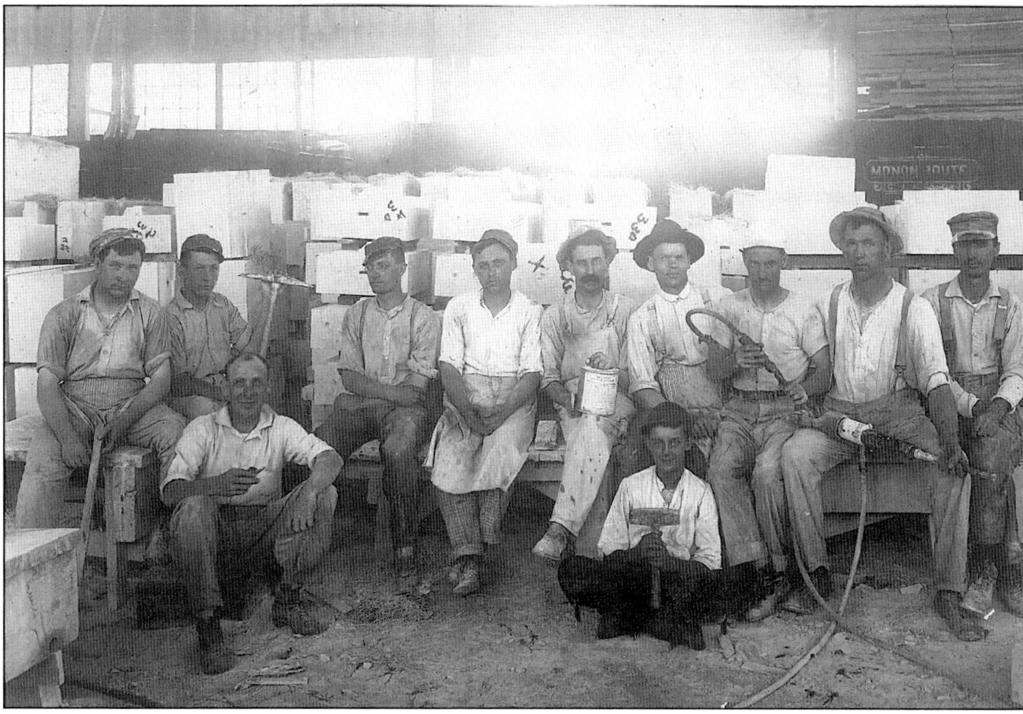

These stone workers are preparing to ship a load of stone on the Monon Route. It is not known where the stone is going.

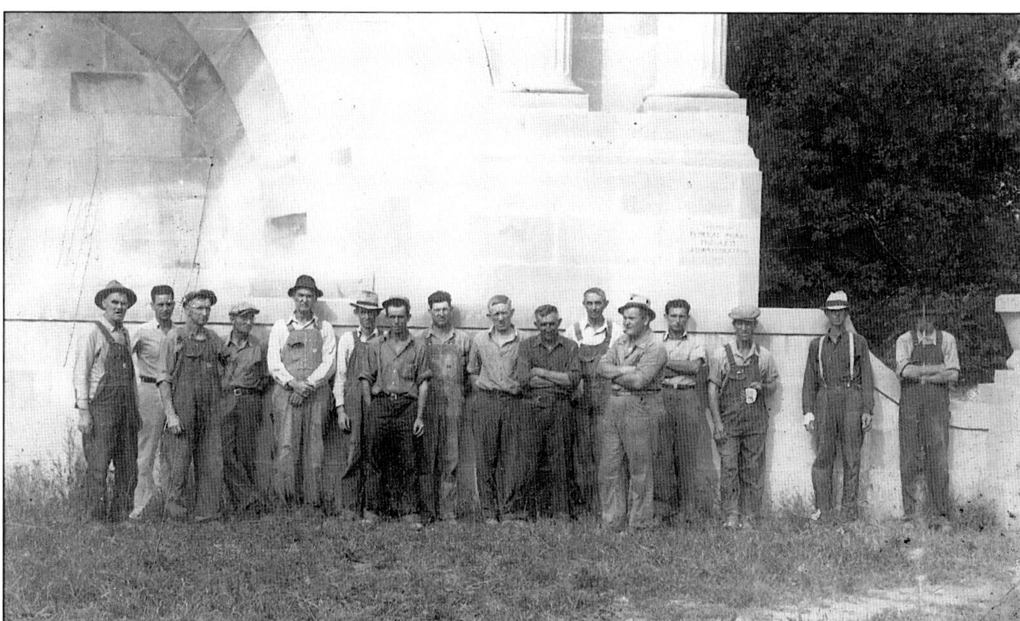

During the Great Depression, this WPA crew worked on the Otis Park Band Shell.

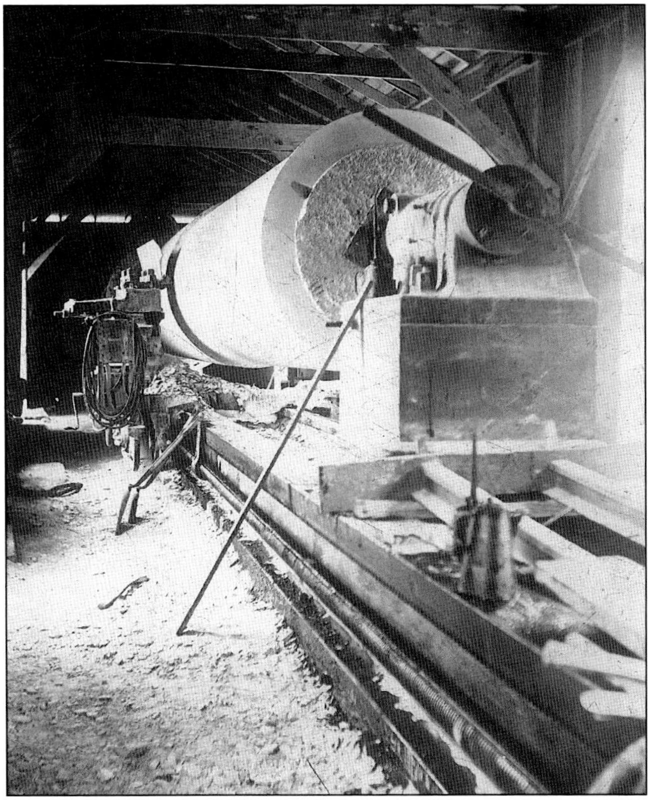

This photo was taken inside one of the mills, *c.* 1920. It shows the process of making columns.

After the columns are turned they are ready to be shipped, once the order is completed. This picture shows them outside the mill.

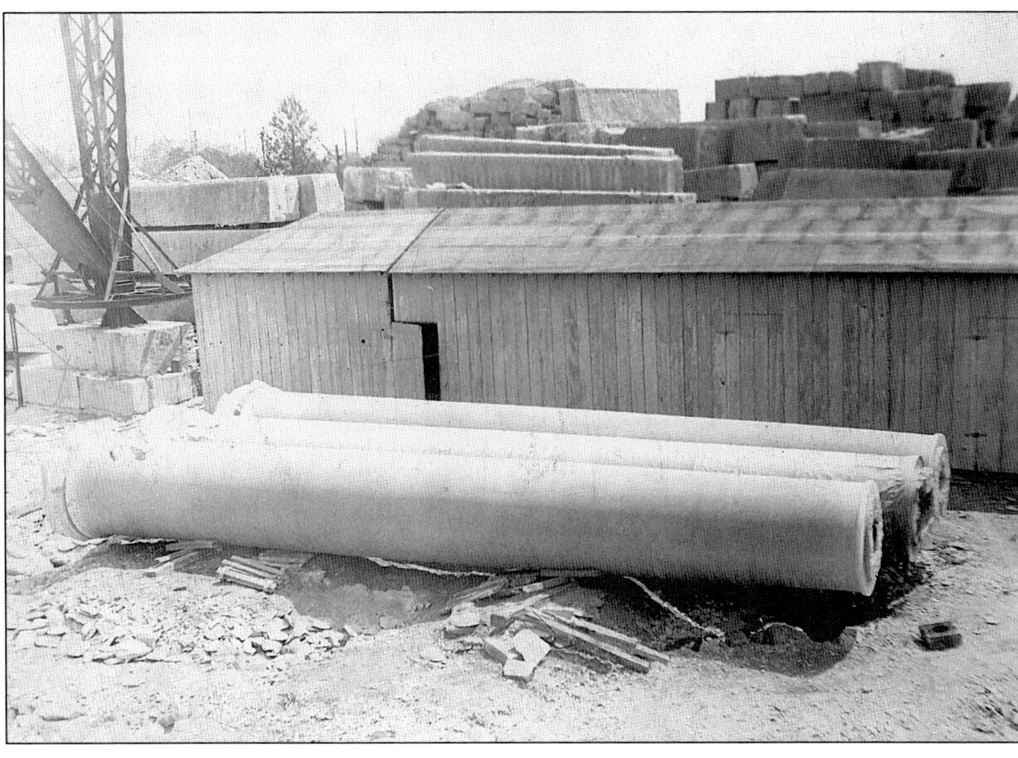

These natural stone steps lead to the PM&B Quarry. Notice the railroad track running near the quarry.

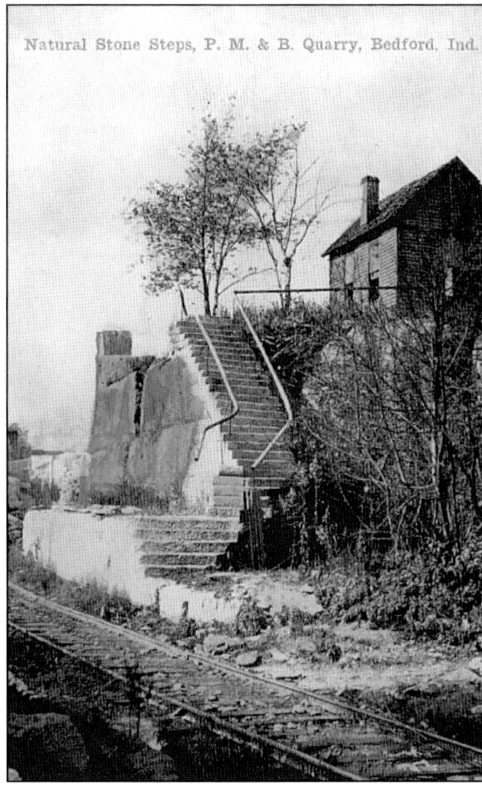

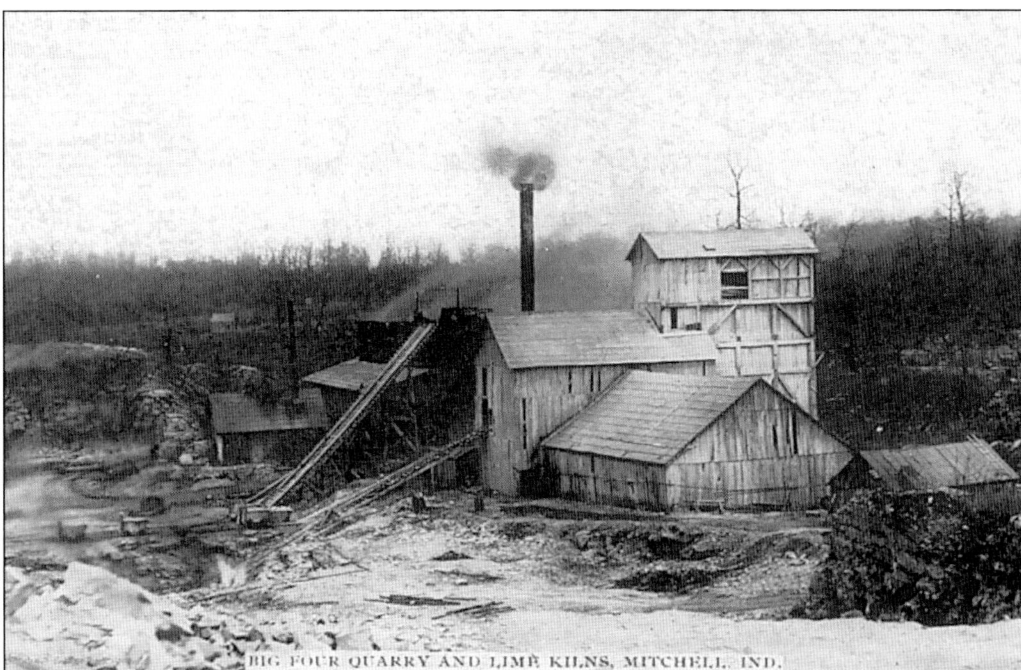

The heart of the limestone belt had many mills and quarries during the first half of this century. Here is a picture of the Big Four Quarry and Lime Kiln in Mitchell, Indiana

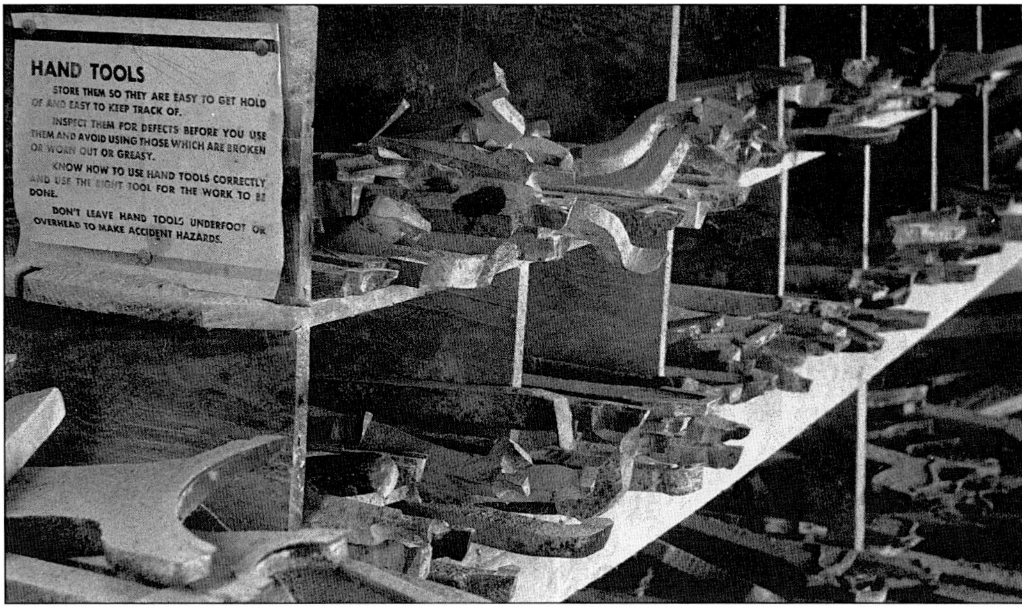

.This picture shows some of the tools that a stonecutter uses in his trade.

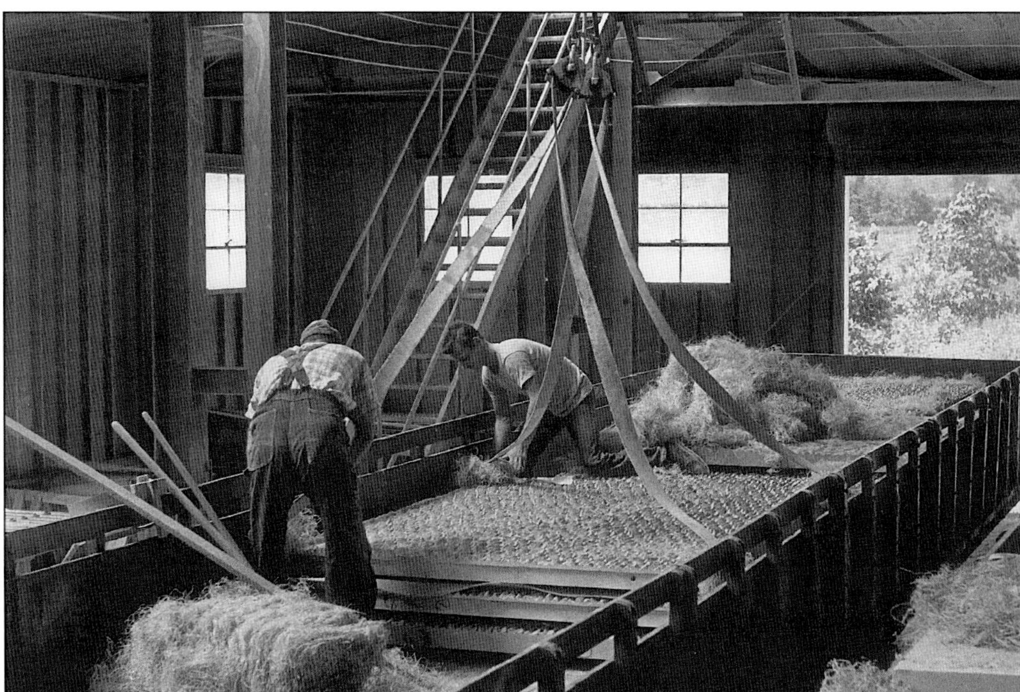

Workers are preparing stone for shipment. Excelsior is placed between the slabs of stone to keep them from breaking during shipment.

Stone carvers are artists who make all kinds of artifacts out of limestone. Here is a group of unusual carved pieces.

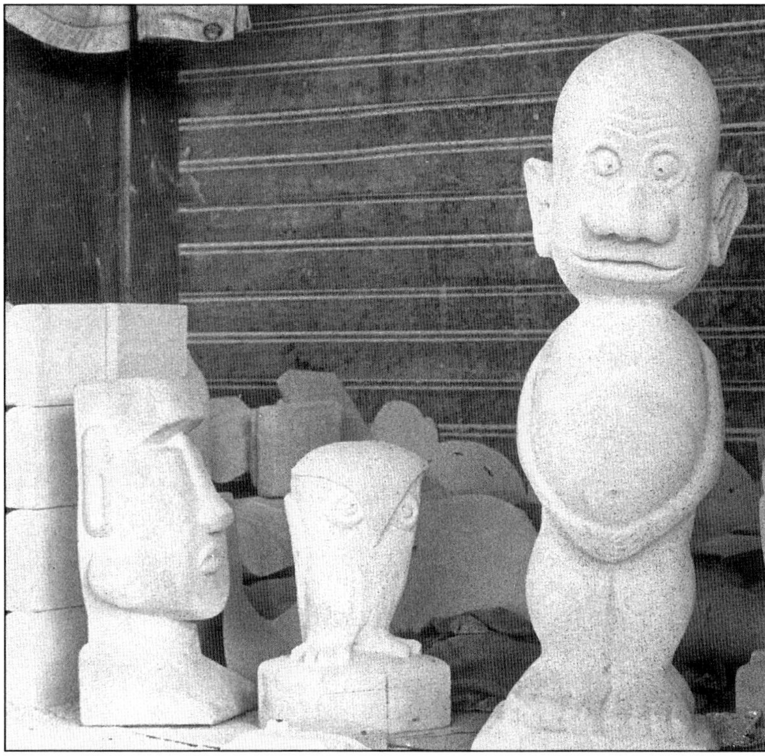

Here is the beginning of an early quarry. The derrick is lifting the keystone, which is the first to be taken from the ground.

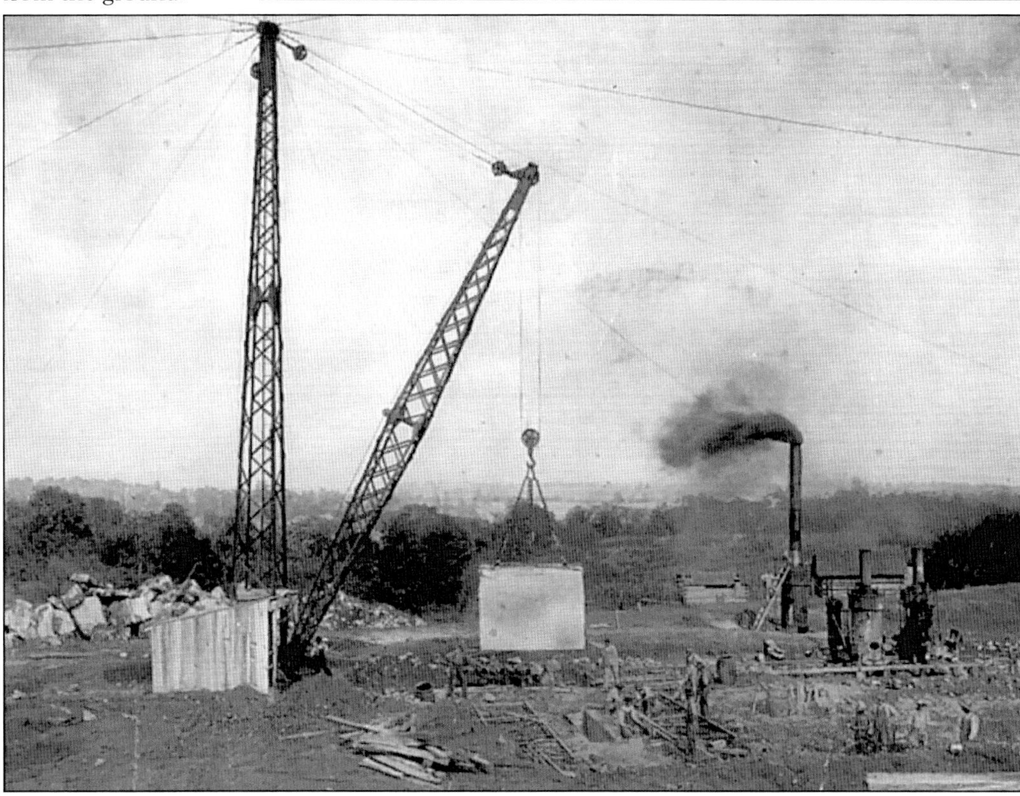

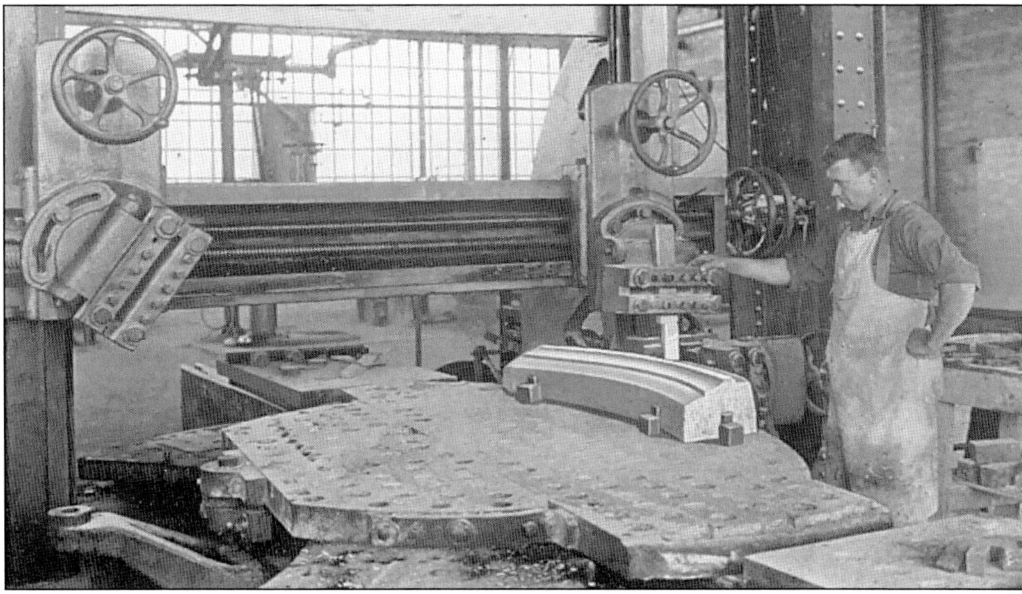

Here is a planer cutting curved moldings in one of Indiana Limestone Company's mills. This photo was taken c. 1928.

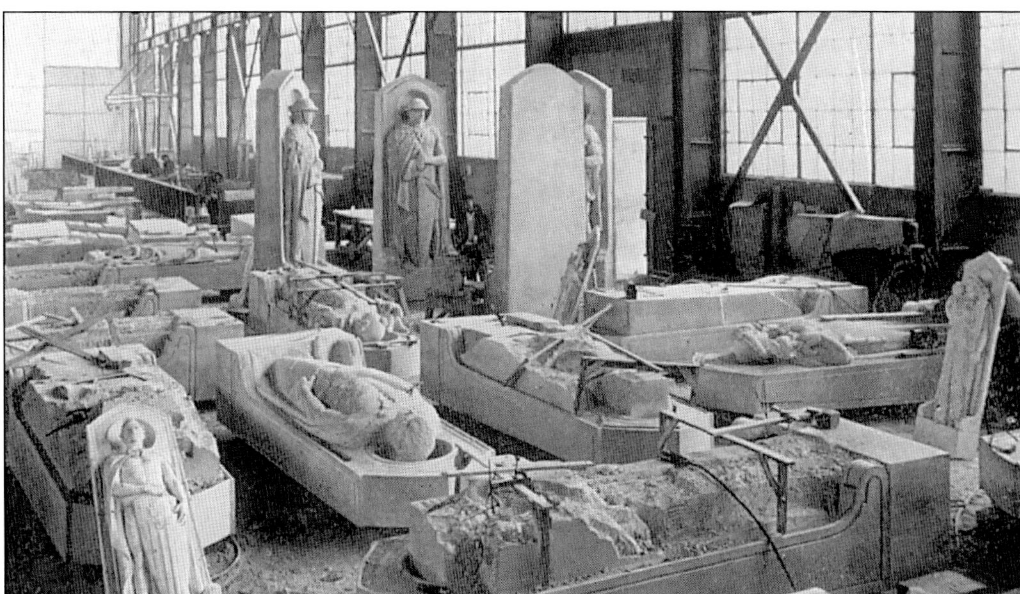

This is the interior of the carving department at one of the local mills. In the early half of this century, each mill had master stone carvers.

Here is a quarry scene during the 1920s. The Hoosier Mill in Bedford owned this quarry.

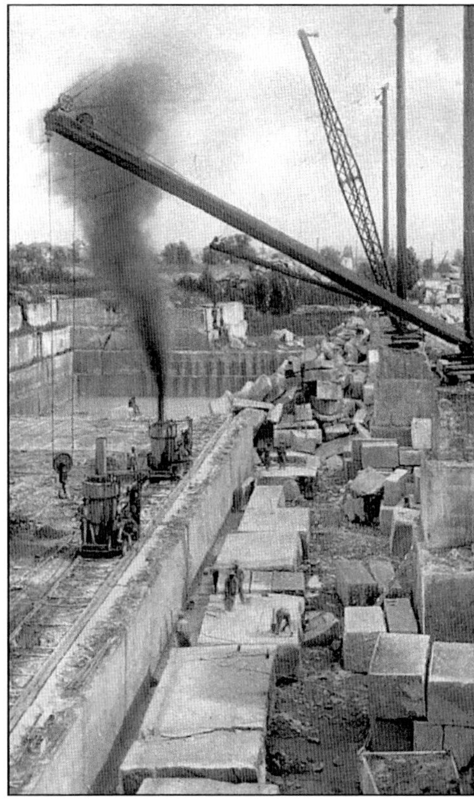

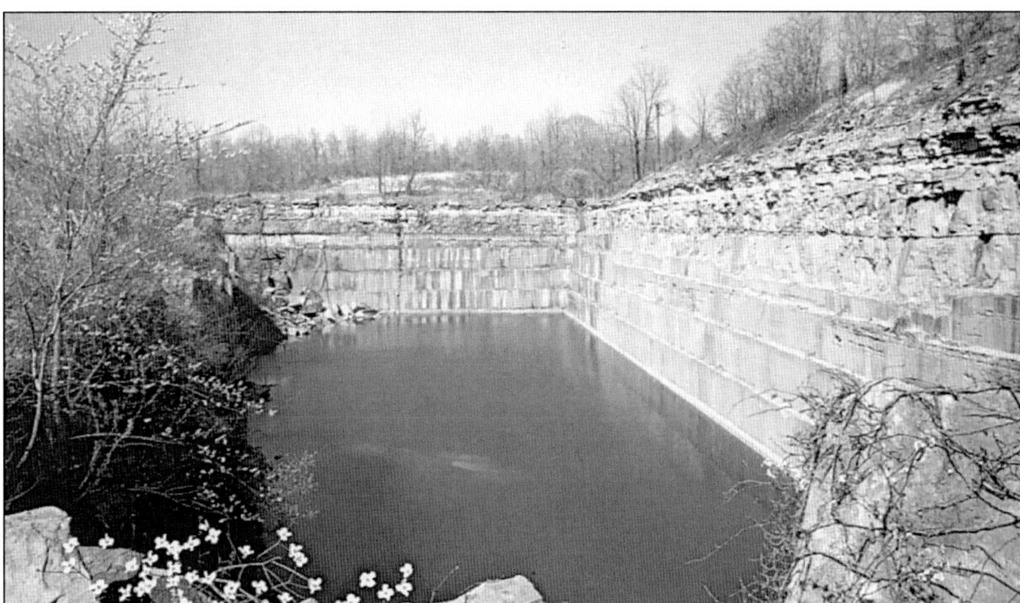

The most famous quarry hole is the Empire State Quarry Hole, photographed in 1930. The stone for the Empire State Building was the only stone to come out of this quarry.

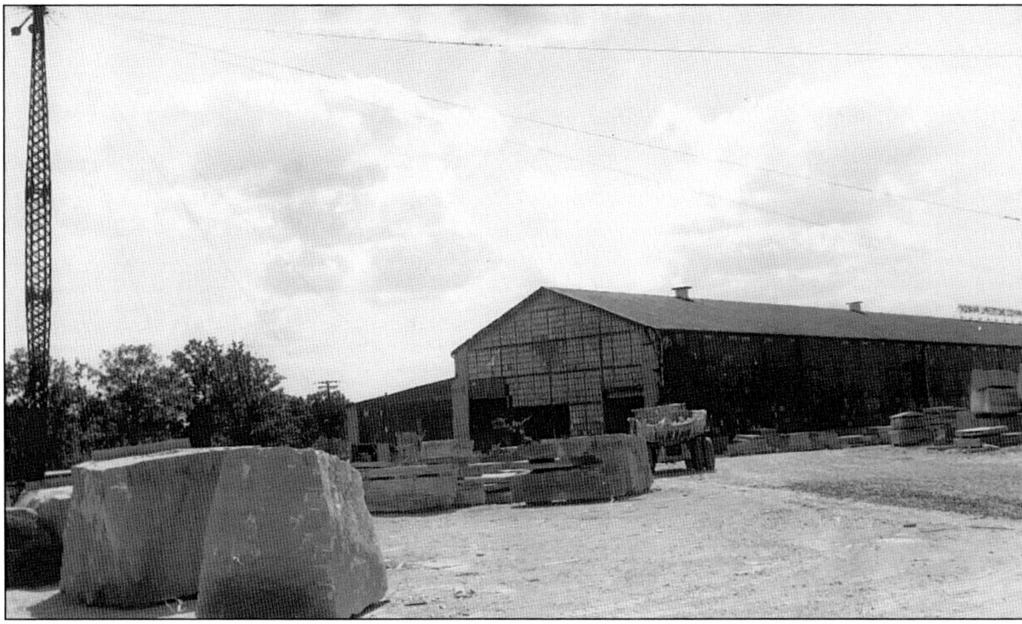

Here is a picture of a local stone mill in Lawrence County. The area outside the mill is called a stacking yard.

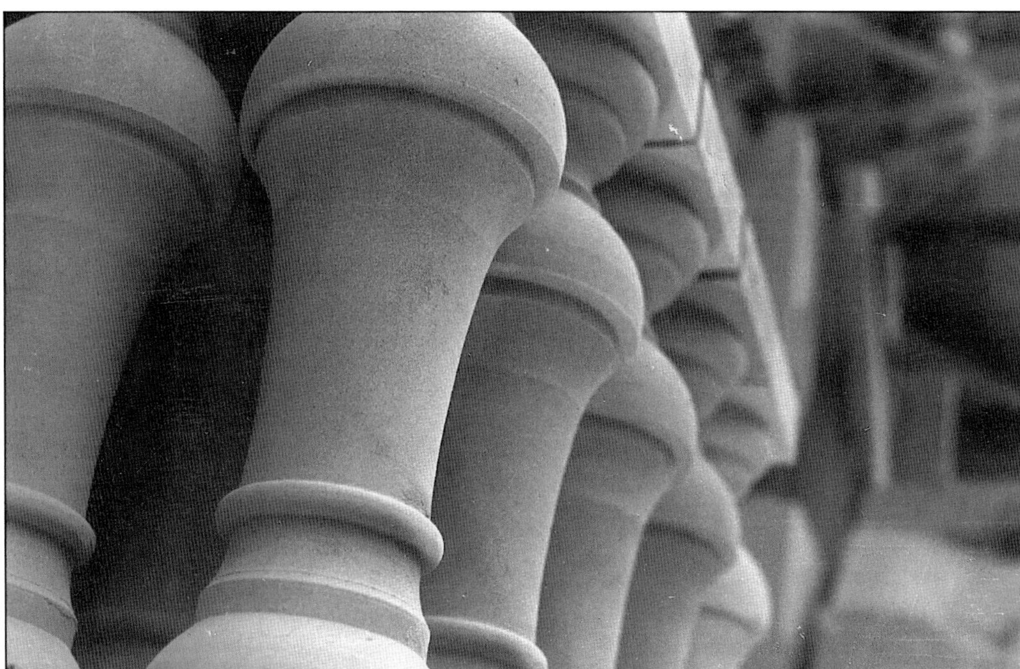

This group of carved pedestals is awaiting shipment to the east. The market for stone remains strong in the eastern states.

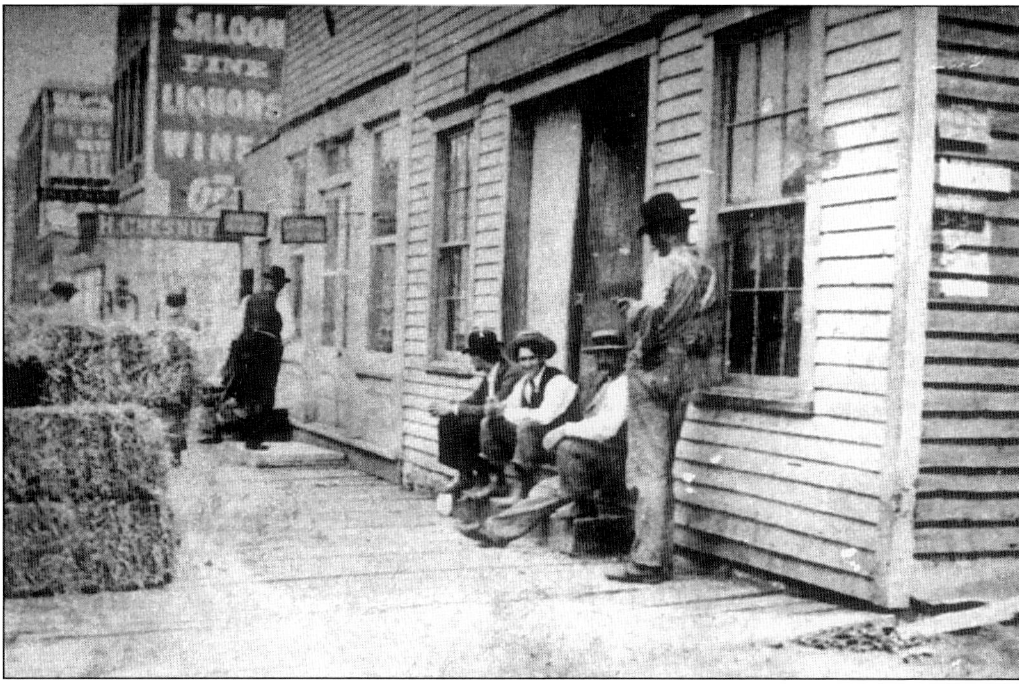

This is a photo of an early saloon, located on 16th Street between J and K Streets in Bedford.

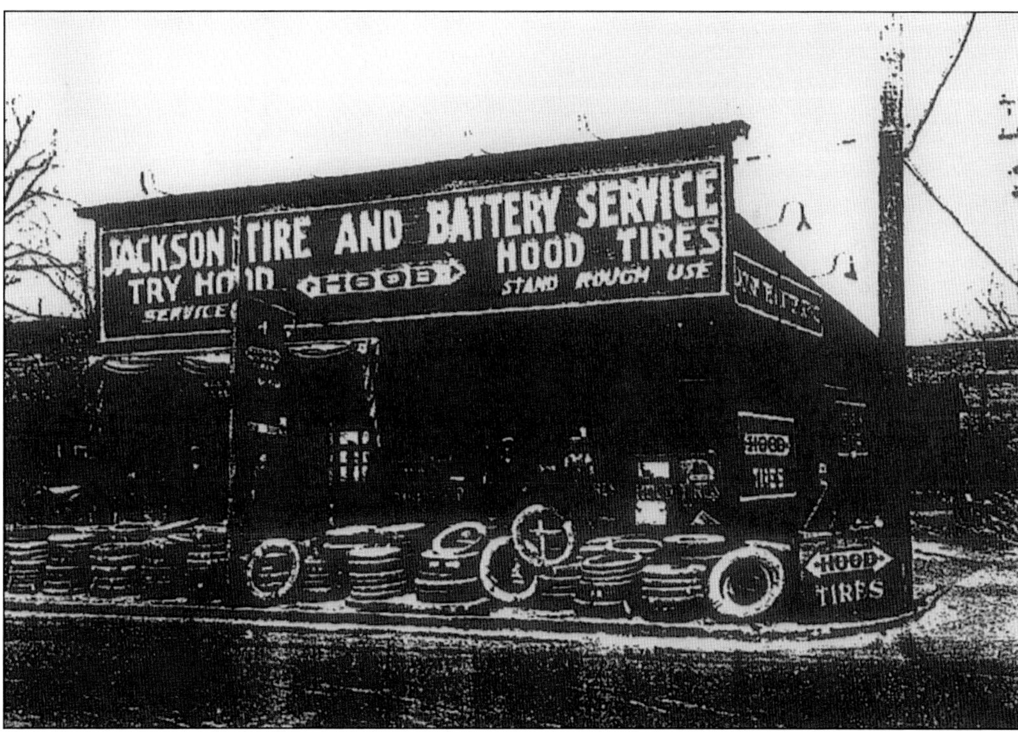

Jackson Tire and Battery Service was in business at this location during the 1930s and 1940s. It was located on 16th Street, across from the current Times Mail Newspaper building in Bedford.

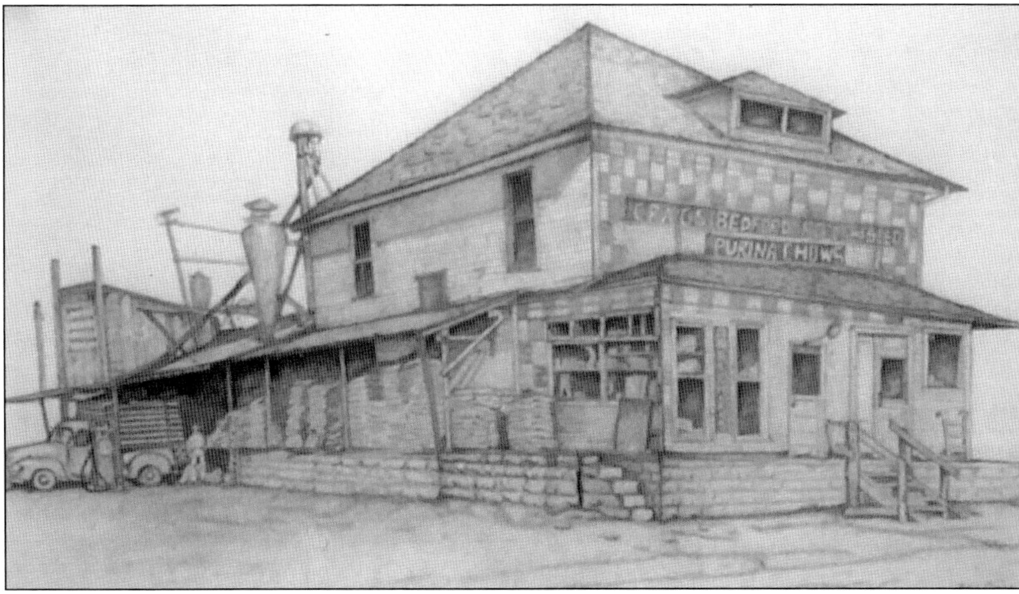

Buck Craig's Bedford Feed and Seed Store is still in business. It is pictured here in the 1940s.

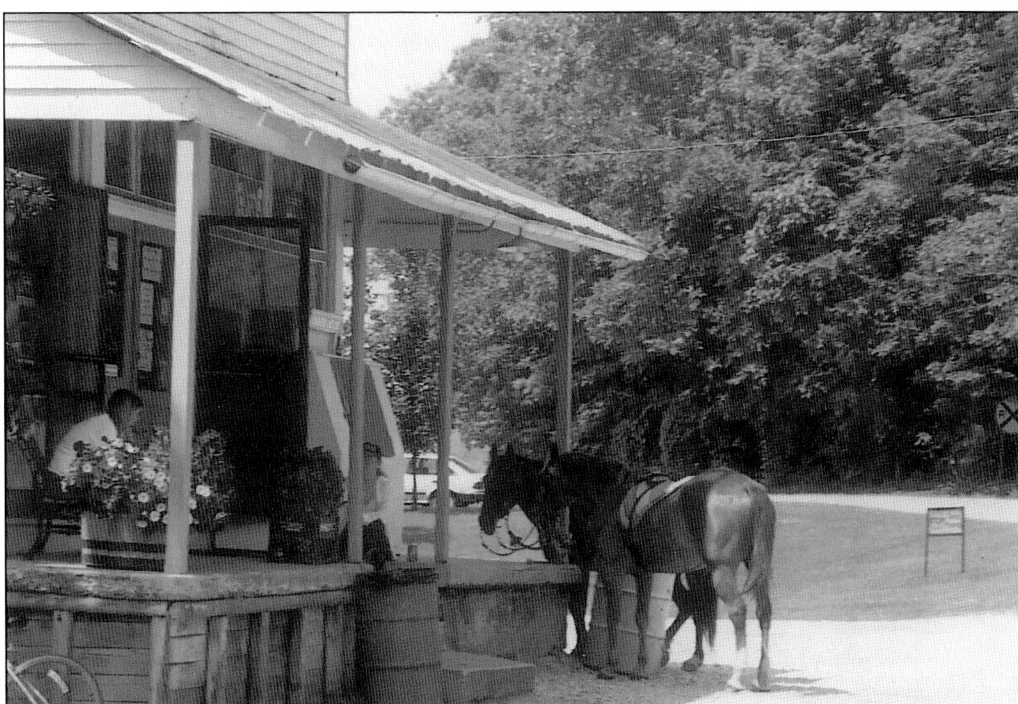

The general store and post office is a popular place in Fort Ritner. It is also a museum with pictures and artifacts of earlier times. It has been in this location since the mid 1860s.

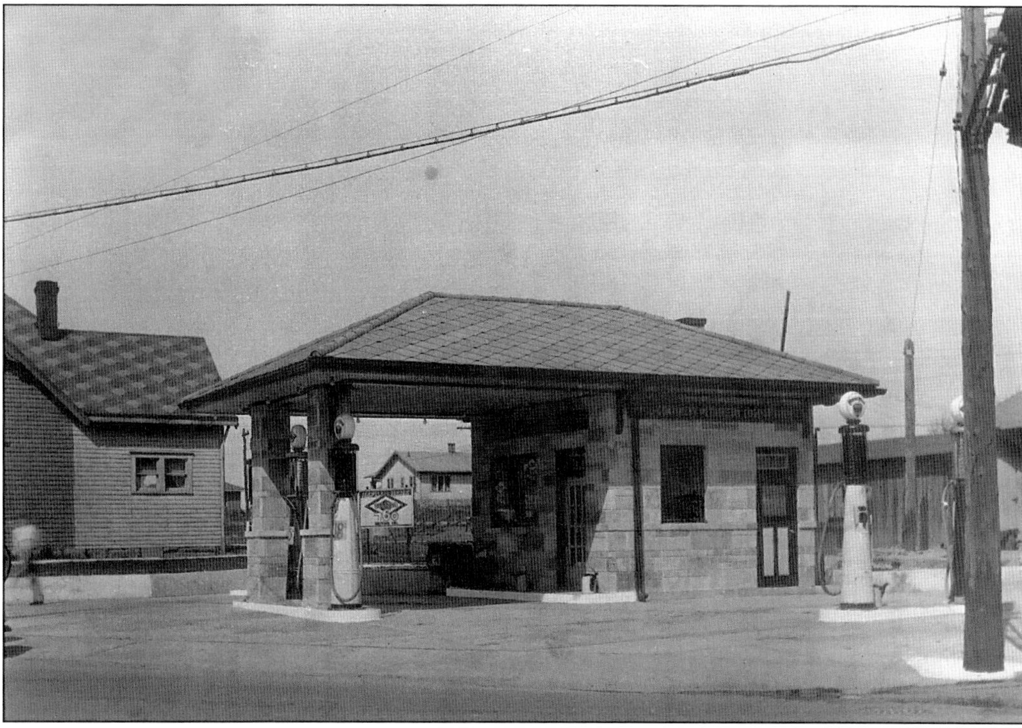

This filling station, built in the early 1920s, was located at 5th and Lincoln in Bedford. Gas was 18.2¢ per gallon at the time this photo was taken. It was torn down in the 1950s.

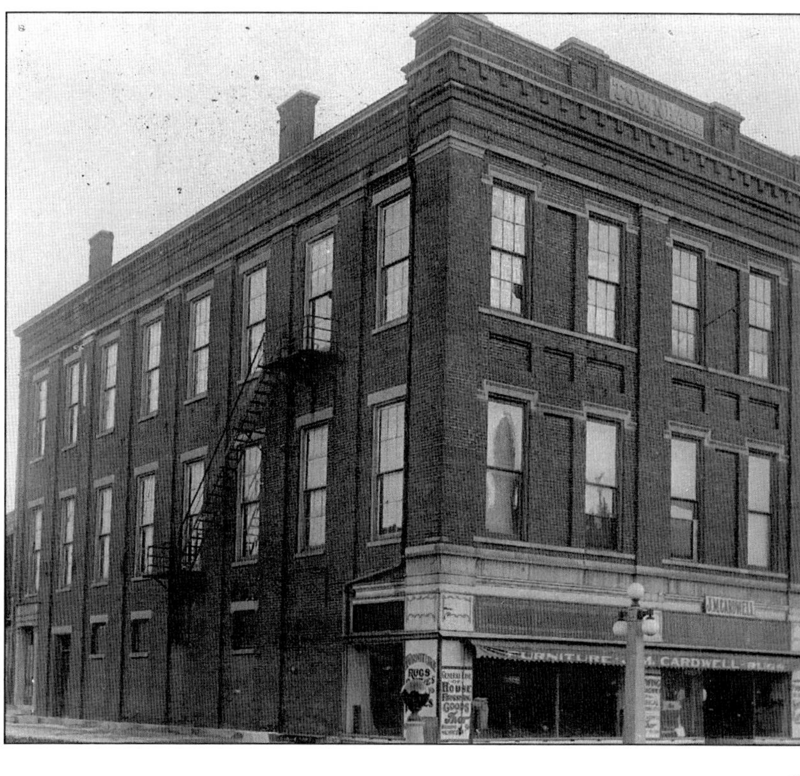

Pictured here is a furniture and rug retail store. The upstairs was used as a Town Hall until about 1922, when it was rebuilt into four stories. The main floor was retained for the Stone City Bank.

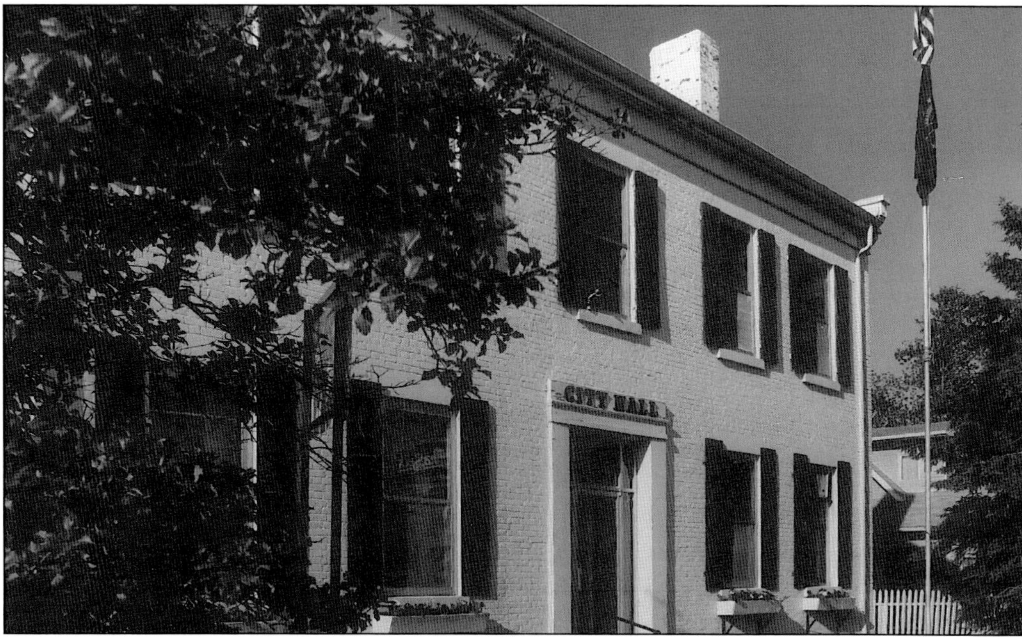

This is a picture of City Hall, the former home of Dr. Joseph Gardner. His friend and co-worker, Clara Barton, founded the American Red Cross. This house was built in 1850, and is still in use today.

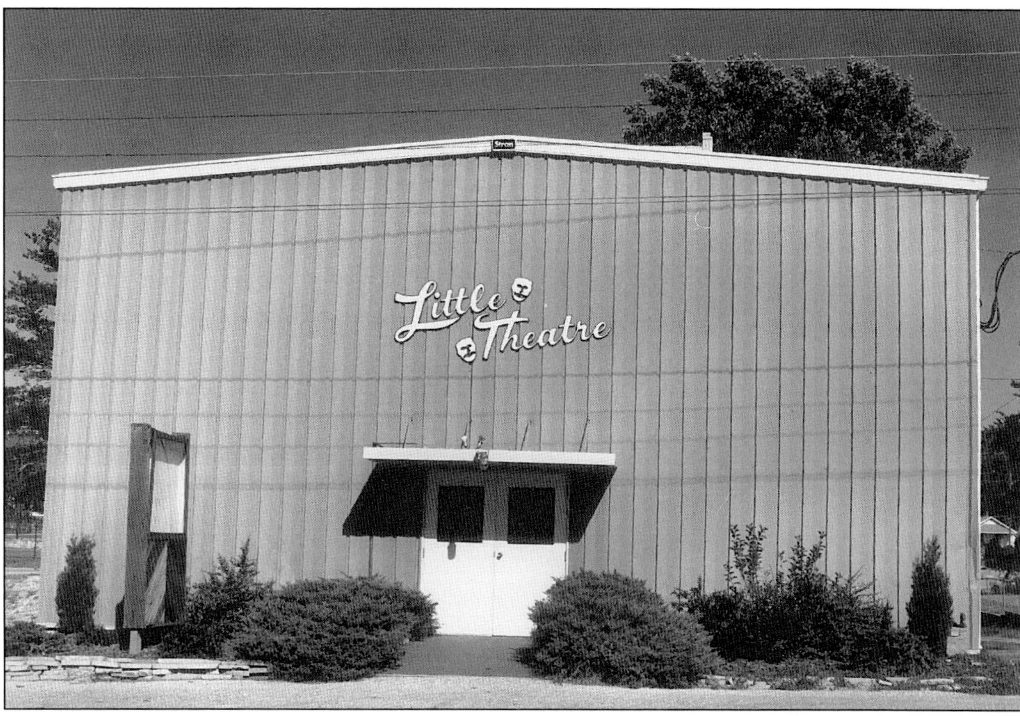

The Little Theater has produced many productions since its beginning about 30 years ago. The group is now raising money for renovations. This is their second building. The first was destroyed by fire.

Four
CHURCHES

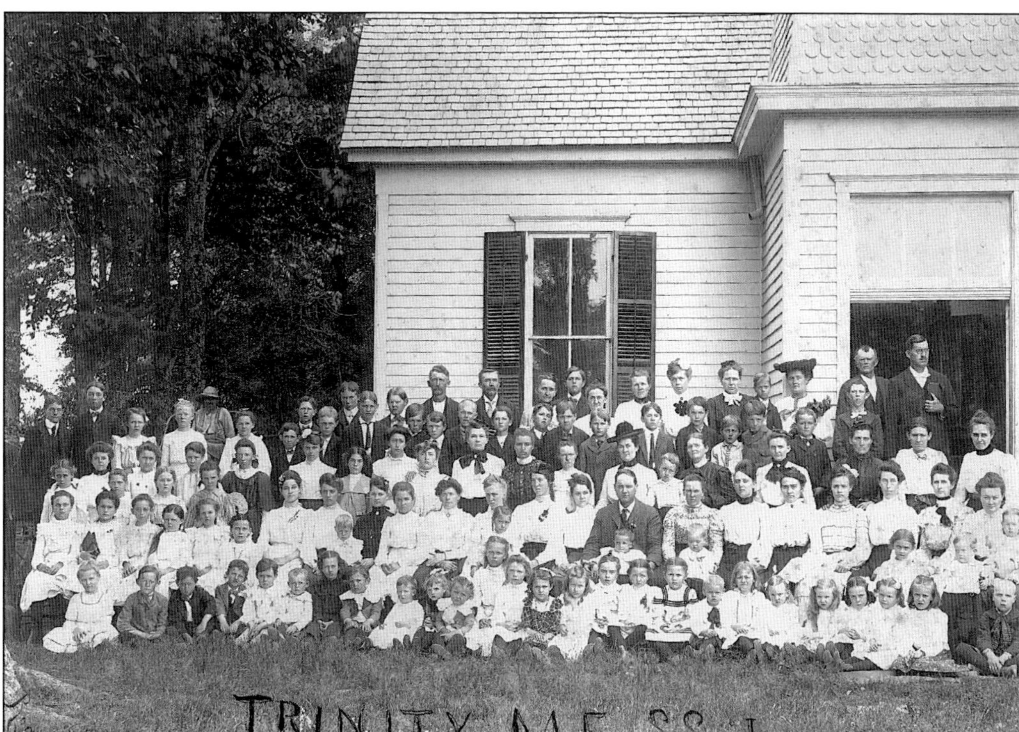

In 1903, this picture was taken of a Sunday school group in front of the Trinity M.E. Church. It is located on Tunnelton Road.

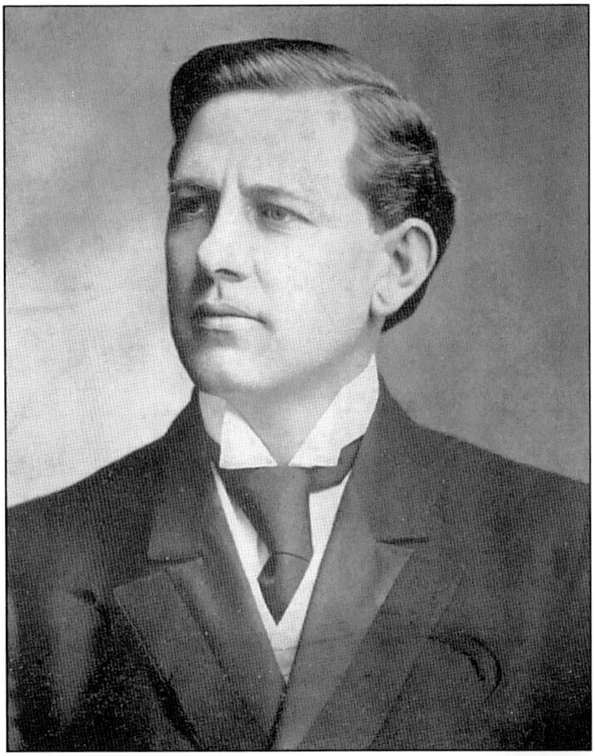

R.Scott Hyde was one of the early Methodist ministers in Bedford. This photo was taken c. 1890.

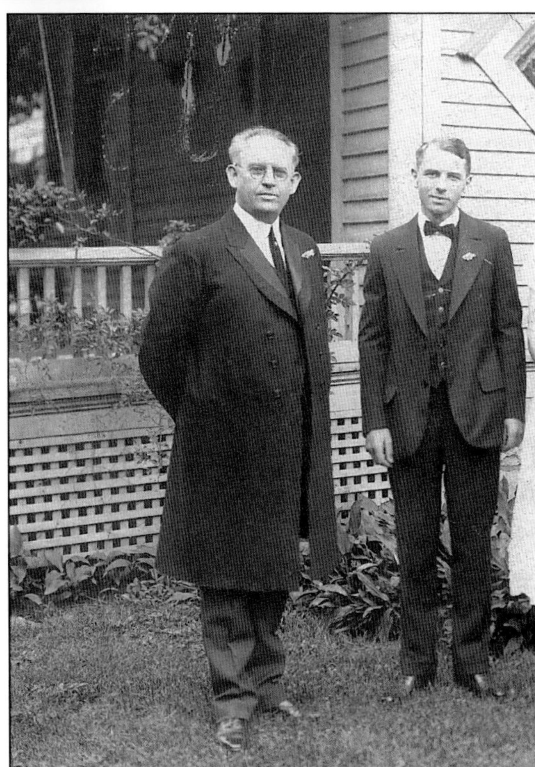

The man on the left is Rev. T.J. Owens, a minister for the Baptist Church. This photograph was taken c. 1940.

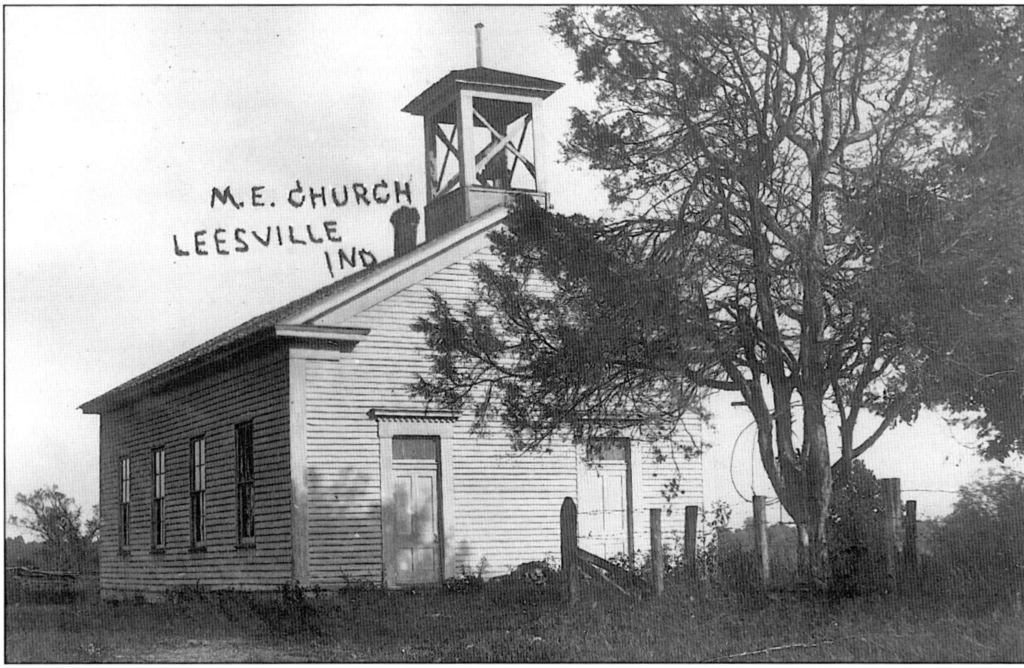

This is the M.E. Church at Leesville in the early 1920s.

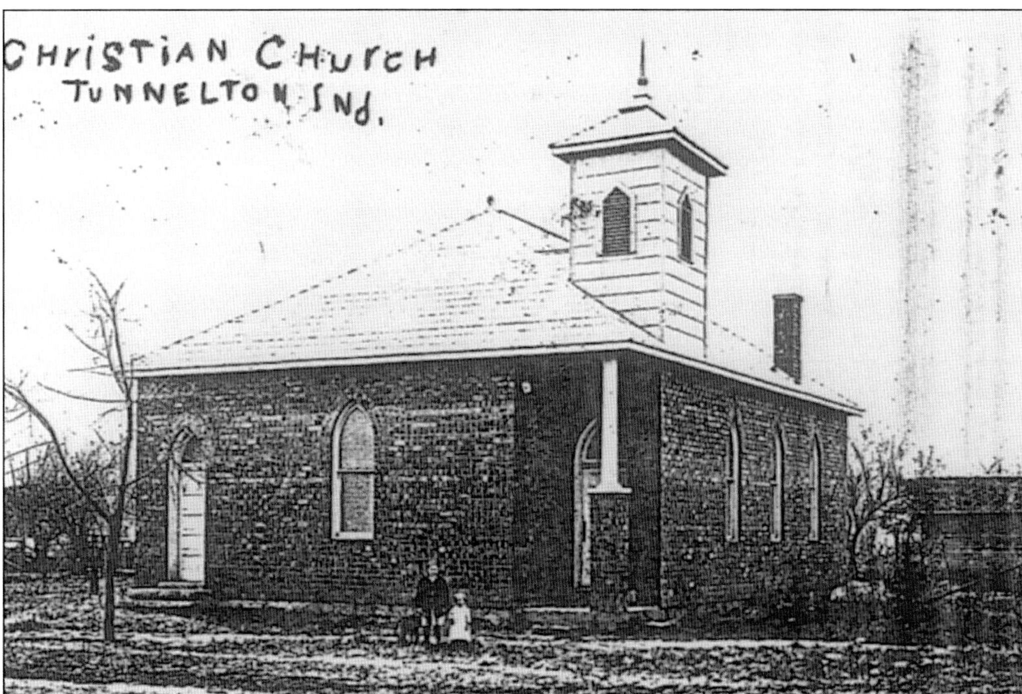

This Christian Church once stood in Tunnelton, but in 1930 it became a residence.

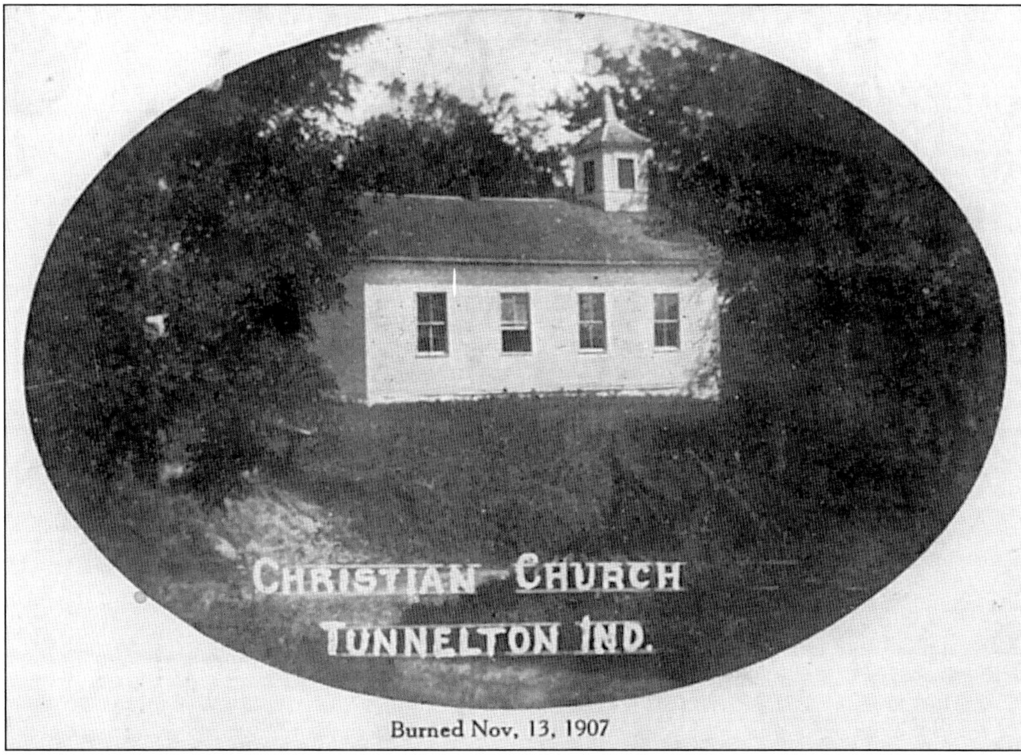

This Christian Church in Tunnelton burned down on November 13, 1907.

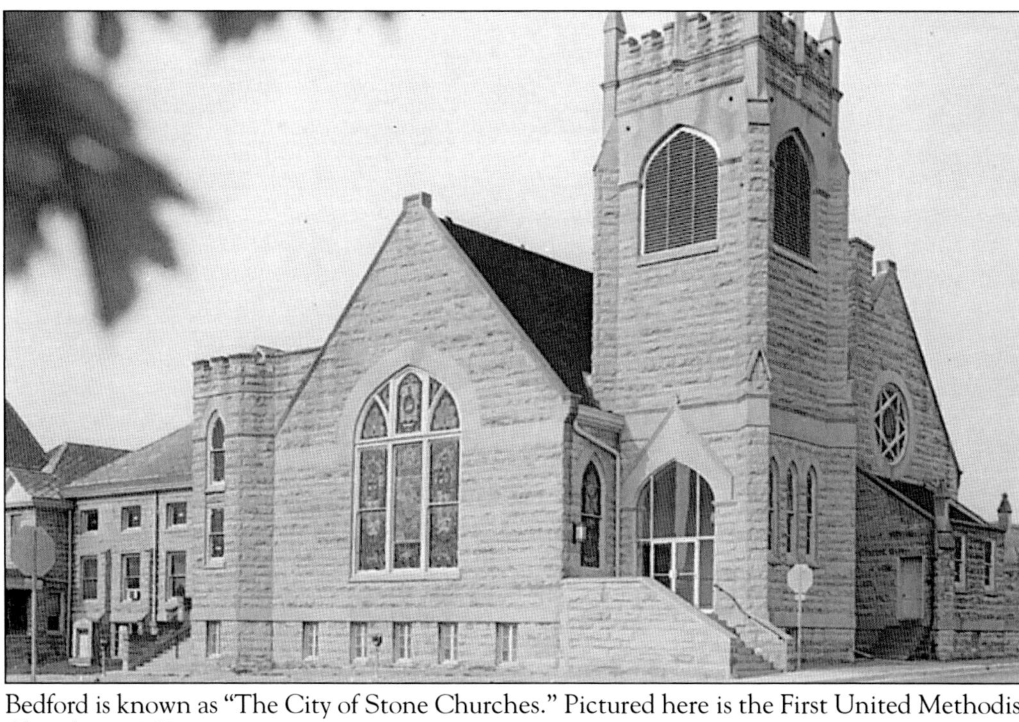
Bedford is known as "The City of Stone Churches." Pictured here is the First United Methodist Church in 1960.

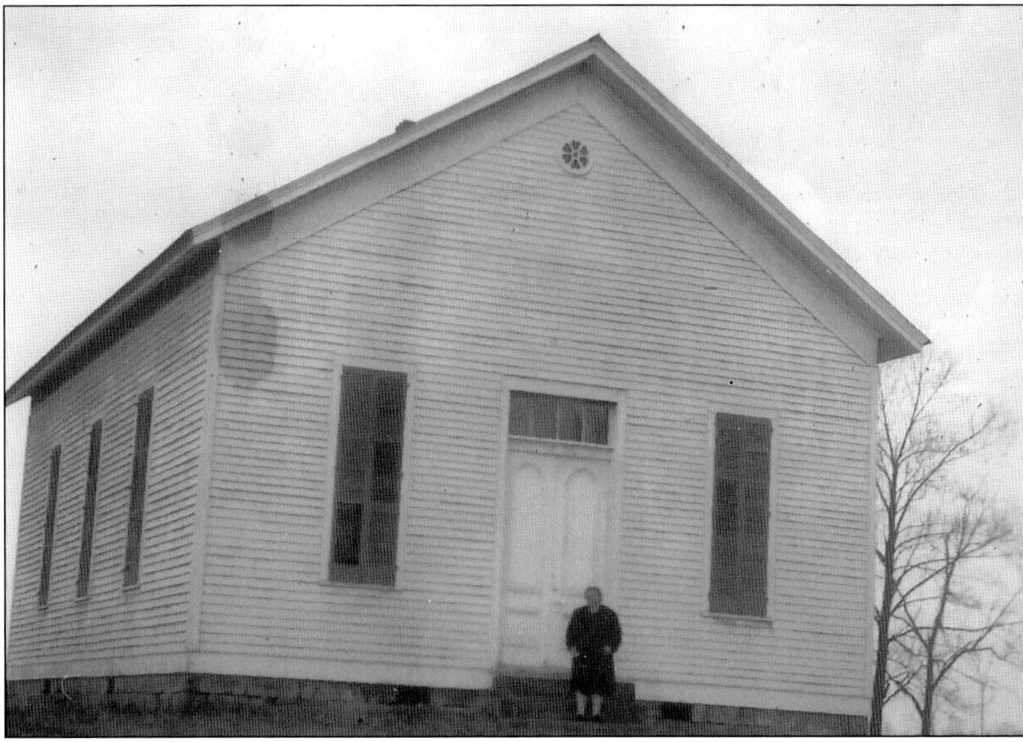

This picture of the Guthrie Creek Hard Shell Baptist Church was taken in 1942. This church is located between Leesville and Clear Springs.

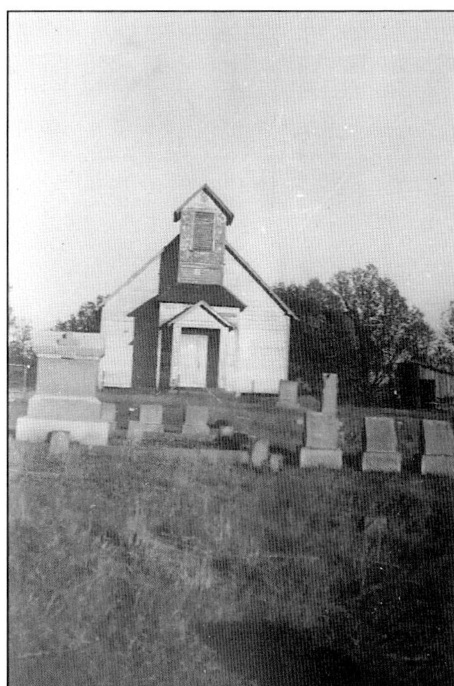

Dixon Chapel Church and cemetery is located near Fort Ritner. This photo was taken in 1939.

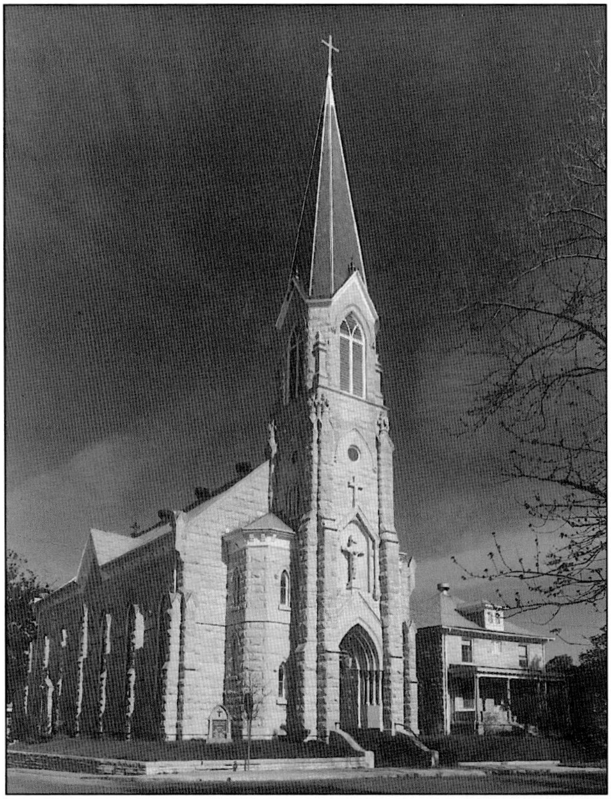

St. Vincent DePaul Catholic Church has beautiful stained glass windows, which were purchased from Belgium near the turn of the century.

Pictured here is the First Presbyterian Church. The present location is on the corner of 15th and L Street.

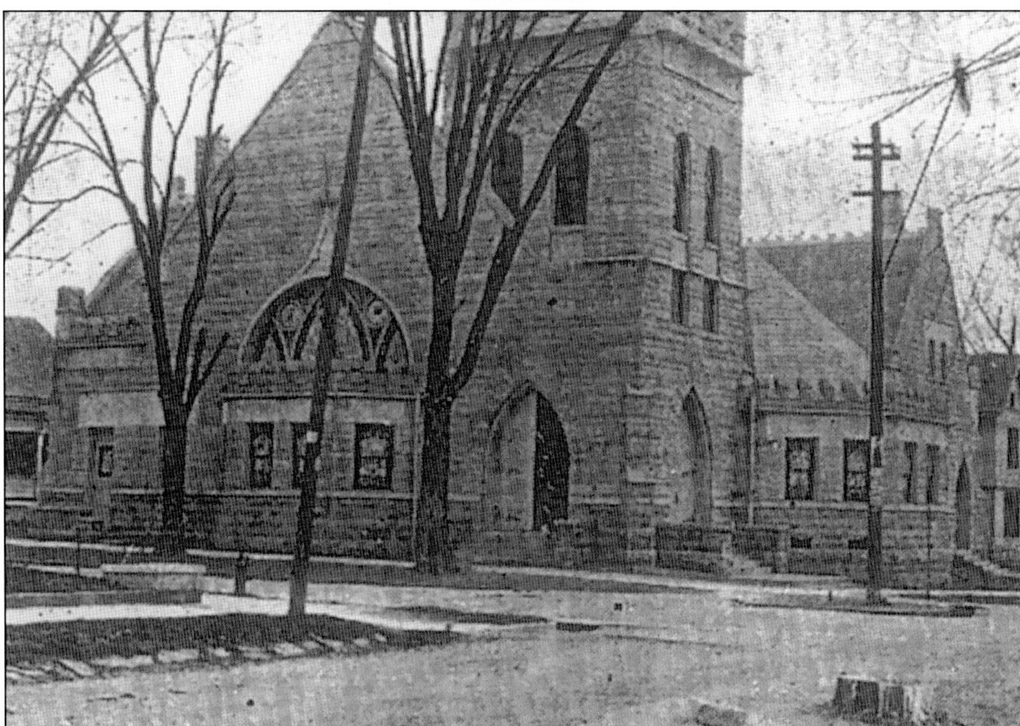

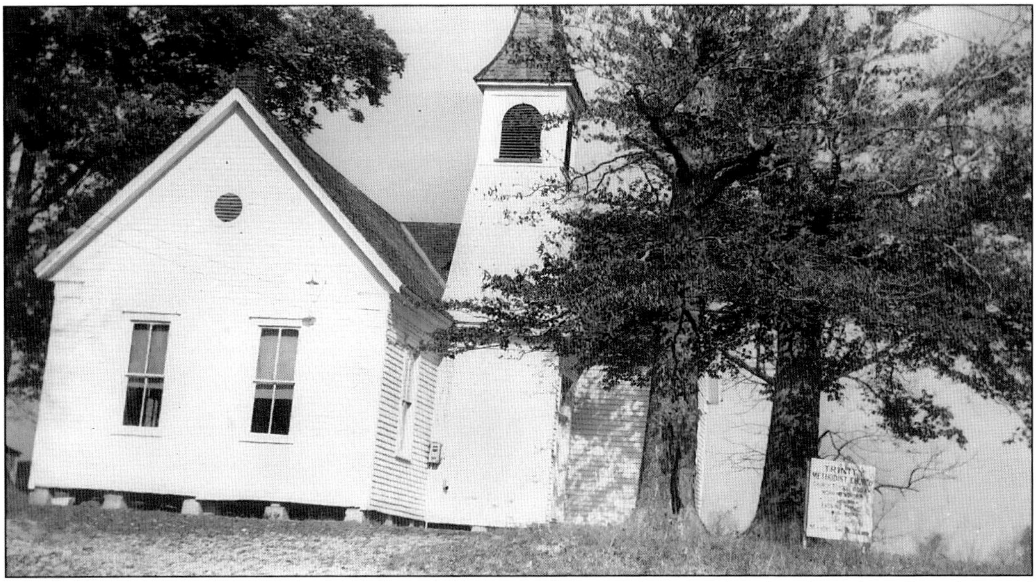

Here is the Trinity Methodist Church, built on A.W. Thomas' land. This church is located on Tunnelton Road, about half way between Bedford and Buddha. This picture was taken in October, 1948.

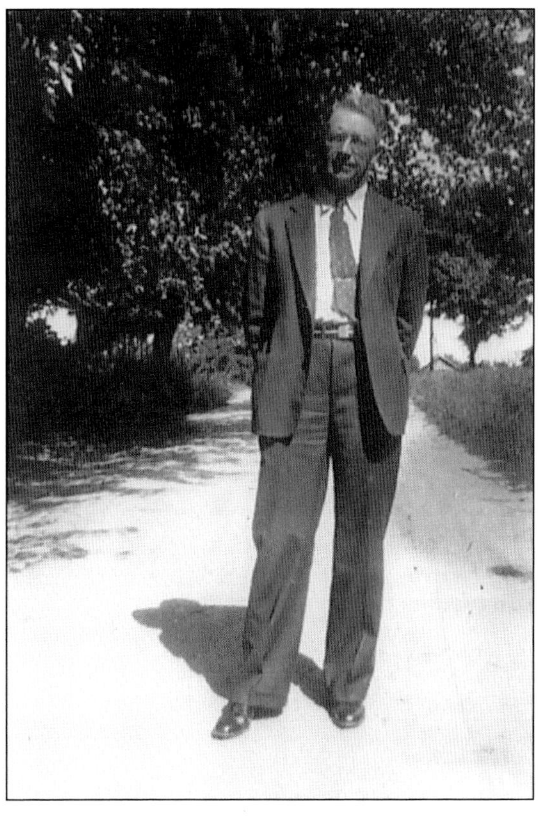

Reverend Haley was the minister of the Methodist Church in Tunnelton during the late 1930s. He is pictured here on the road just in front of the church.

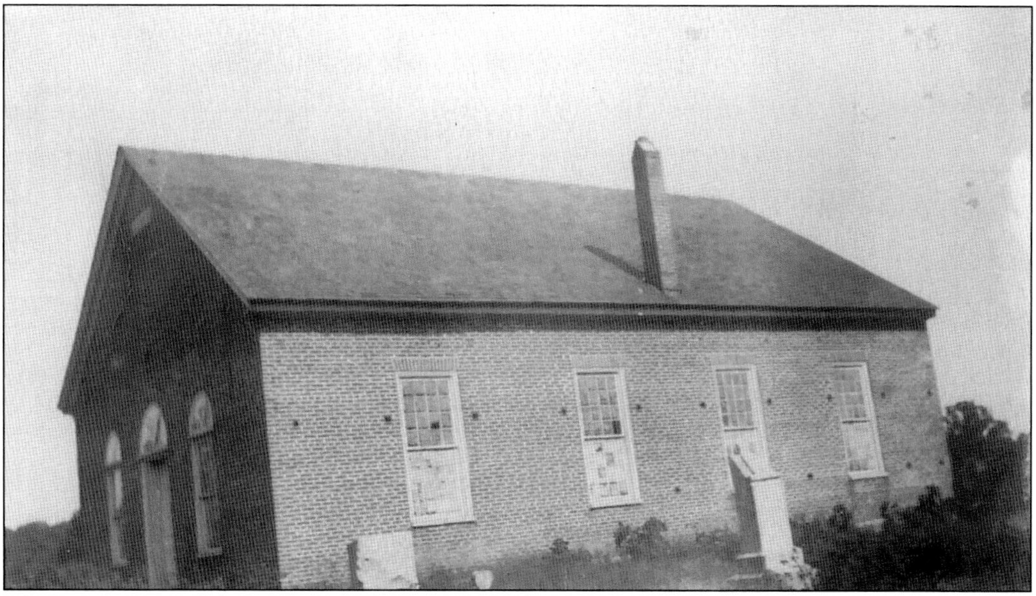

This is a picture of the Erie Church, which was destroyed by a storm in 1922.

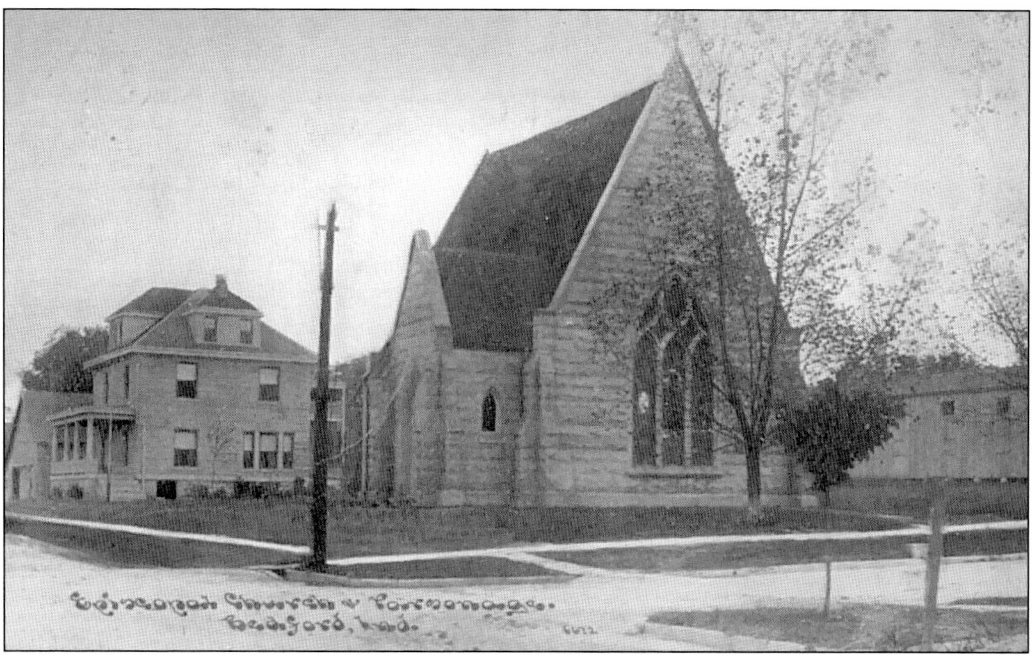

In the early 1900s, the Episcopal Church and Parsonage in Bedford looked like this. The church has been enlarged at its original location on 14th and M Street.

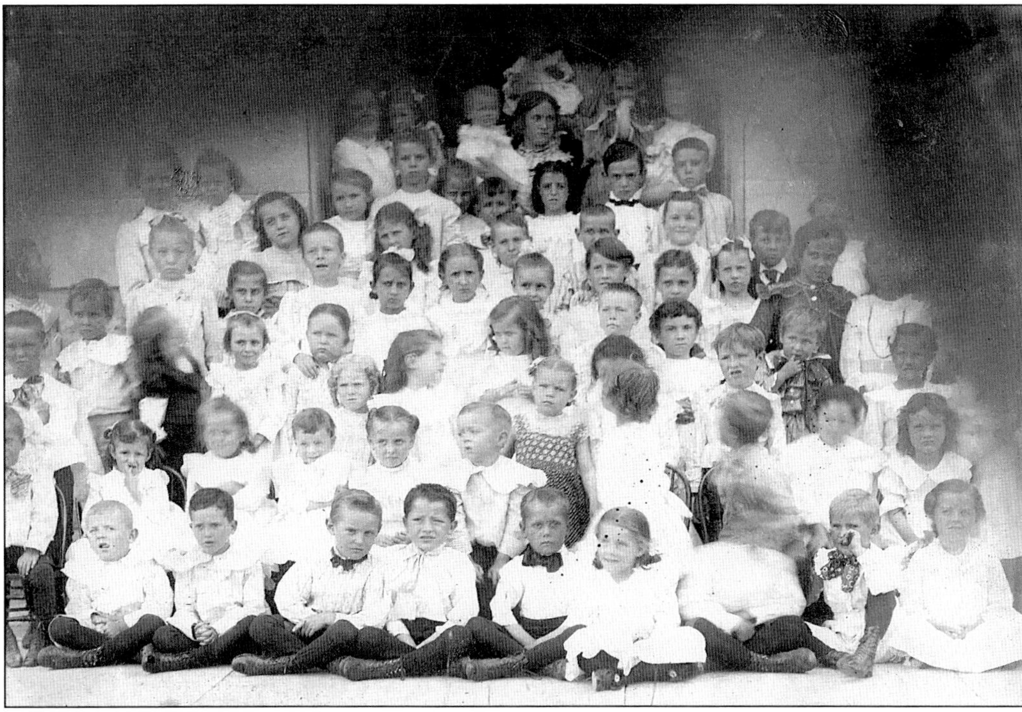

A group of Sunday school children from the First Baptist Church in Bedford pose for this picture in 1902.

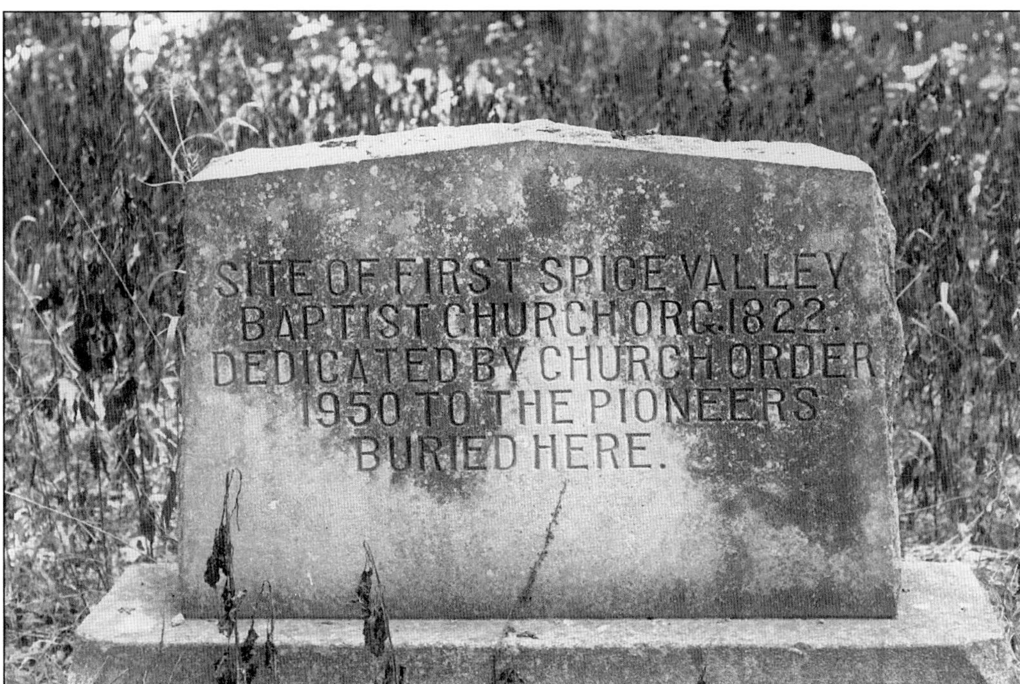

This stone marks the spot of the first Spice Valley Baptist Church, originating in 1822. It was dedicated to the early pioneers buried in the cemetery by members in 1950.

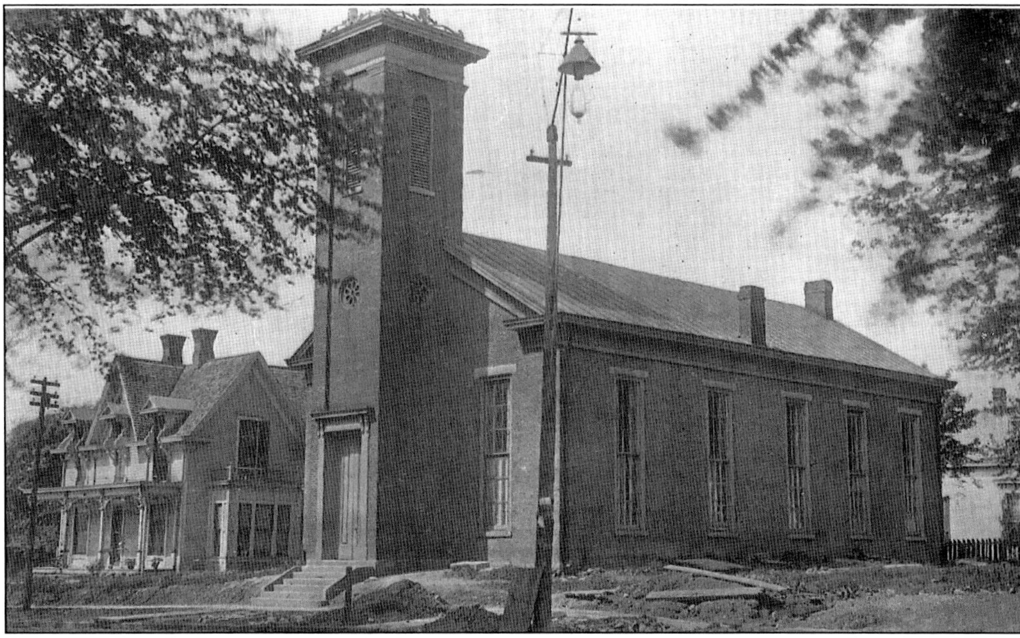

This picture is of the First Methodist Church in Bedford after the first church had been remodeled in 1867.

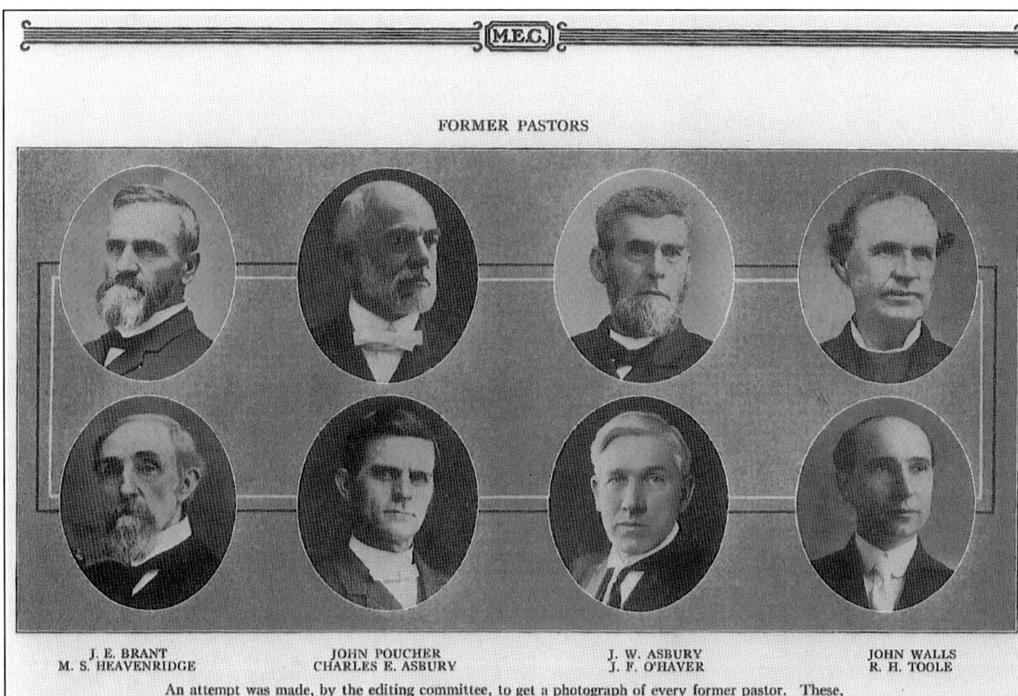

Here are photographs of some of the early pastors of the First Methodist Church in Bedford. This picture was taken in 1923, and is not a complete listing.

Five

EARLY SCHOOLS

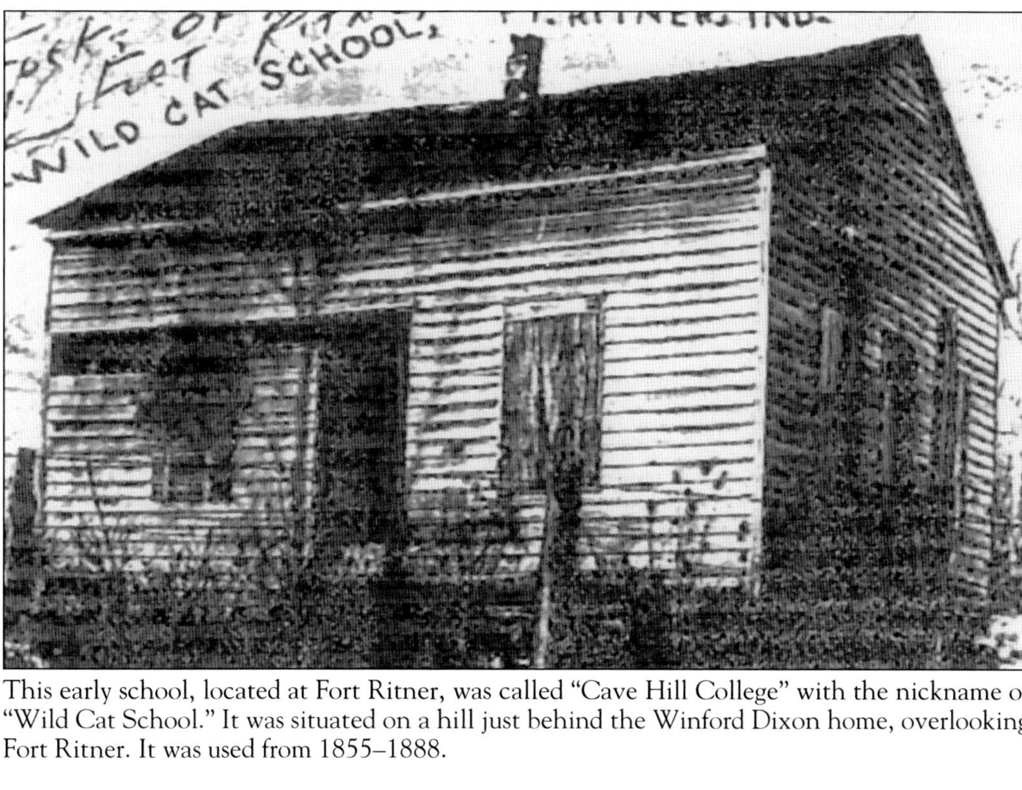

This early school, located at Fort Ritner, was called "Cave Hill College" with the nickname of "Wild Cat School." It was situated on a hill just behind the Winford Dixon home, overlooking Fort Ritner. It was used from 1855–1888.

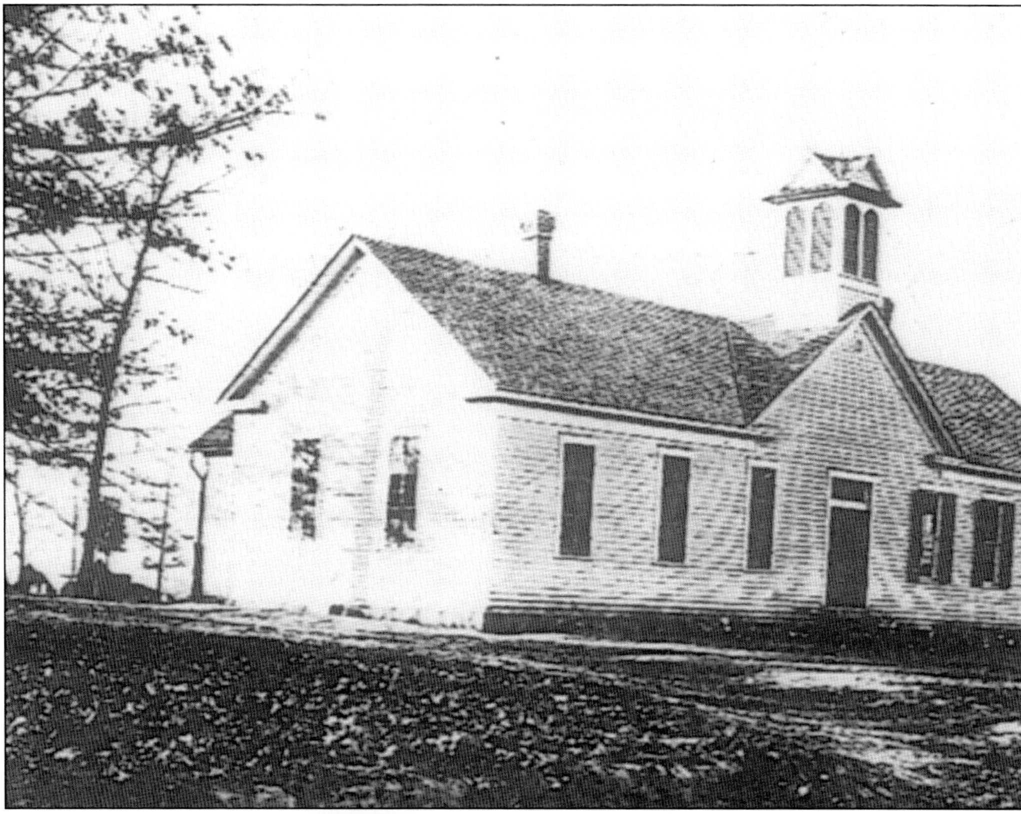

In the late 1890s, this three-room school was located at Stonington. It has since been destroyed.

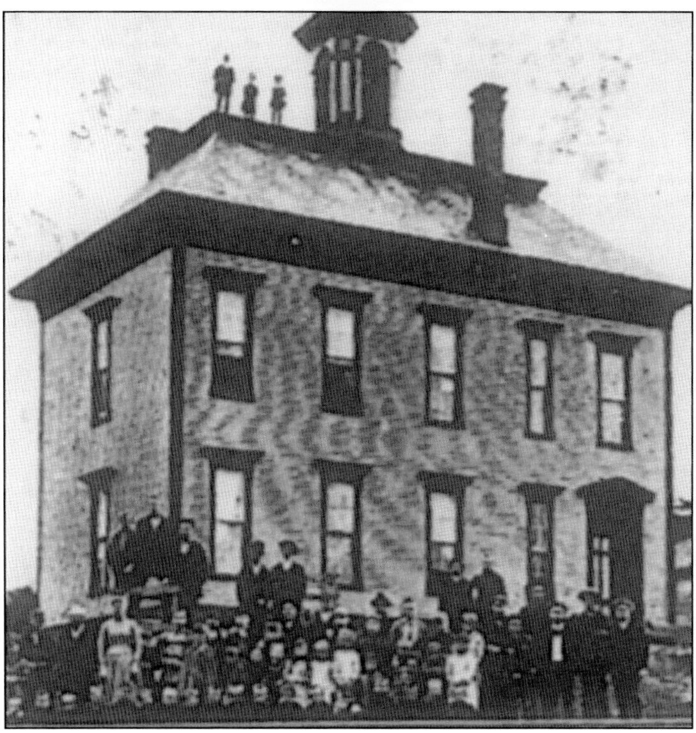

This school is no longer in existence, but at one time it stood in the town of Springville. This picture was taken *c.* 1890.

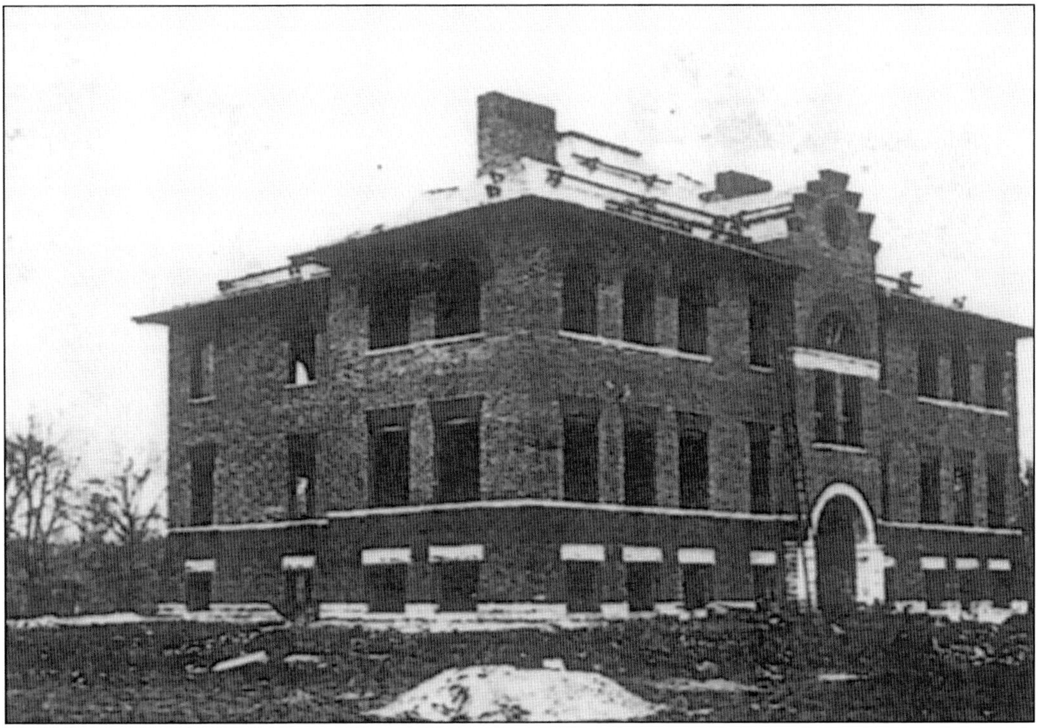

Consolidation of the schools in Lawrence County did away with some of the many high schools. Here is an early picture of Mitchell High School.

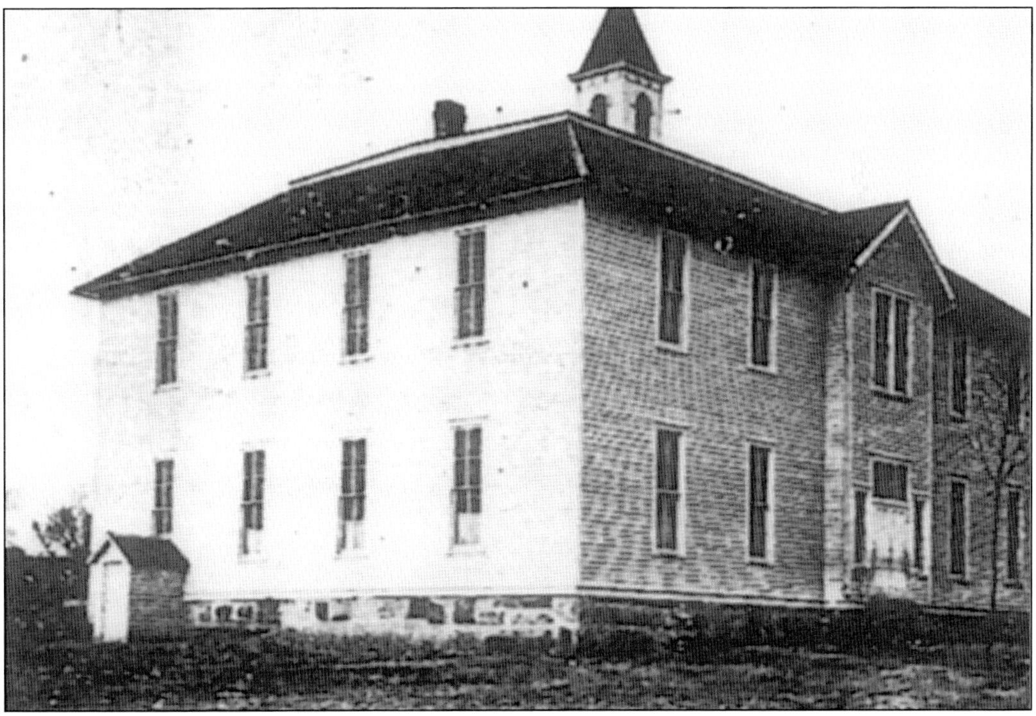

Here is a picture of Oolitic School taken c. 1890. It is no longer in existence.

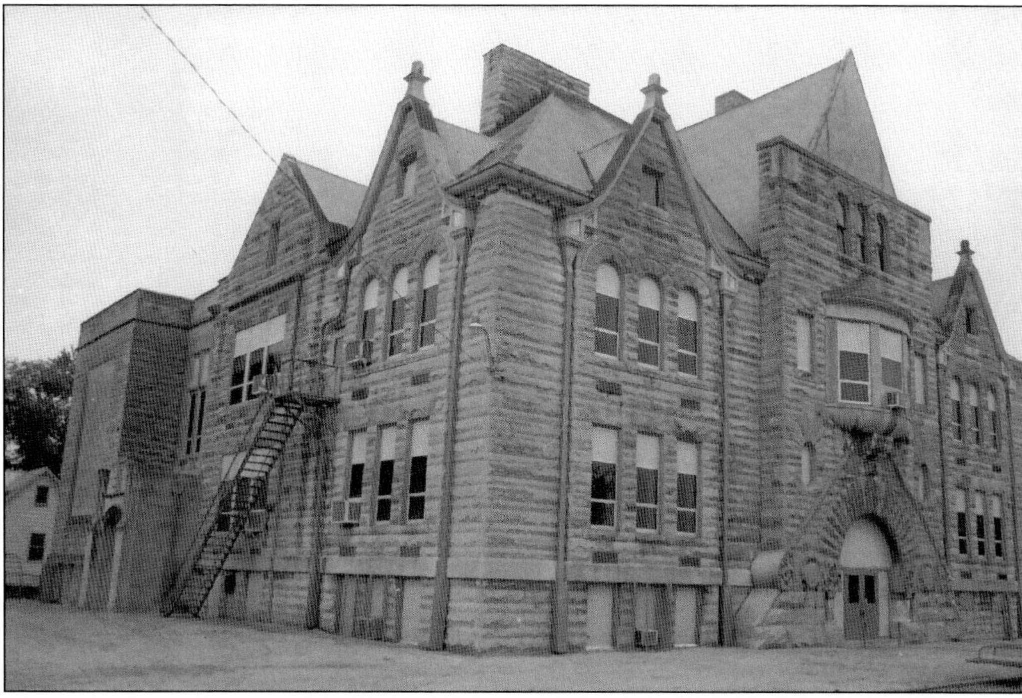

Stalker School, named after an educator in the school system, is pictured here in 1900. It is built of solid limestone and is now used as an apartment building.

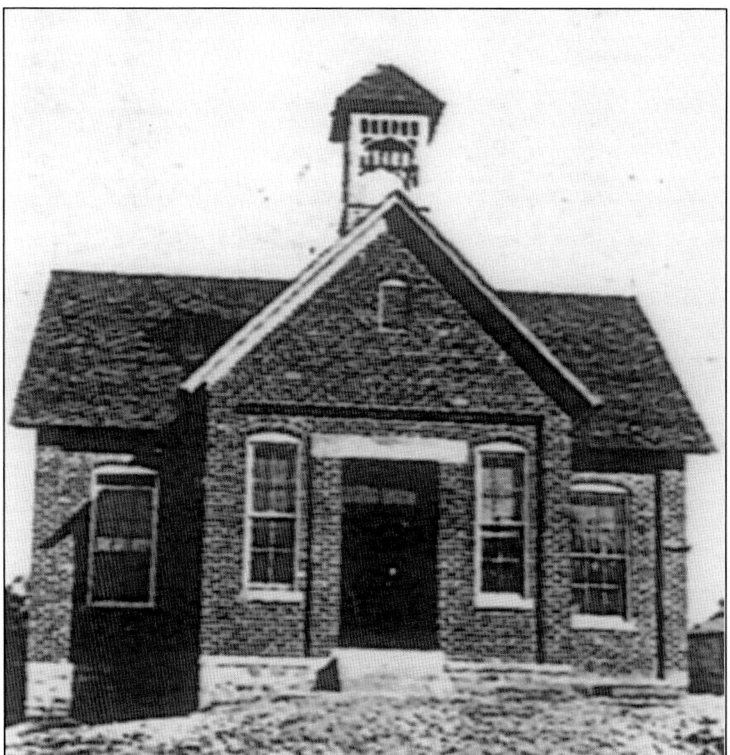

One of the early schools in Marion Township was school No. 15. This grade school is no longer in use.

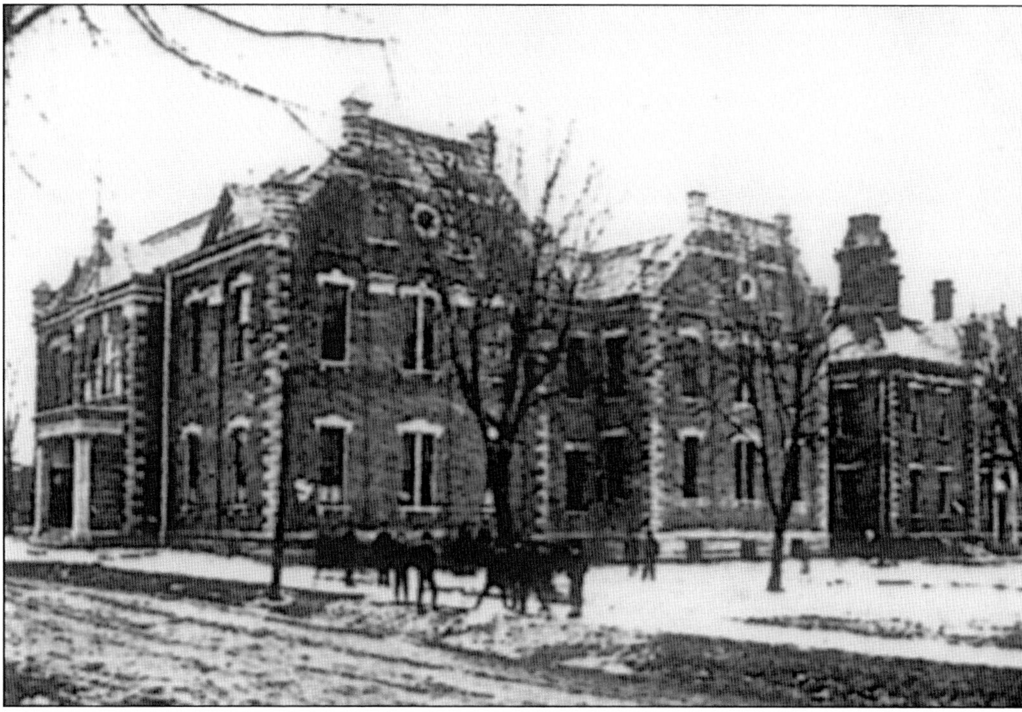

This is a picture of Bedford High School, taken in 1890. It later became the junior high after the new high school was built in the early 1920s.

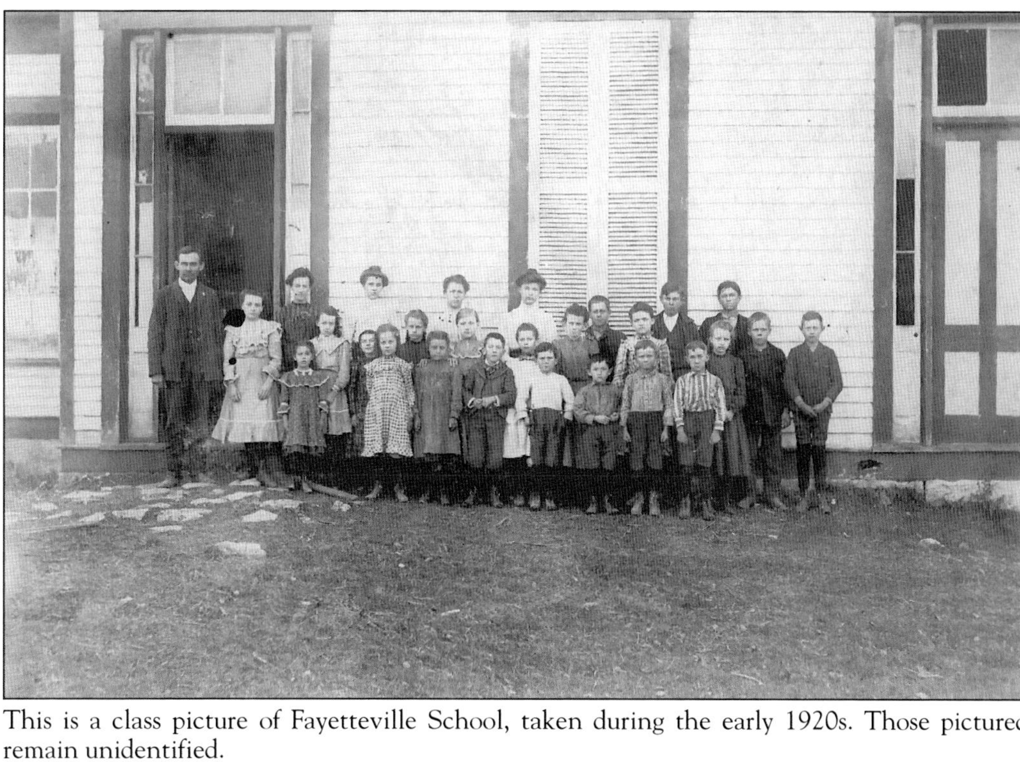

This is a class picture of Fayetteville School, taken during the early 1920s. Those pictured remain unidentified.

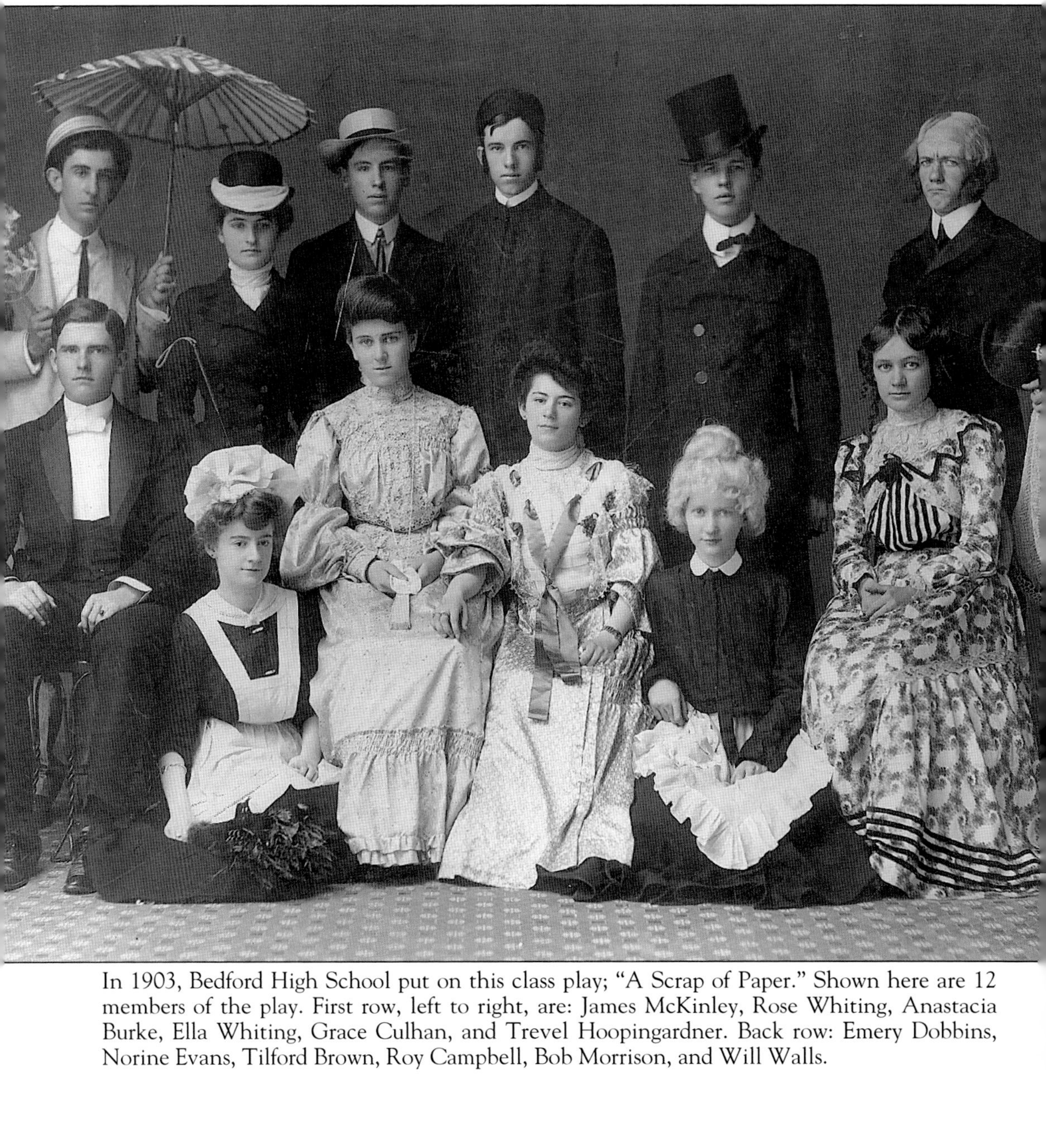

In 1903, Bedford High School put on this class play; "A Scrap of Paper." Shown here are 12 members of the play. First row, left to right, are: James McKinley, Rose Whiting, Anastacia Burke, Ella Whiting, Grace Culhan, and Trevel Hoopingardner. Back row: Emery Dobbins, Norine Evans, Tilford Brown, Roy Campbell, Bob Morrison, and Will Walls.

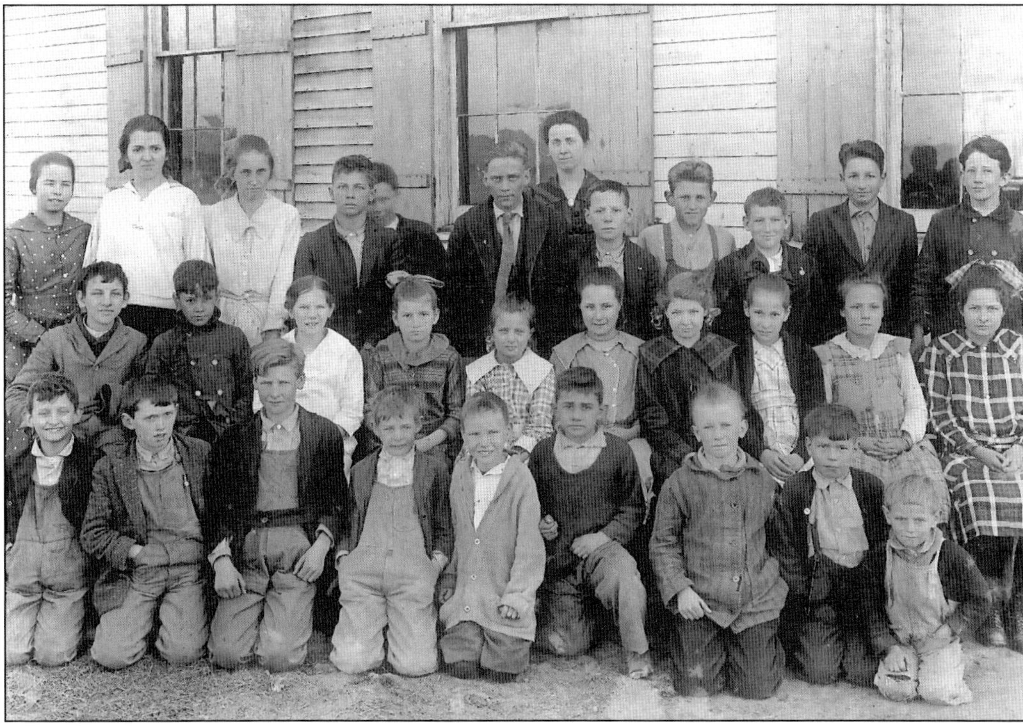

In 1918, this picture was taken of the students of Cross Lanes School. Edna Miller was the teacher at that time. The names of the students are unknown.

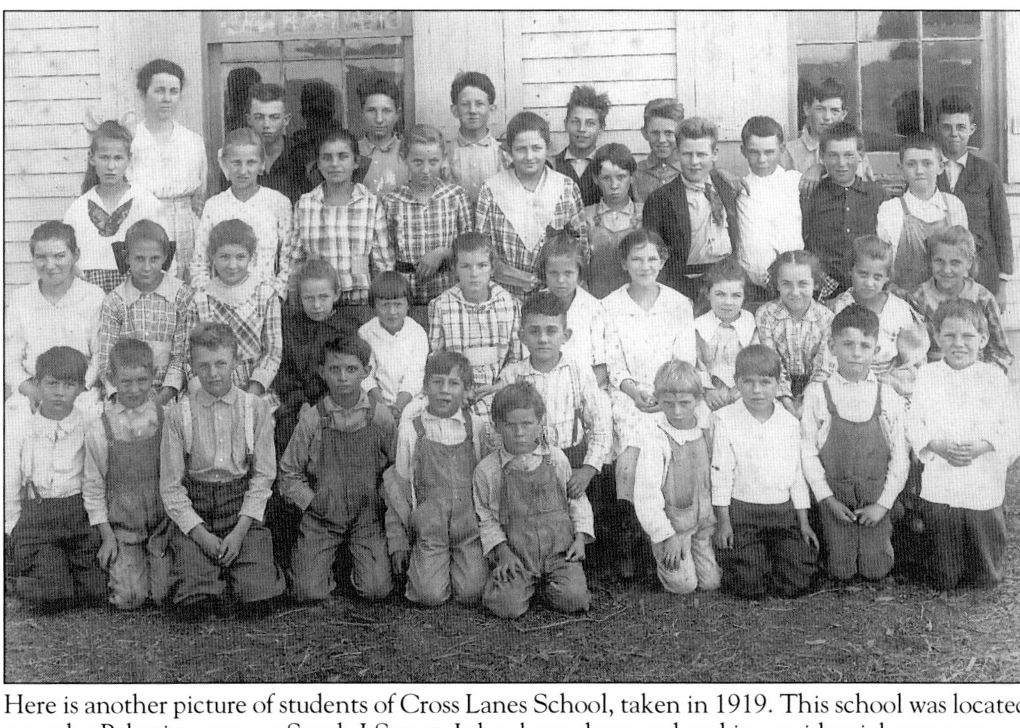

Here is another picture of students of Cross Lanes School, taken in 1919. This school was located near the Palestine area on South I Street. It has been destroyed and is a residential area now.

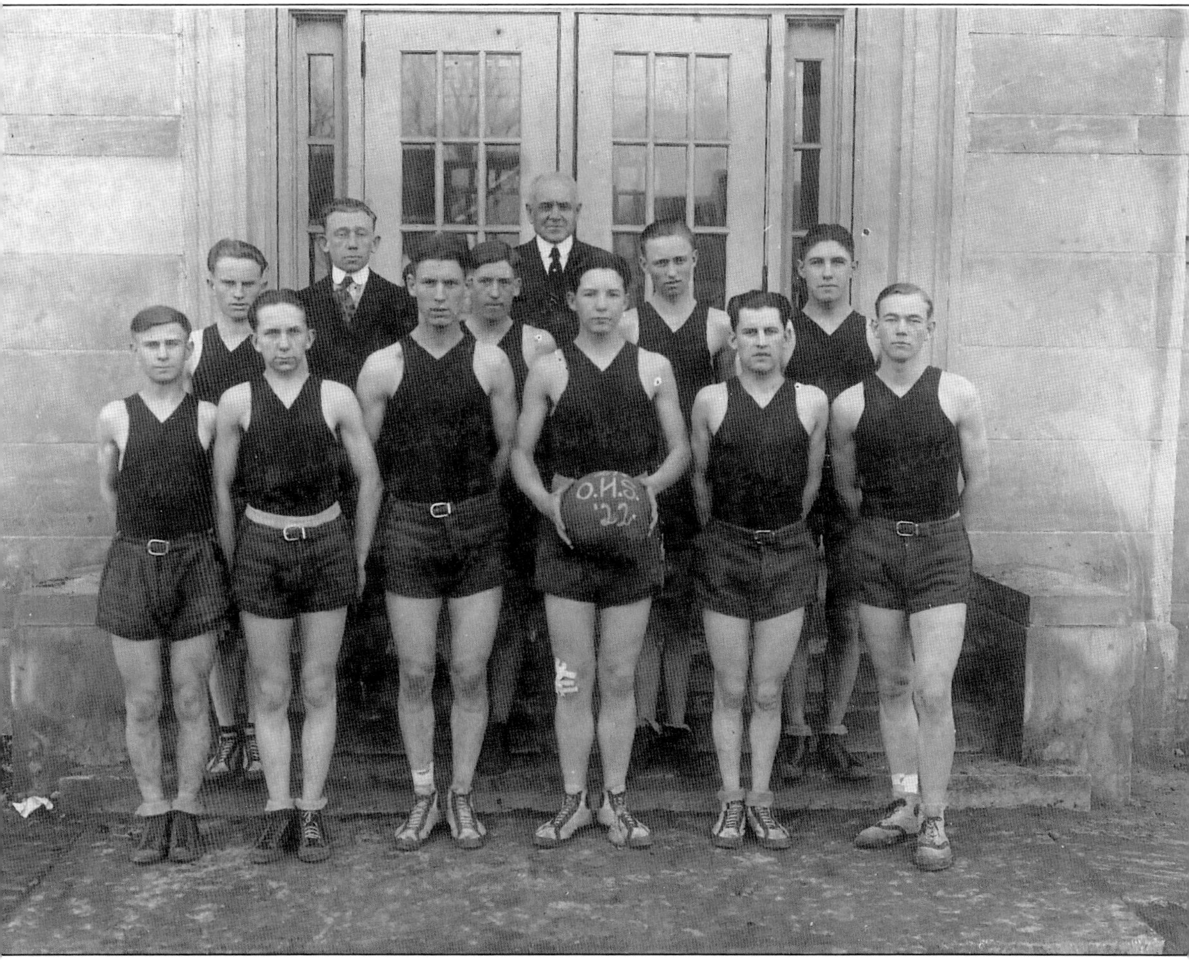

This is Oolitic's basketball team in 1922. Only two people can be identified. Ted Jones is holding the ball. John Anderson is the last one on the right, in the back row.

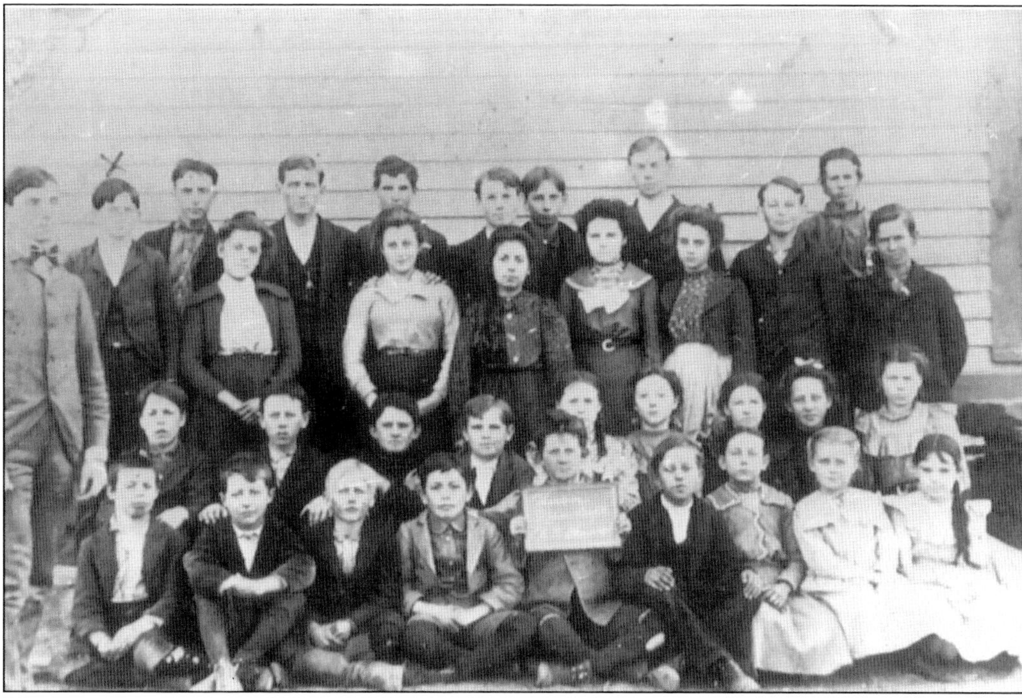

This is a class picture of Huron School, which is no longer in use. The children in this 1904 photograph cannot be identified.

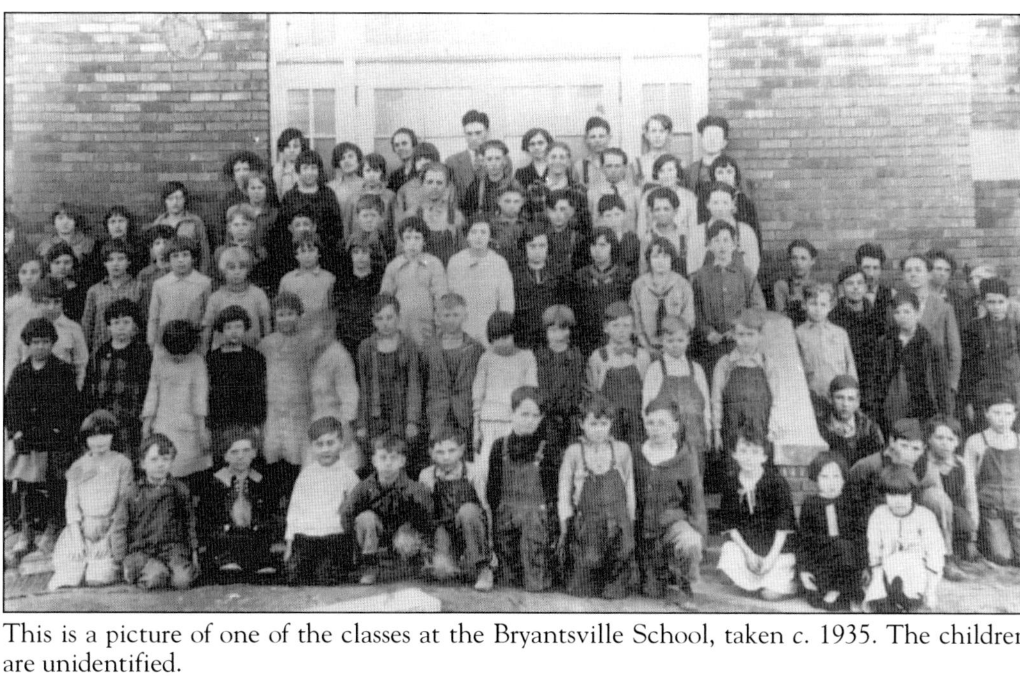

This is a picture of one of the classes at the Bryantsville School, taken *c.* 1935. The children are unidentified.

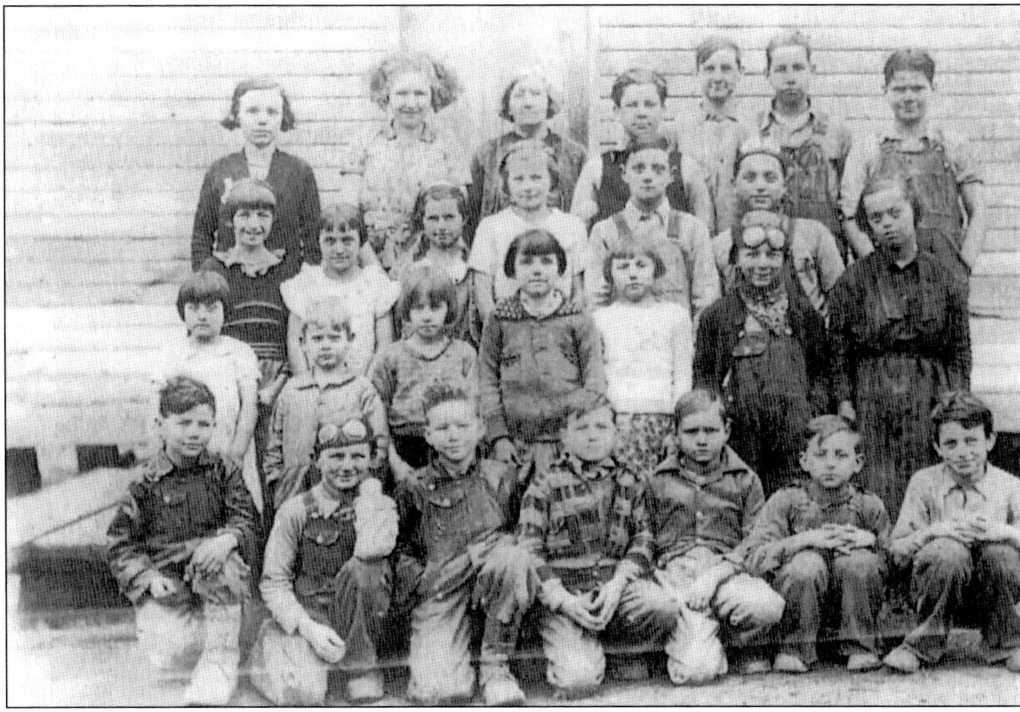

Henderson Creek School is no longer in use as a school. This is a class picture of the class of 1936. Some of the family names of the students are: Lane, Stancomb, East, Blackwell, Glassco, Axom, and Pruitt. The teacher was Della Bridwell.

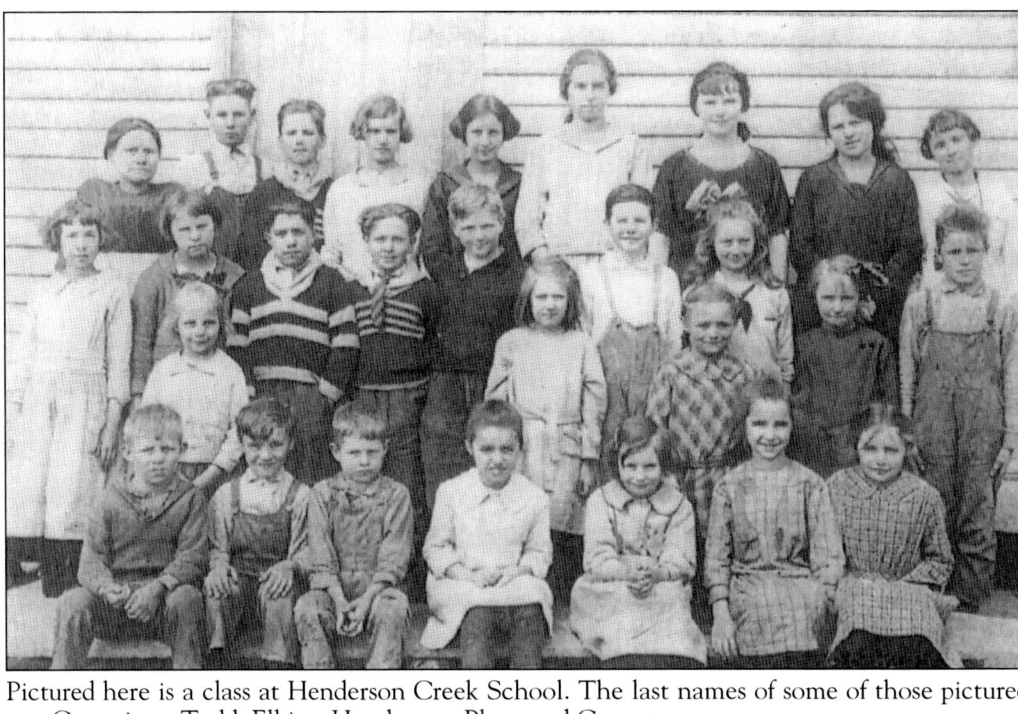

Pictured here is a class at Henderson Creek School. The last names of some of those pictured are: Cummings, Todd, Elkins, Henderson, Pless, and George.

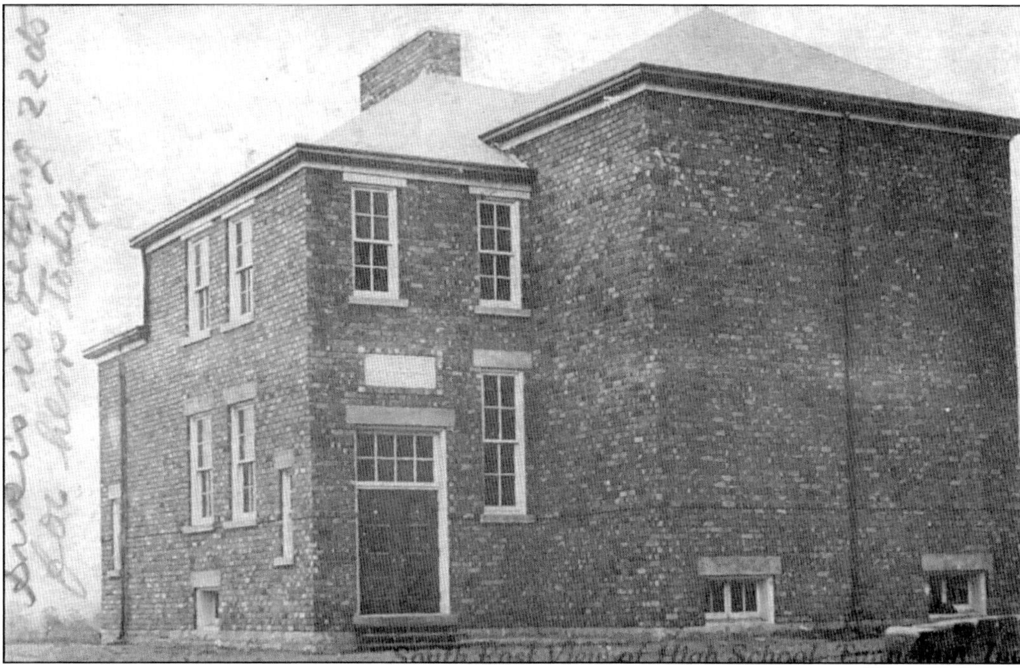

Here is the southeast view of the Tunnelton High School in 1920. During consolidation, this school building was torn down, and children now go to Bedford North Lawrence.

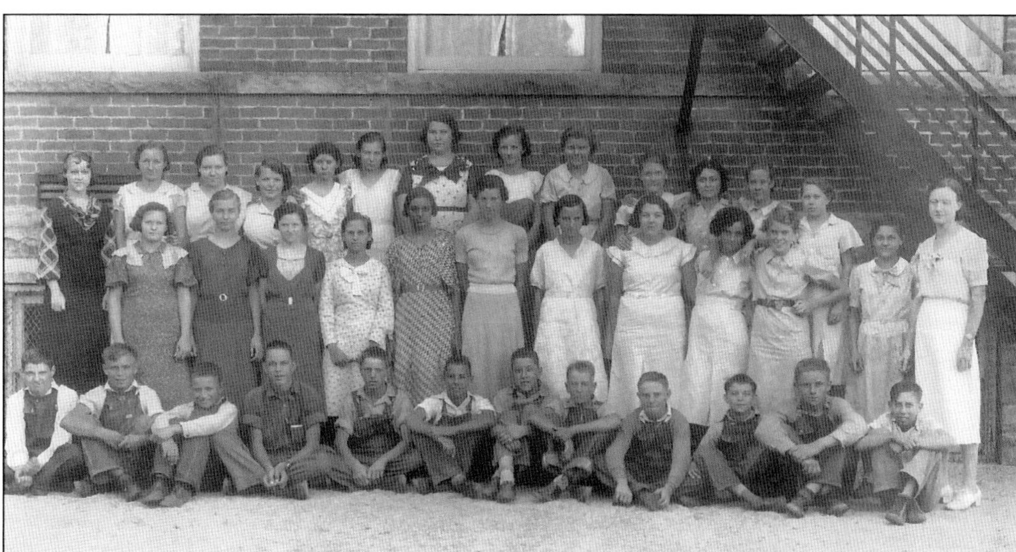

Here is the freshman class of 1934-35 of Tunnelton High School.

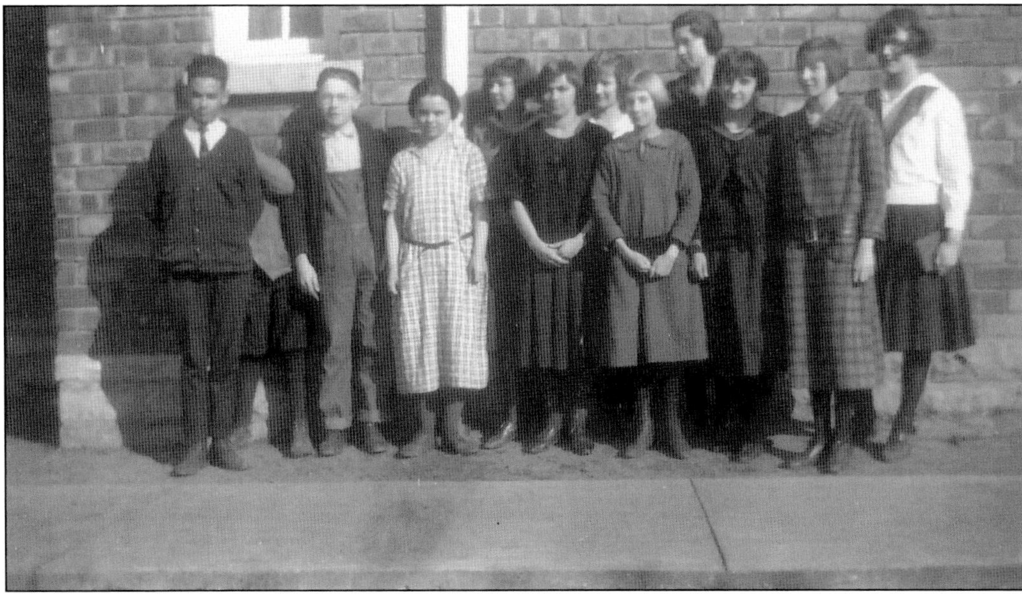

In 1925, this photo was taken of the junior class of Tunnelton High School. The students are not identified.

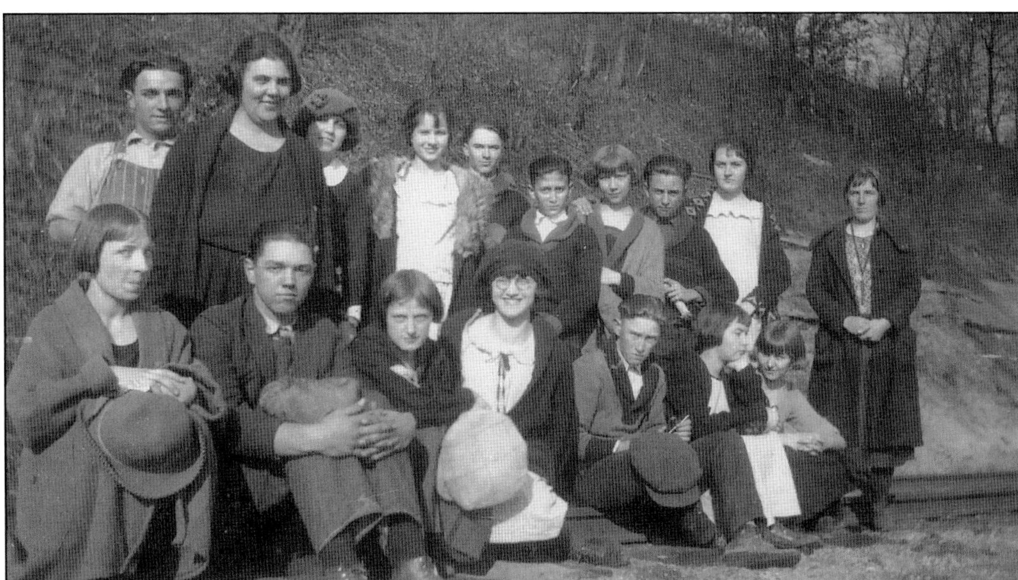

These students in the Tunnelton High School botany class of 1923, pose for this picture on one of their outings.

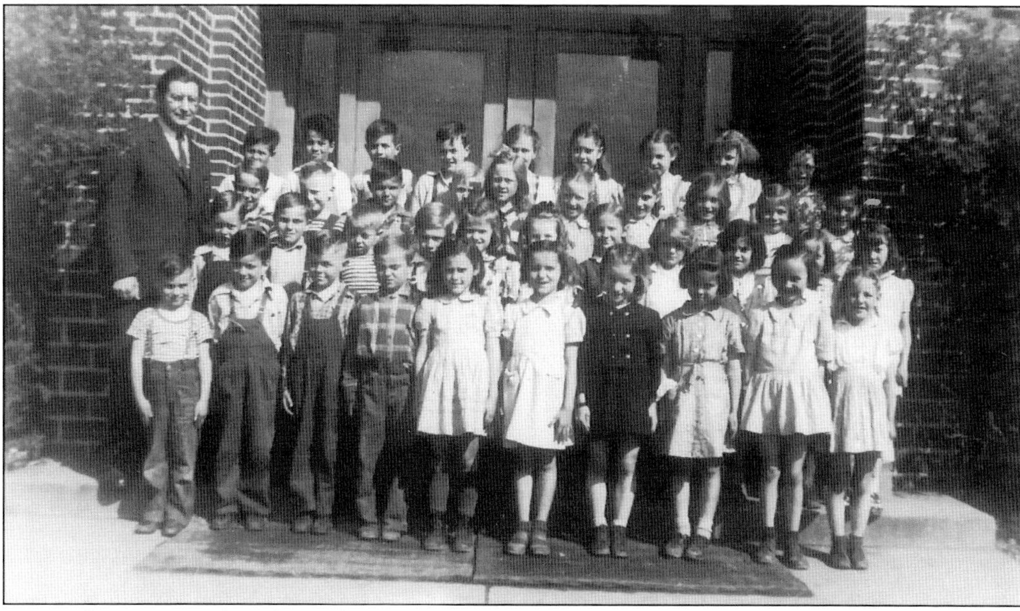

Don Allen, pictured at the right, was a teacher at Tunnelton School during the 1930s. This photo is one of his unidentified classes, and was taken before consolidation when many of the smaller schools disappeared.

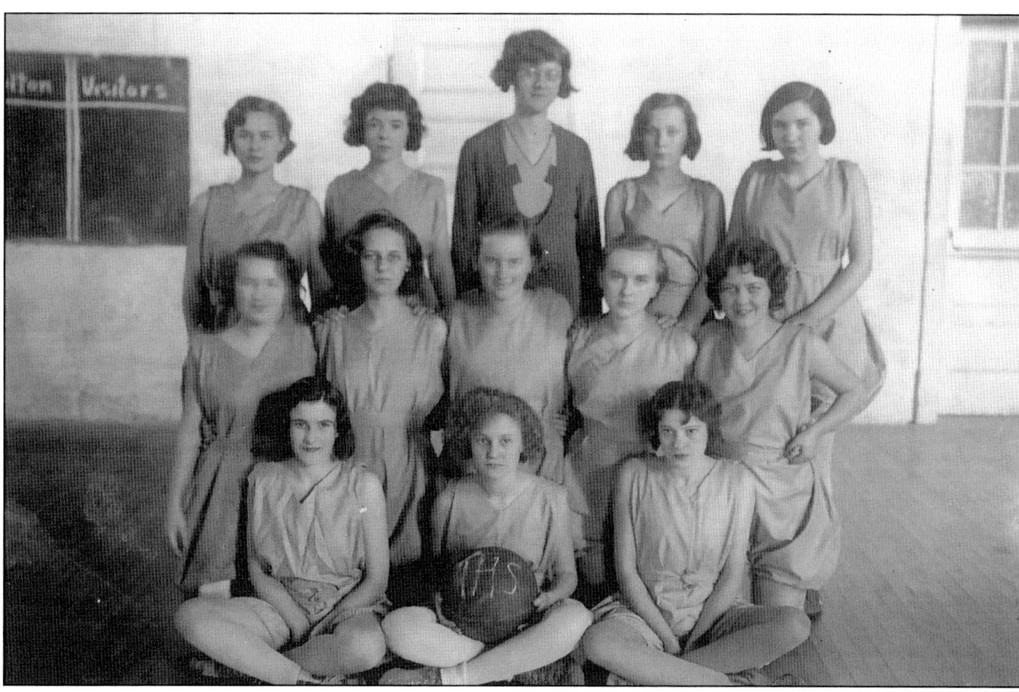

This is a picture of Madge Crane's gym class, Tunnelton High School c. 1929. The girls cannot be identified.

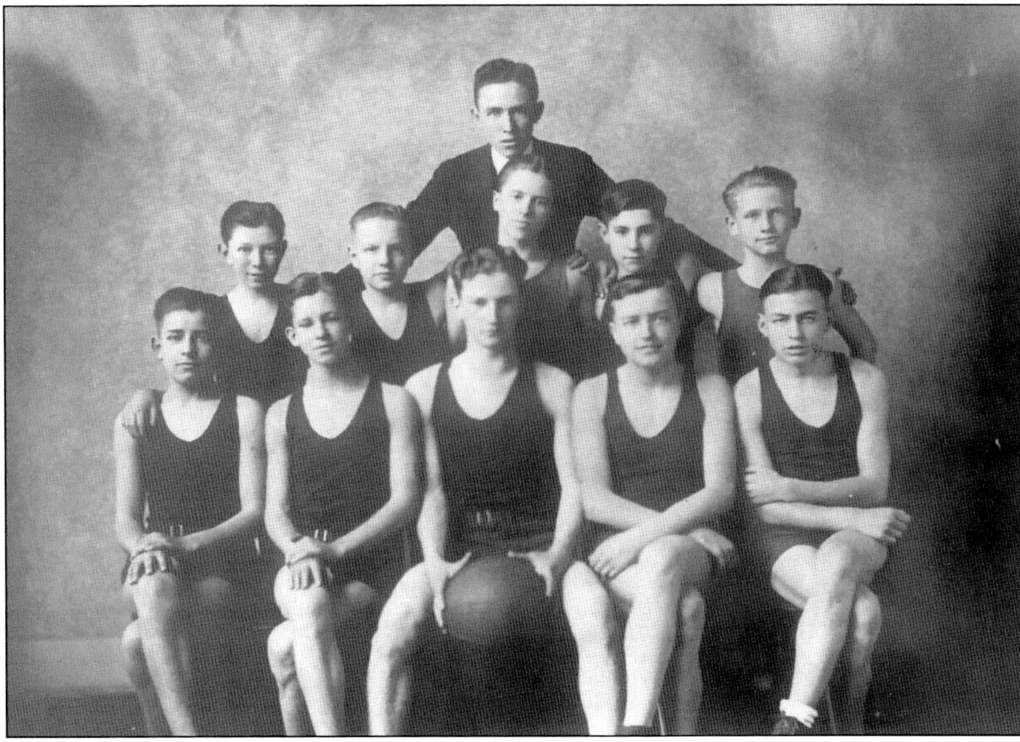

This is the Bedford Junior High Basketball Team in 1924. Pictured in the front row are: Jim Askew, Harold Gould, Chris Schmidt, Sam Miller, and Art Wells. Back row: Yank Terry, Don Wallis, John Abbott, Kenny Reath, Bob Nunn, and Coach Lex Combs.

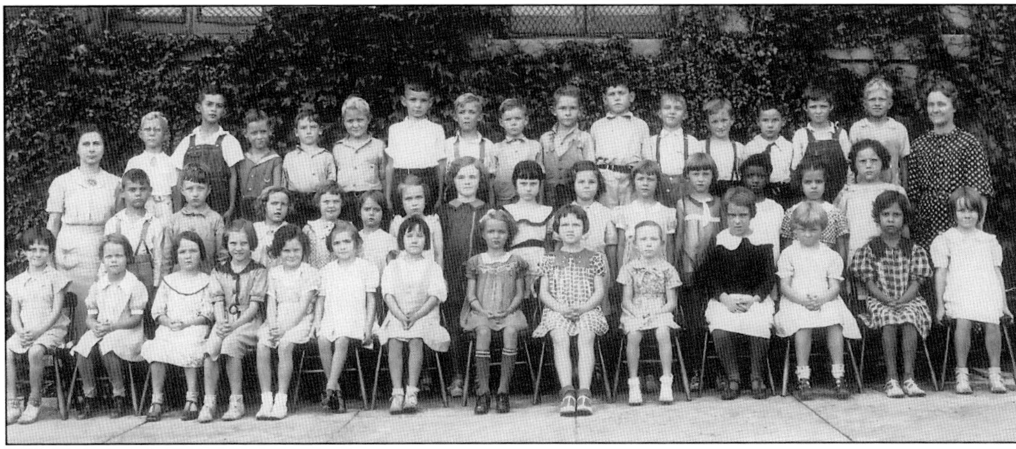

This is the 1937 second grade class of Lincoln School. It was torn down, making space for a fire station.

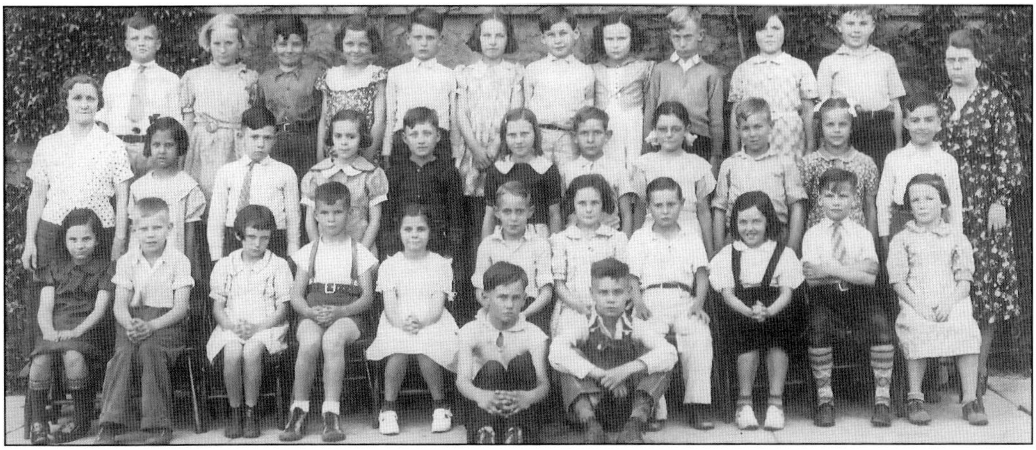

This photo is the third grade 1938 class of Lincoln School. The teacher on the far right is Mrs. Blaze. The principle on the far left is unknown.

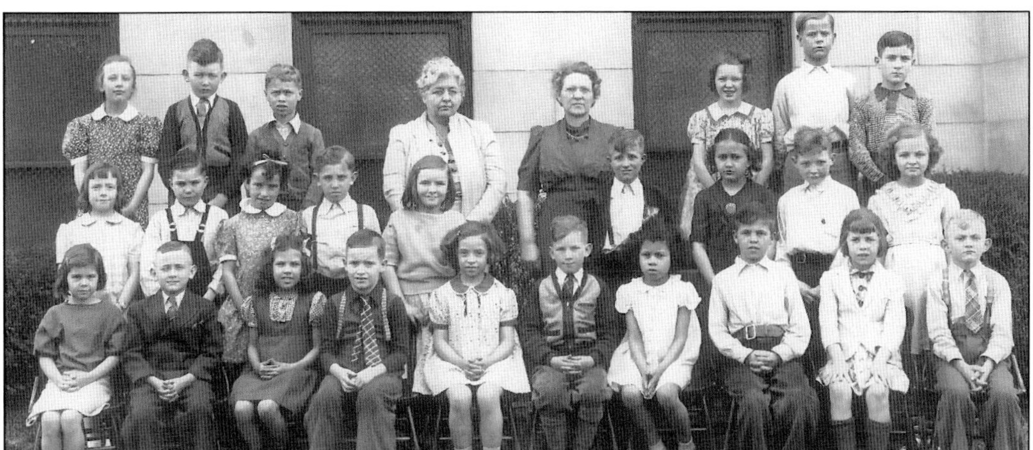

Madden School was located in northern Bedford. Pictured here is the third grade class of 1938. This building is no longer used as a school. Mrs. Martindale (left) is the teacher and Mrs. Kirk (right) is the principal.

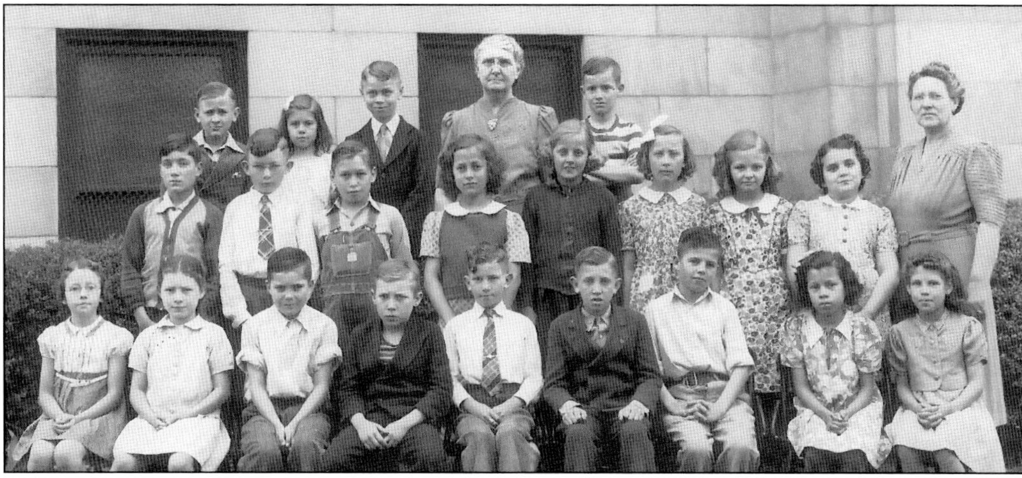

This is a picture of the 1939 fourth grade class at Madden School. Mrs. Dusard, in the back, is the teacher, and Mrs. Kirk, at right, is the principal.

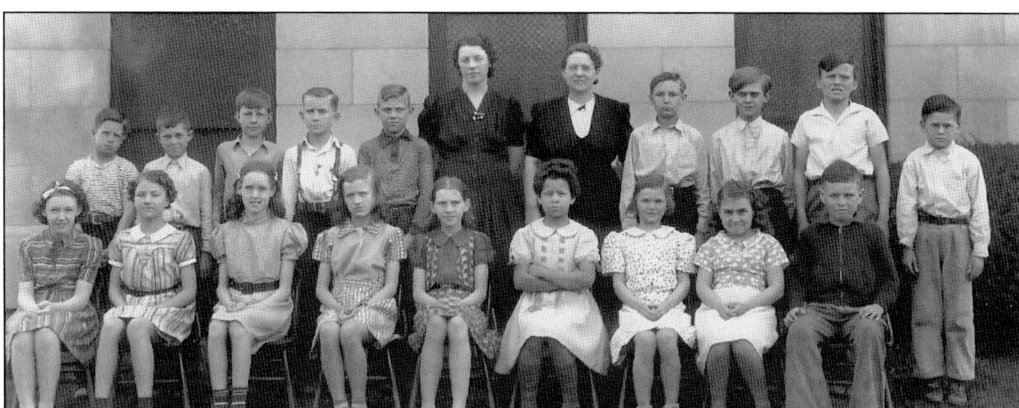

In 1940, this photo was taken of the 5th grade class at Madden School. The teacher, back row and left, is Mrs. Peed.

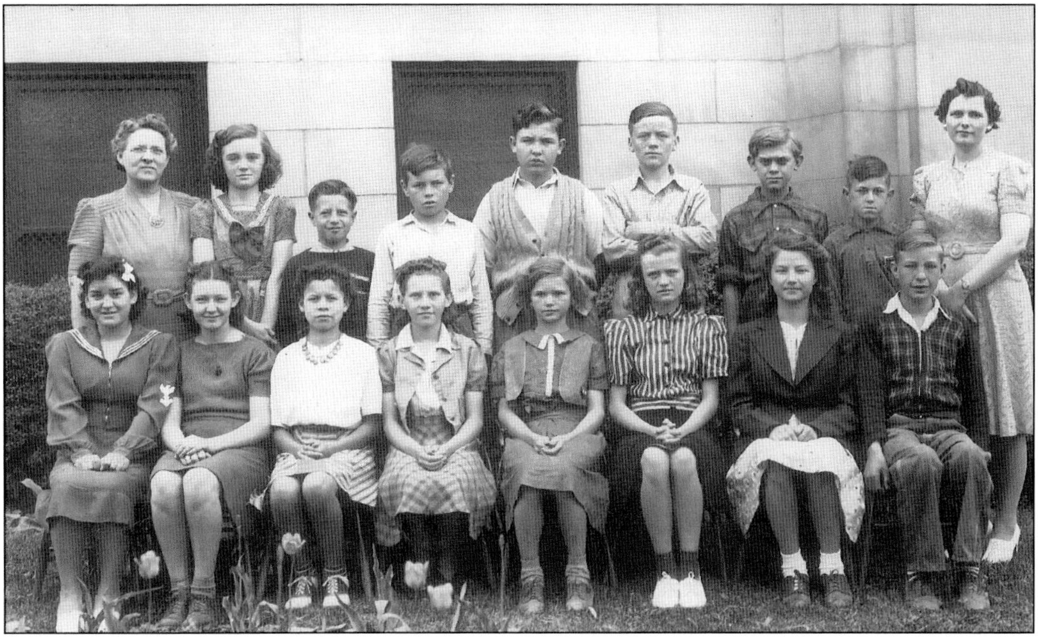

This is a picture of the sixth grade class at Madden School, taken in 1941.

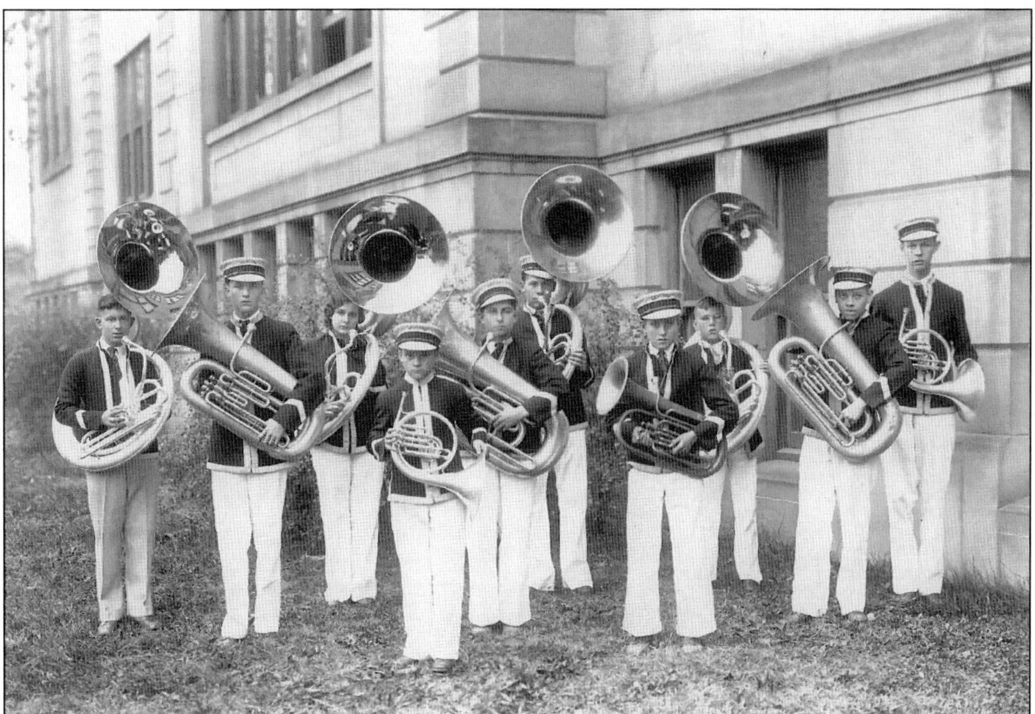

This picture was taken of the Bedford High School Band c. 1930. The identity of those shown is not known.

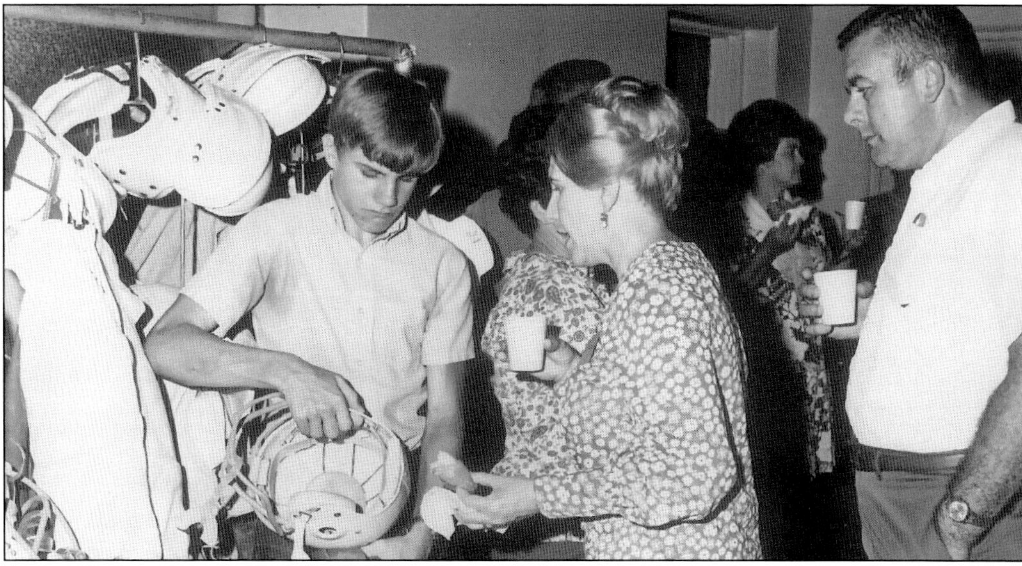

Mr. and Mrs. Sam Kruse talk to their son in the locker room just before a football game. This photo was taken in 1970.

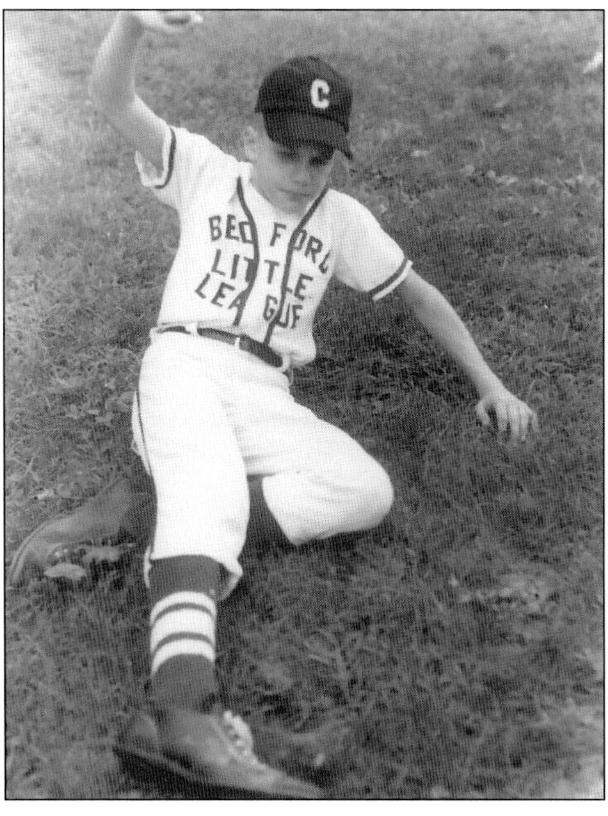

Bedford has always had a very active Boys' Club. This 12-year-old Shawswick School student played softball on the Boys' Club Little League Team.

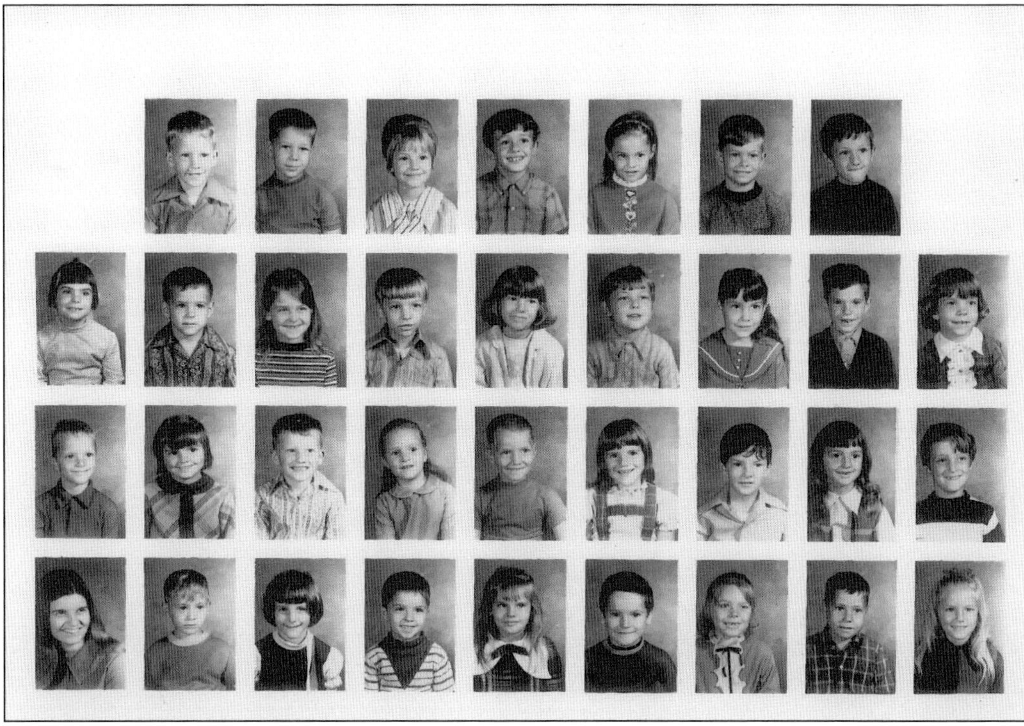

This is a Shawswick School first grade picture taken in 1971.

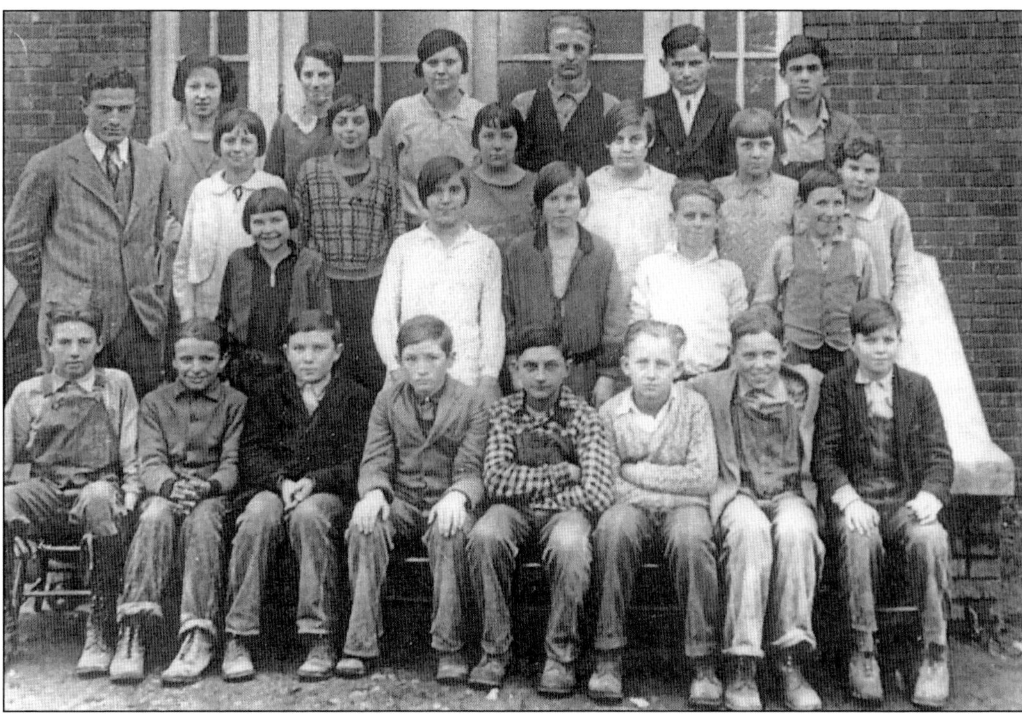

This picture is Bryantsville grades five, six, seven, and eight of 1929. Frank Tincher, left in the picture, is the teacher.

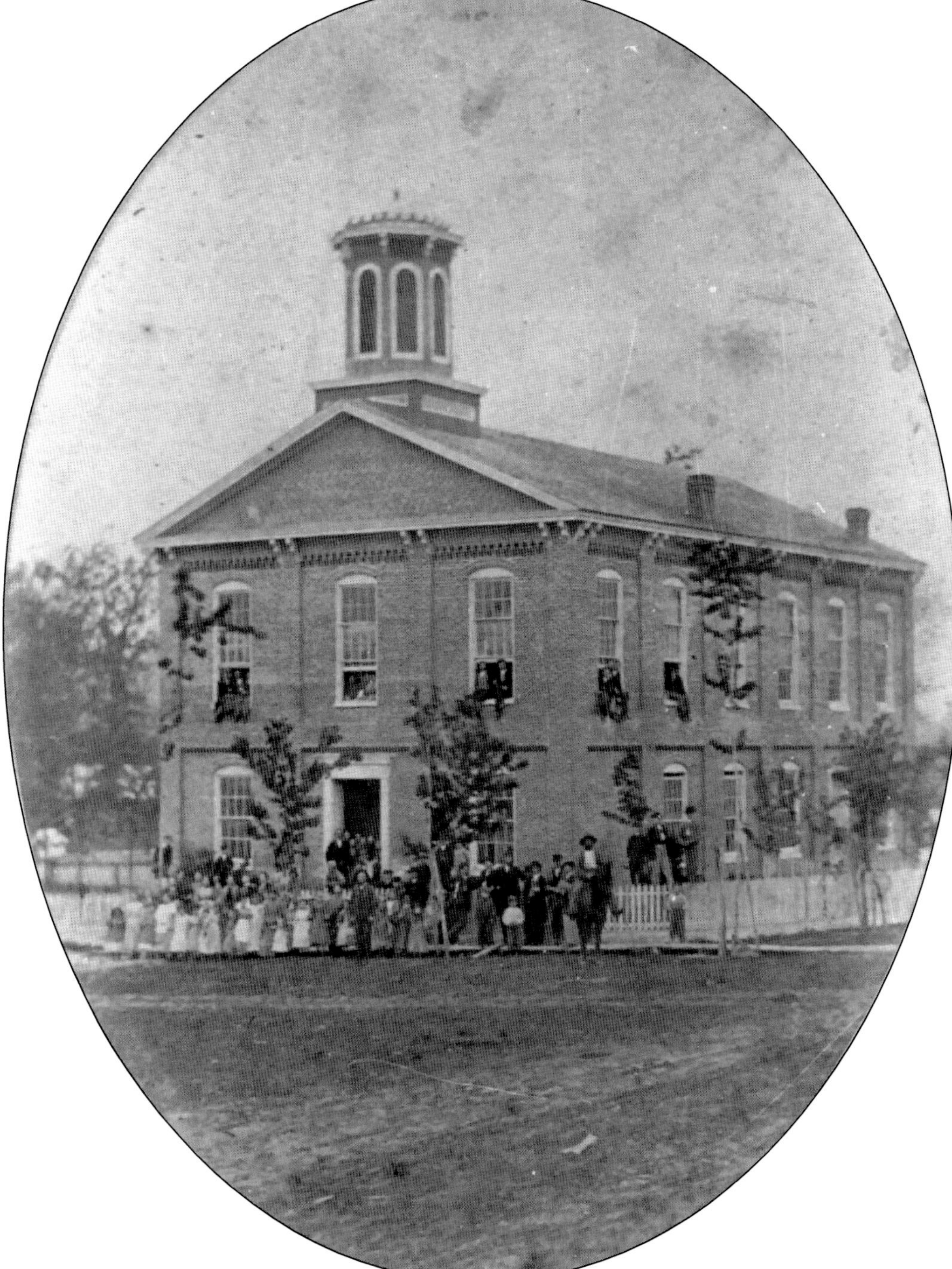

In 1860, this building was erected and known as the Baptist Church. The lower story was used for educational studies (the Mitchell Seminary), and the upper was used for worship as a church. It later became the First Baptist Church on 7th and Frank Street.

Six

Transportation

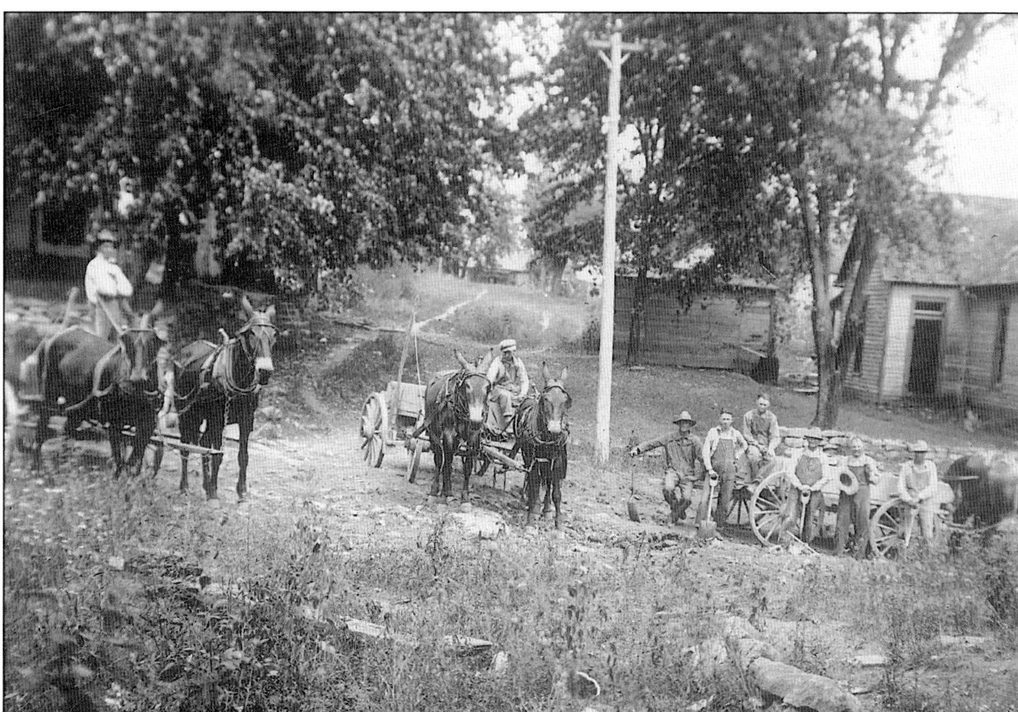

This is a group of farm hands with their mode of transportation, mules and wagons. It is believed that this picture was taken in the early 1900s, on the Miles Standish farm in Lawrence County.

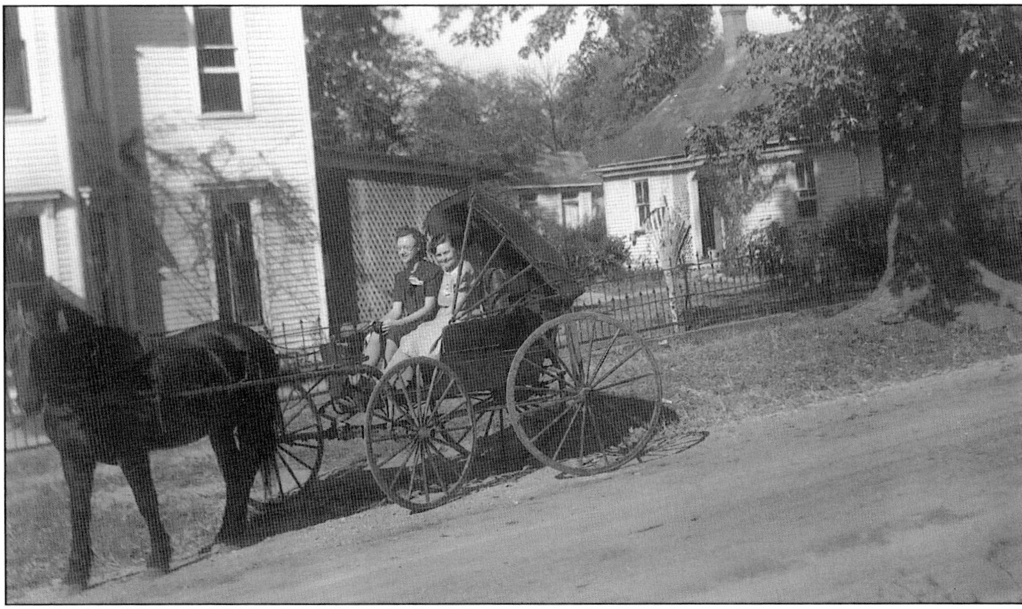

Ella Wright and Madge Crane (driving) are seated in the Wilcox buggy in front of the Wilcox homestead, which was occupied by Miss Wright and her brother Grant Wright. This picture was taken in the 1920s at Tunnelton.

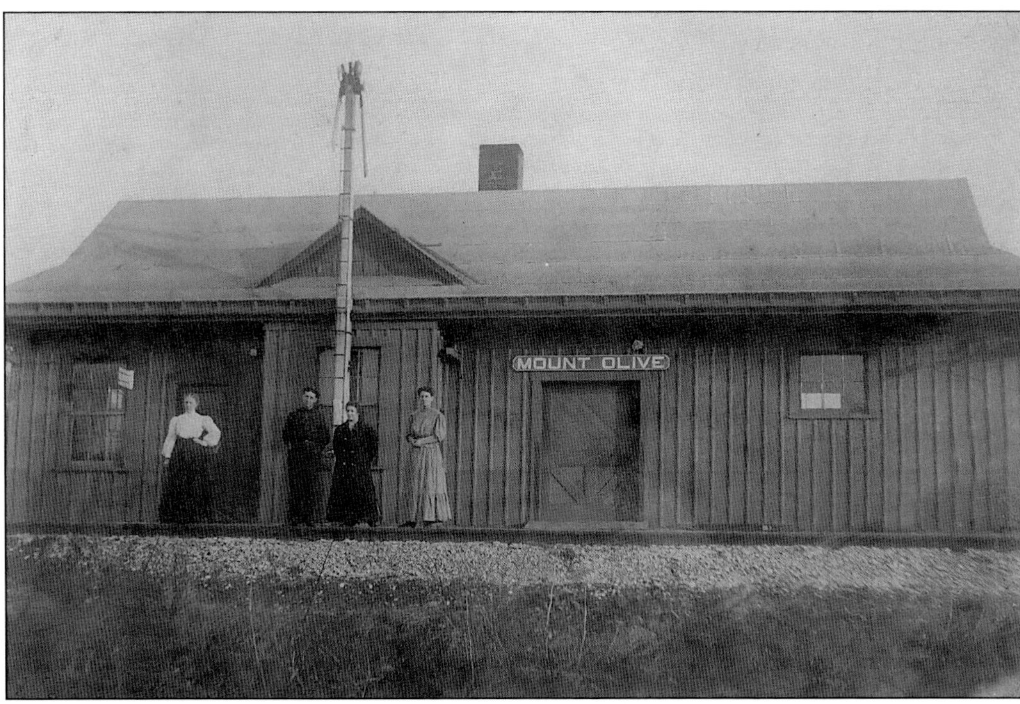

This is a picture of Mount Olive Depot in the early 1900s. Standing on the platform, left to right, are: Carrie Inman, Luther Pierce, Myrtle Clements, and Dell Roush.

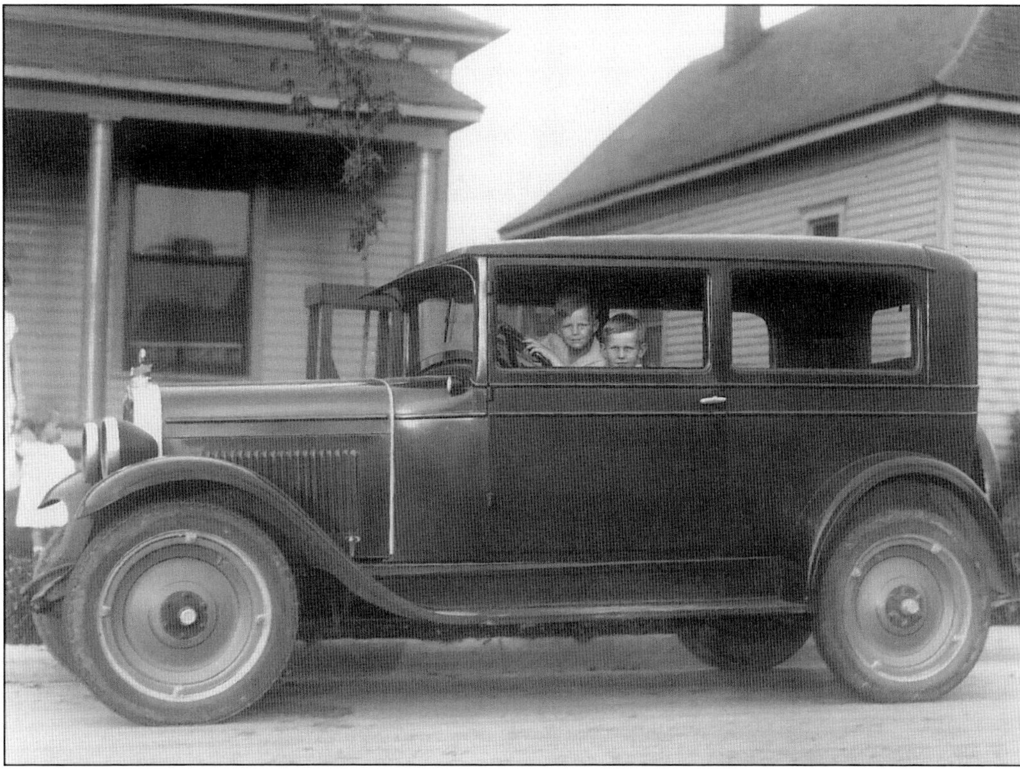

Tom and Gordon Long are shown here in their father's 1930/1931 Chevrolet.

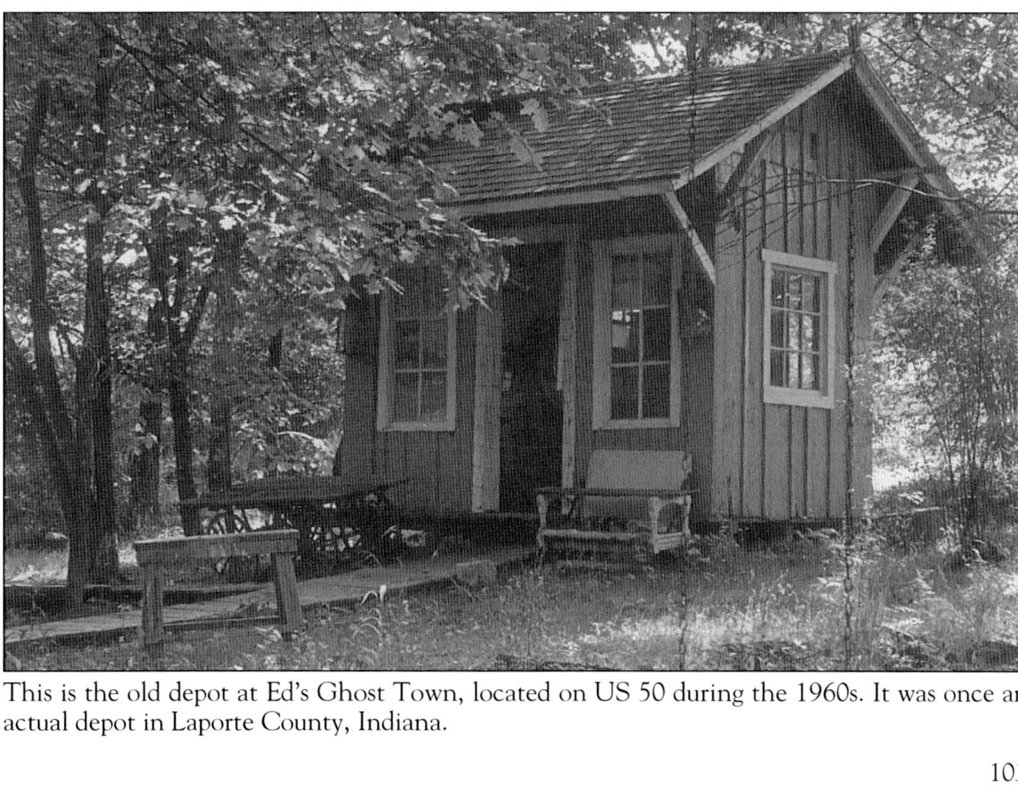

This is the old depot at Ed's Ghost Town, located on US 50 during the 1960s. It was once an actual depot in Laporte County, Indiana.

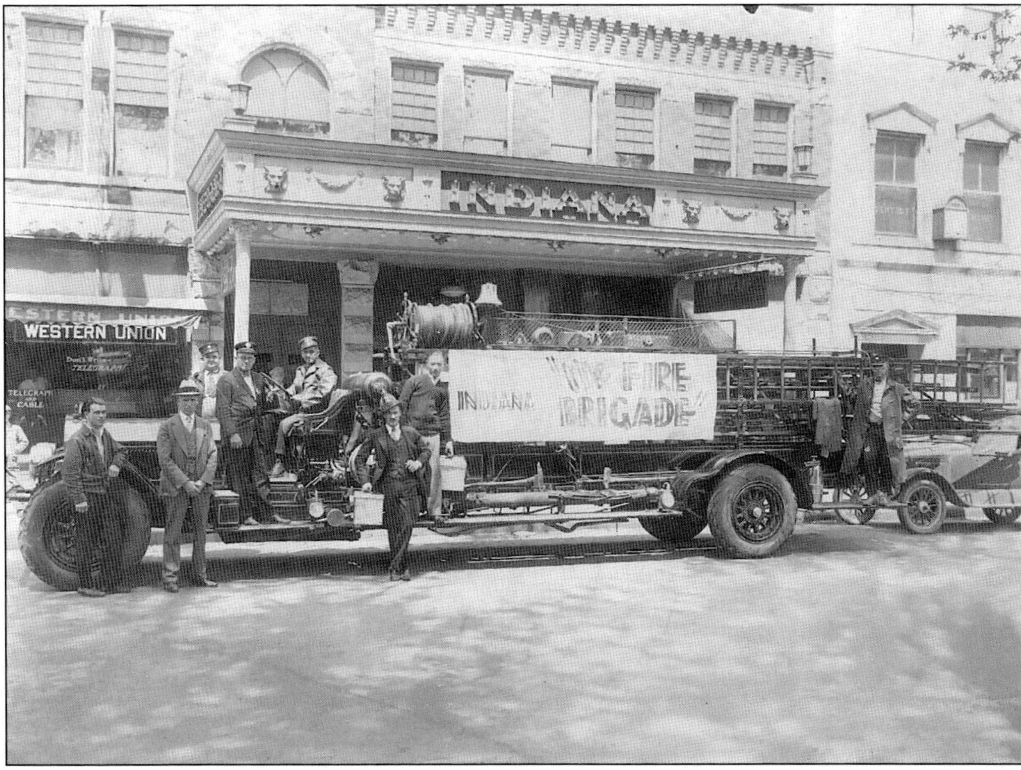

The "Indiana Fire Brigade" is parked in front of the old Indiana Theater in Bedford. This was one of the first fire trucks.

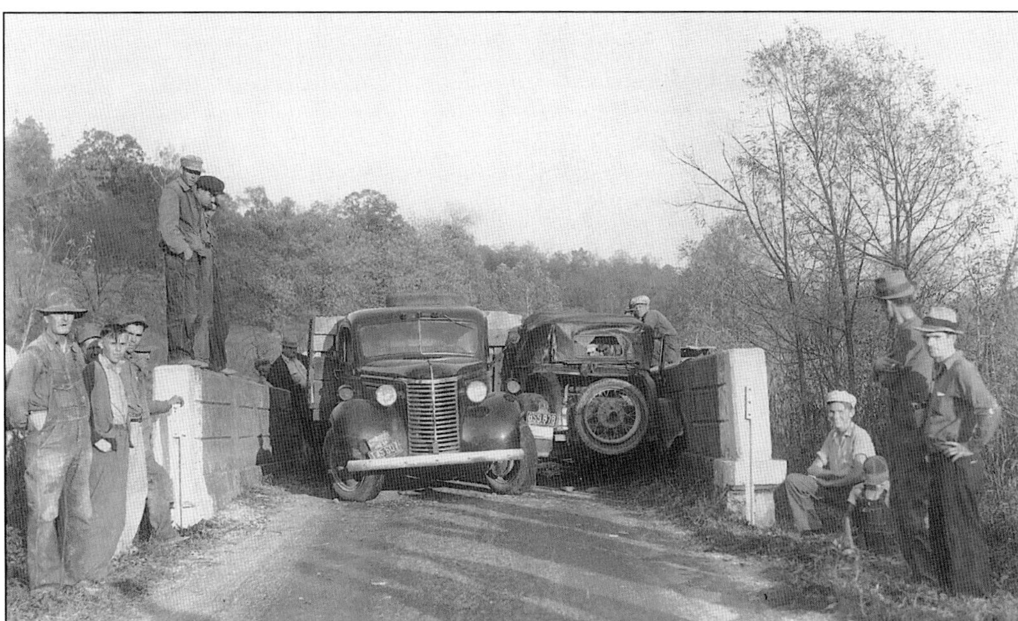

This is an accident that occurred in the late 1930s at the narrow Stump Hole Bridge southeast of Bedford. The onlookers cannot be identified.

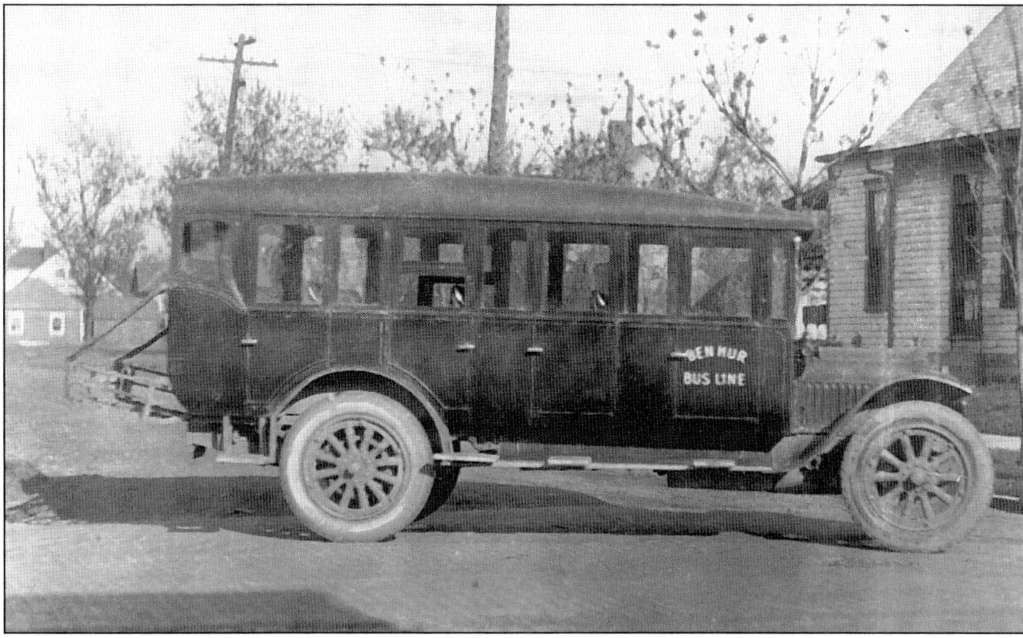

In the early 1900s, this bus belonging to the Ben Hur Bus Line was seen parked on the street in Bedford.

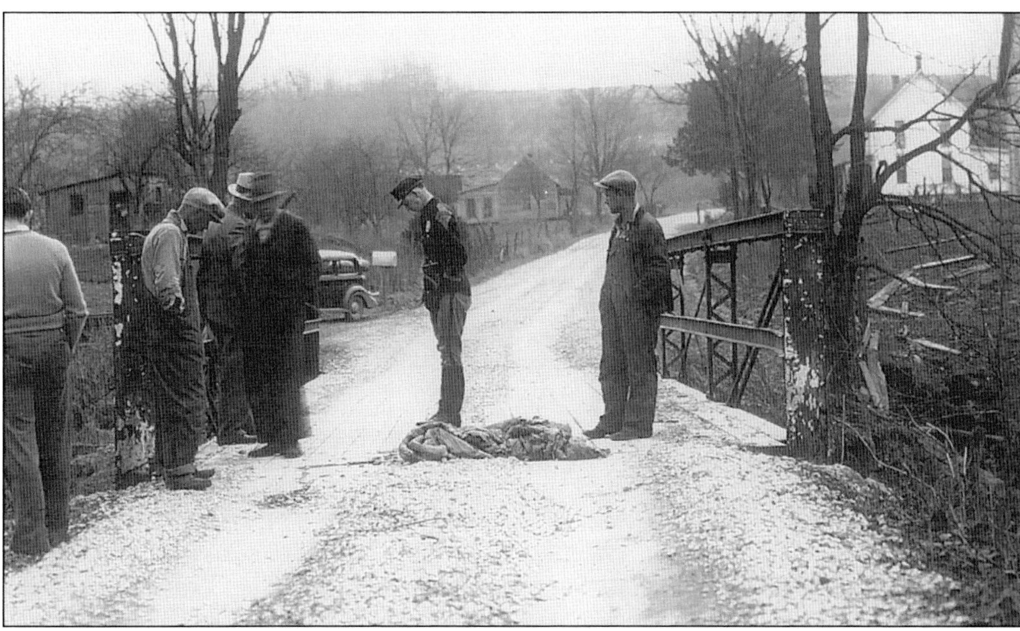

This hit and run accident happened in 1936, where an unidentified man was killed. The accident happened between Fayetteville and Silverville.

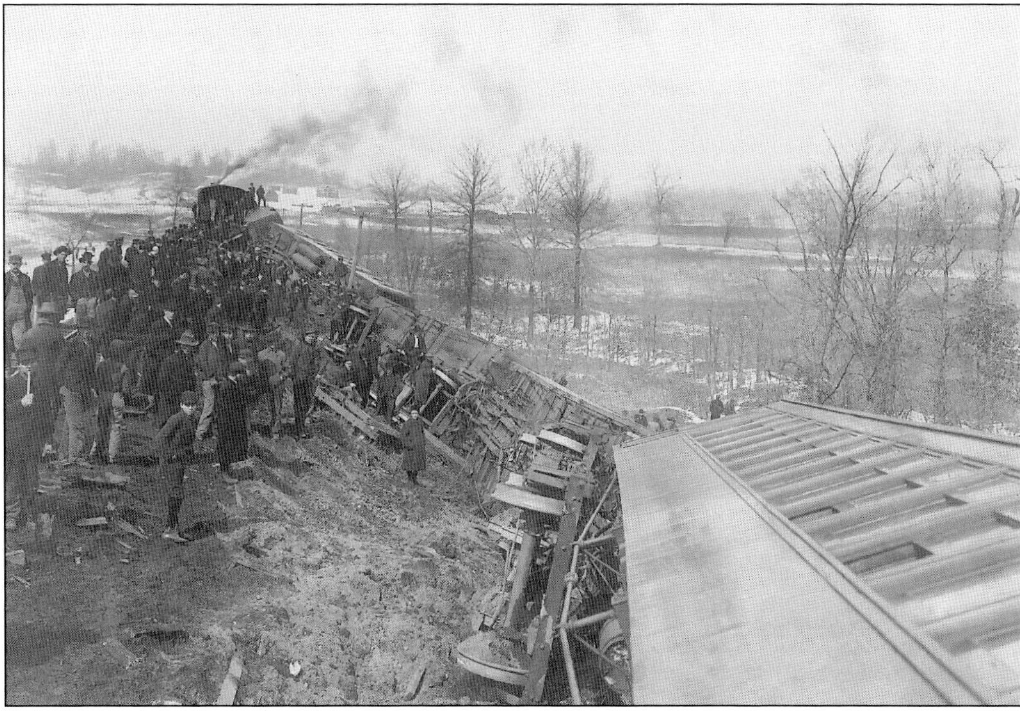

This train wreck was believed to have been on the B&O track in the early 1900s. It is not known if there were any deaths or injuries.

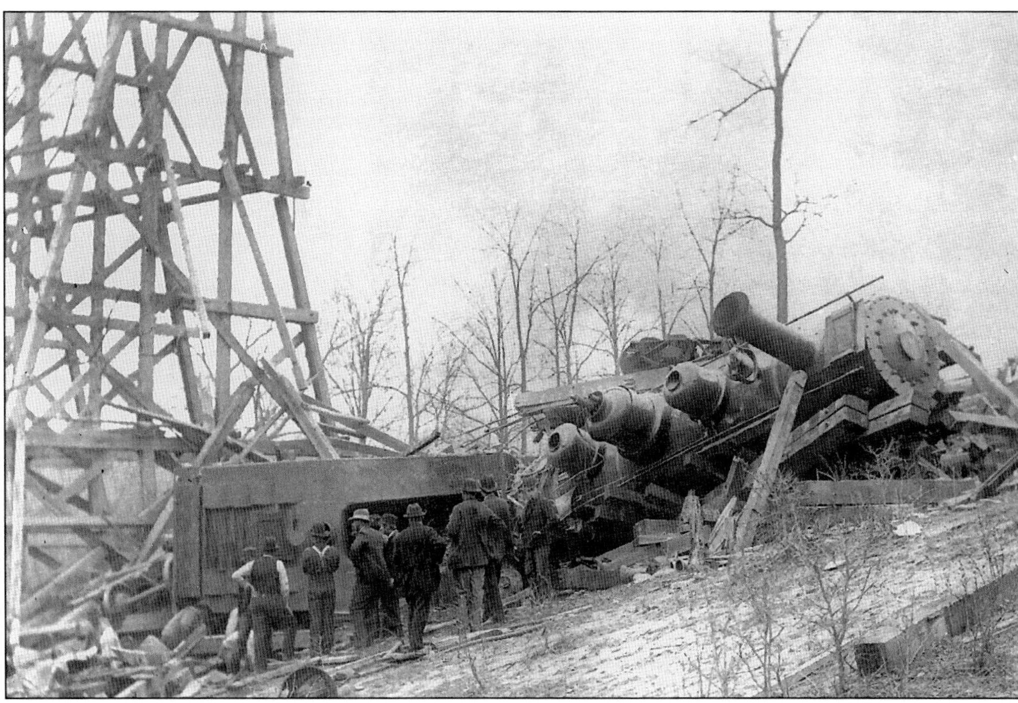

This accident happened April 13, 1896, on the Beford Belt. The five people killed were the conductor, bridge foreman, fireman, and two bridge carpenters. Three people were injured.

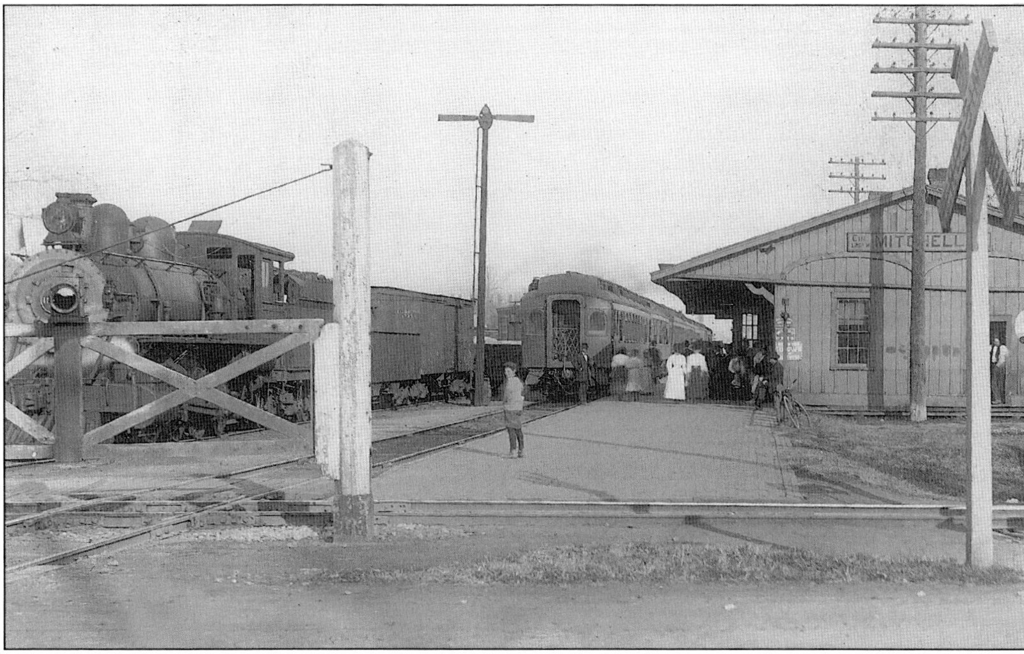

Here is the B&O Train Depot in Mitchell, Indiana. The B&O track played a huge part in the history of Lawrence County. It transported troops in the Civil War, World War I, and World War II.

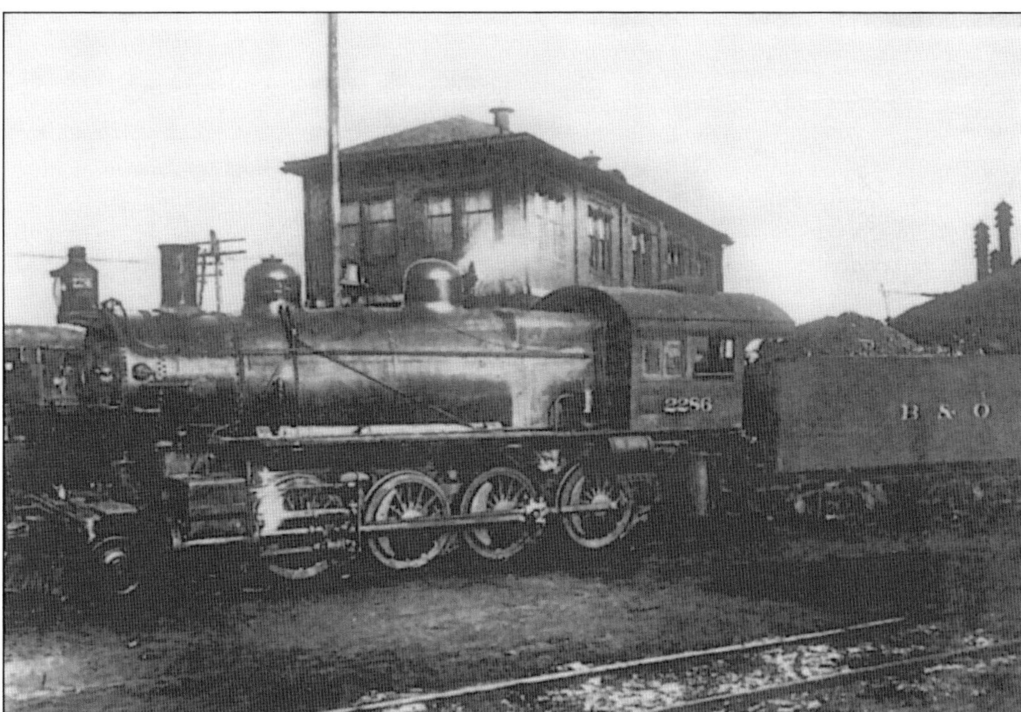

This is B&O Locomotive #2286, the heaviest powered locomotive used on the Bedford B&O line.

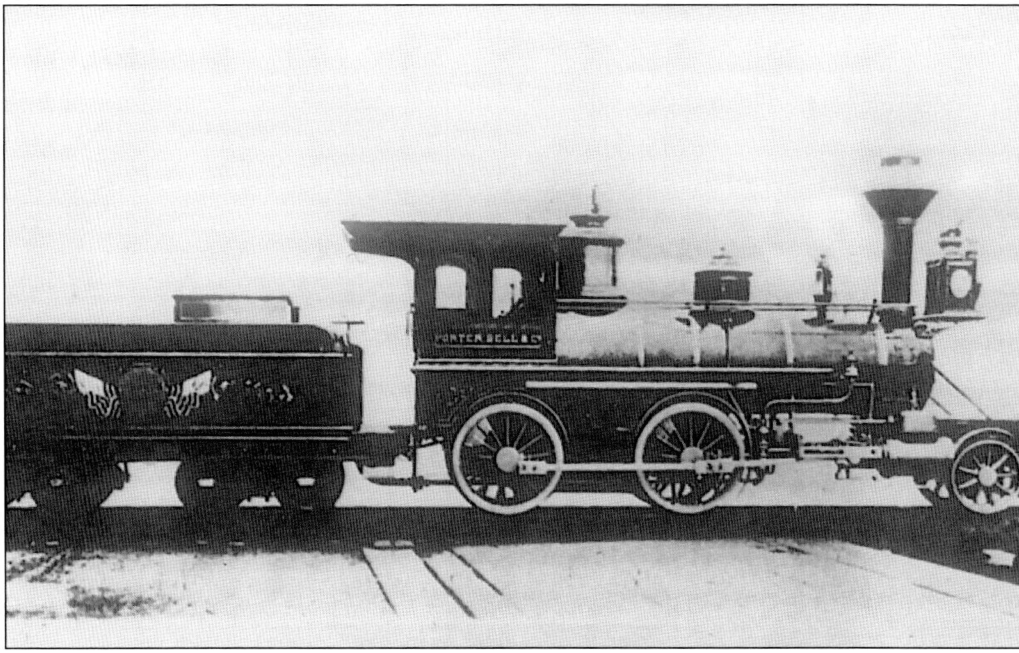

This is a photo of the "Bedford" pride of the narrow gage. It went from Bedford to Bloomfield.

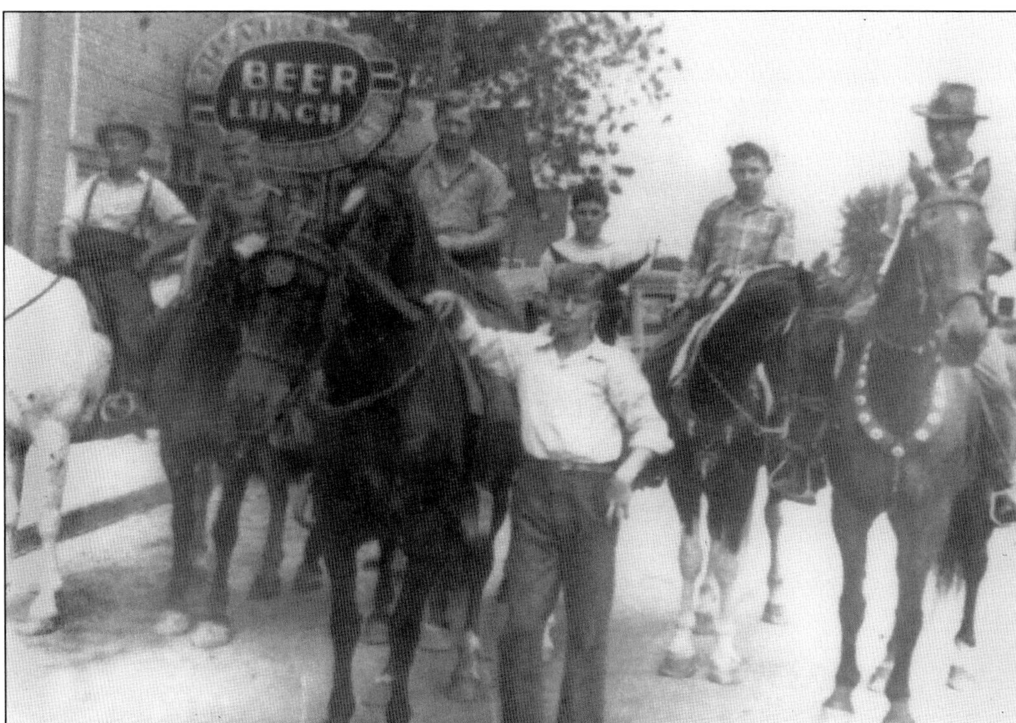

This group of horsemen was headed for a parade at Bedford. Those people shown are: Ross Terrell, Charlie Terrell, George Terrell, Louie Daggy, Hillard Barlow, Bill Crane, and Carl Terrell.

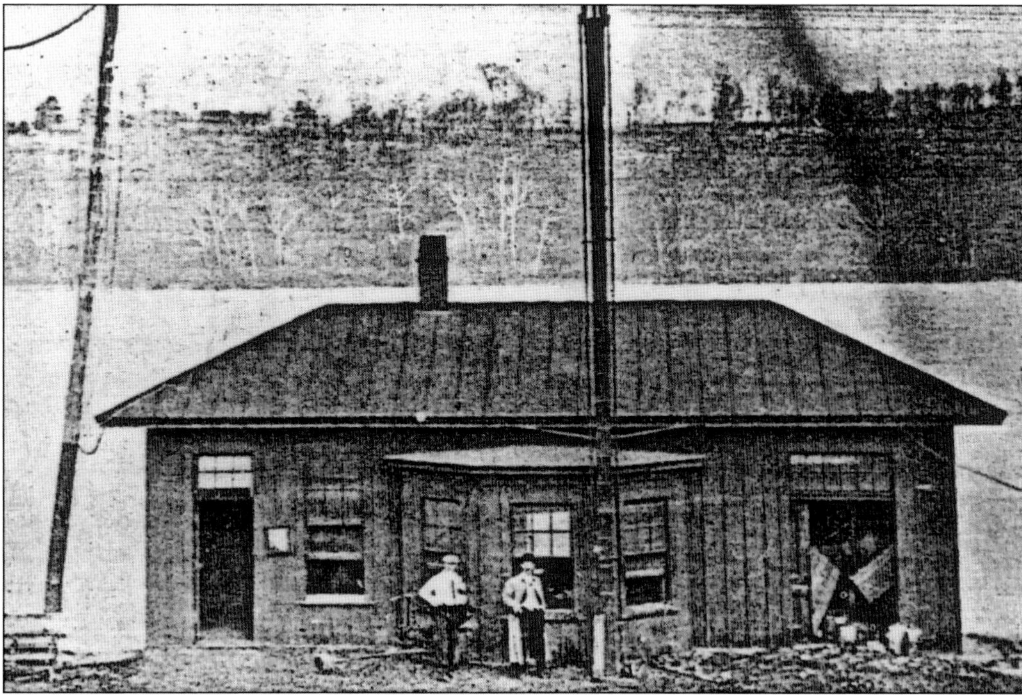

This is a picture of the old Rivervale Rail Road Station as it looked in 1913.

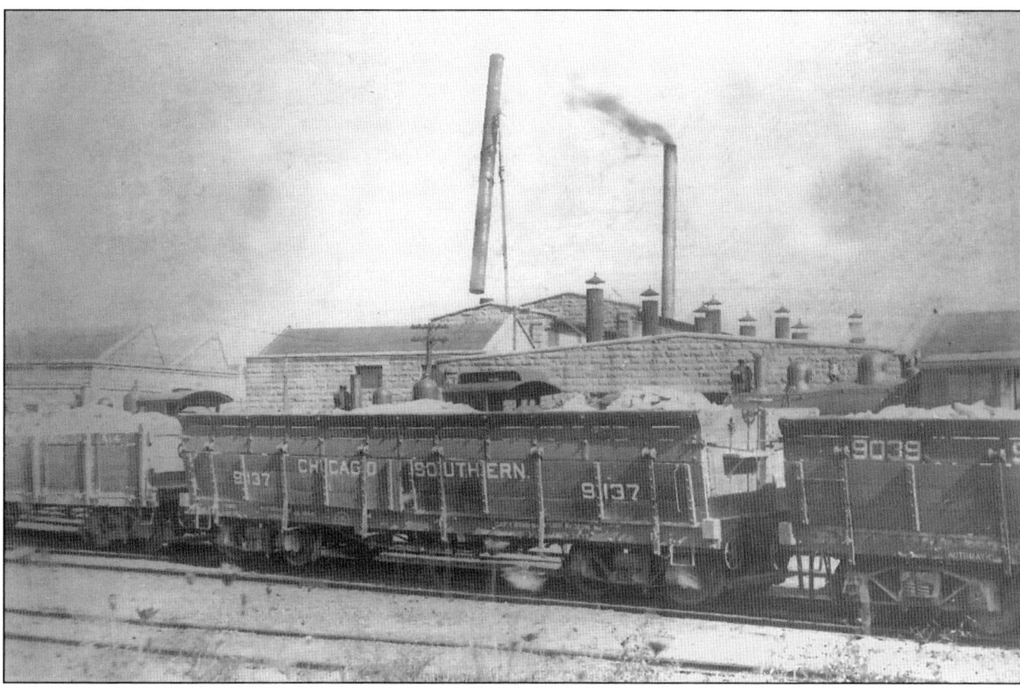

The Milwaukee Rail Road Yard was in the north end of Bedford. There was a prisoner holding camp near this area during the Civil War near this area.

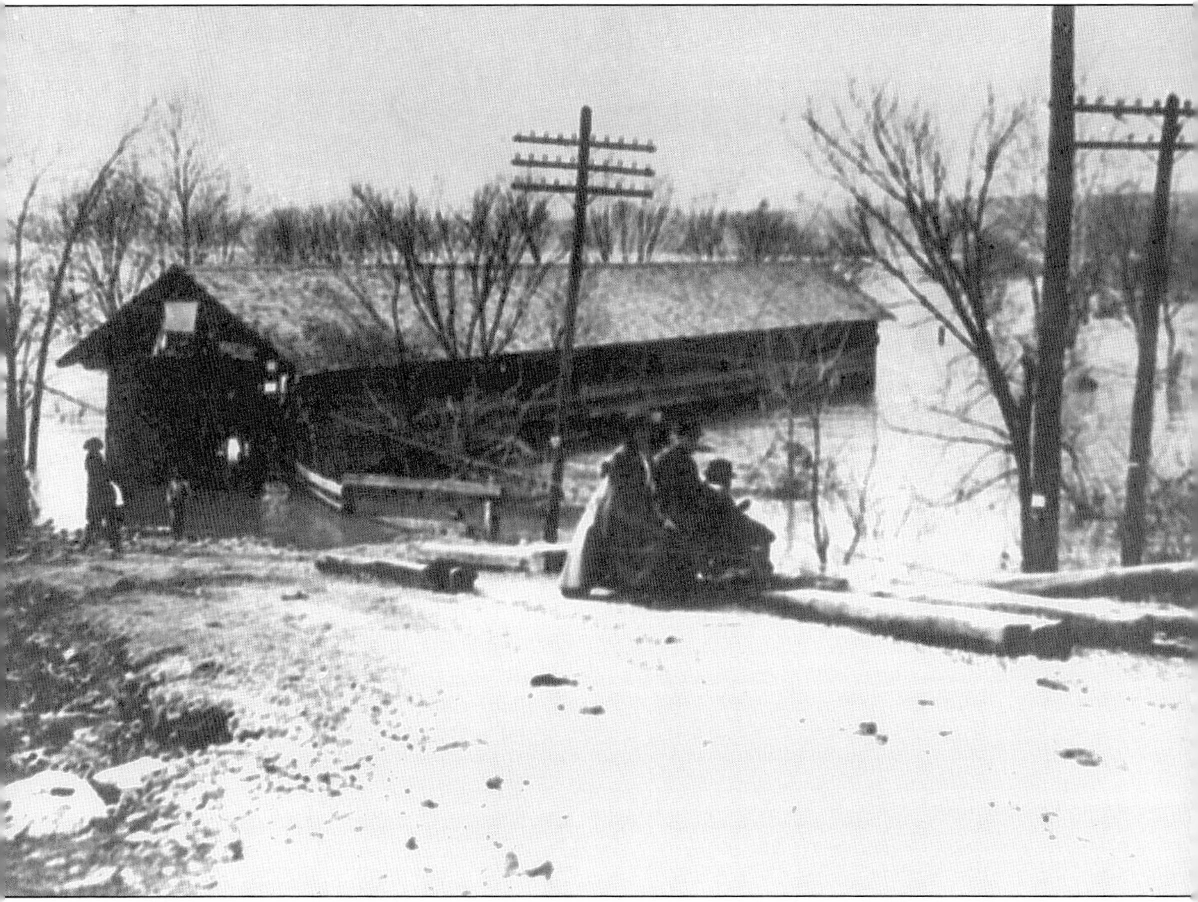

This covered bridge, no longer in existence, was located between Bedford and Oolitic. The flood of 1913 was disastrous to the people of Lawrence County. This photo shows how high the water rose.

Seven

HOUSES AND BUILDINGS

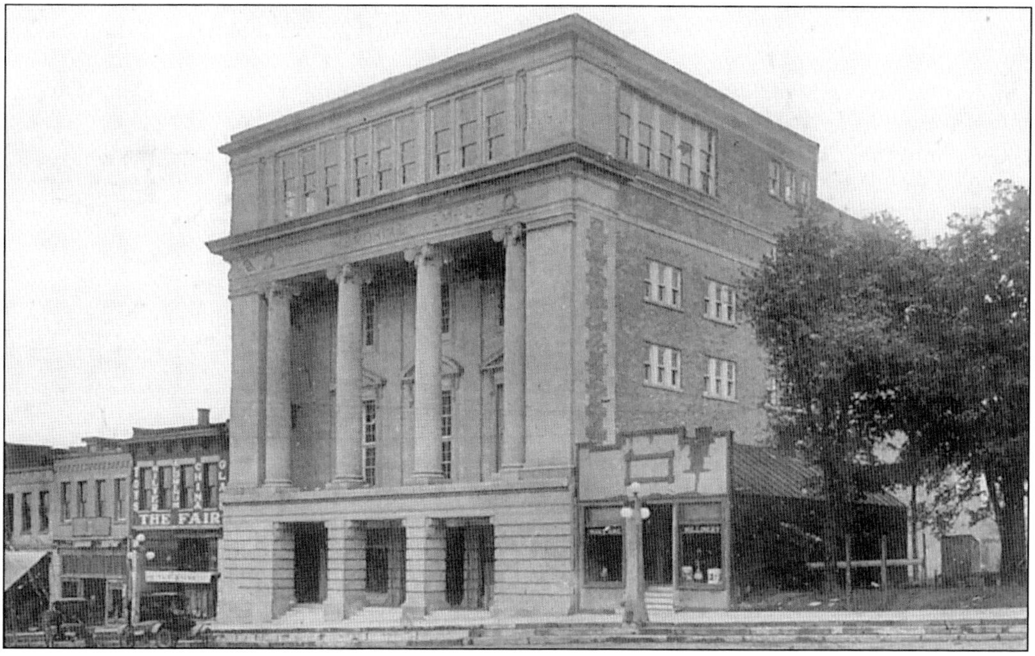

Moses Fell Dunn, an early businessman, donated the Masonic Temple on the north side of the square in Bedford. This photo was taken in the 1920s, before the Greystone Hotel was built on the square.

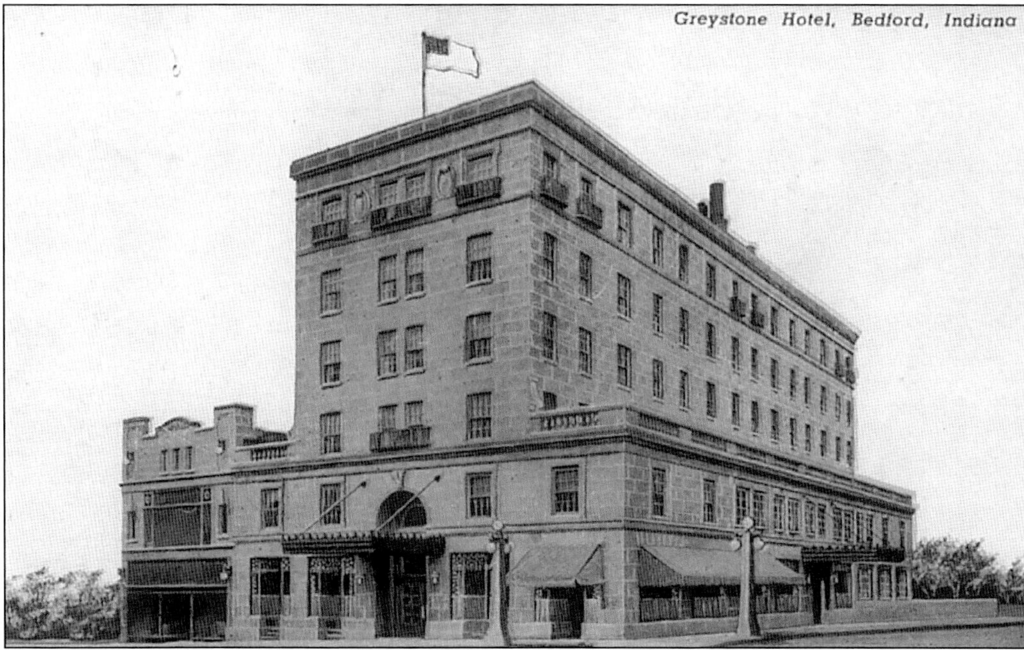

The Greystone Hotel was advertised as "the finest hotel in southern Indiana" just after it was build about 1920. It caught on fire three times, and the building was razed in the early 1990s.

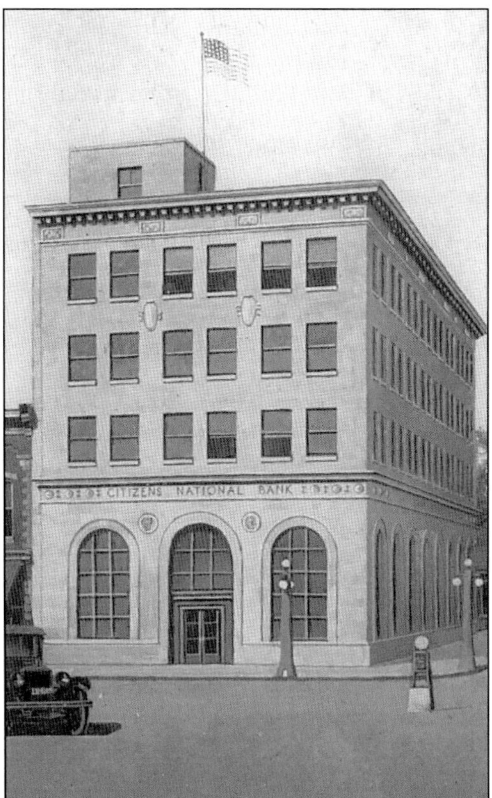

Pictured here is the Citizen's National Bank building in the 1920s. The stone light fixtures around the square in Bedford are no longer in use. The building is now occupied by Union Planters Bank.

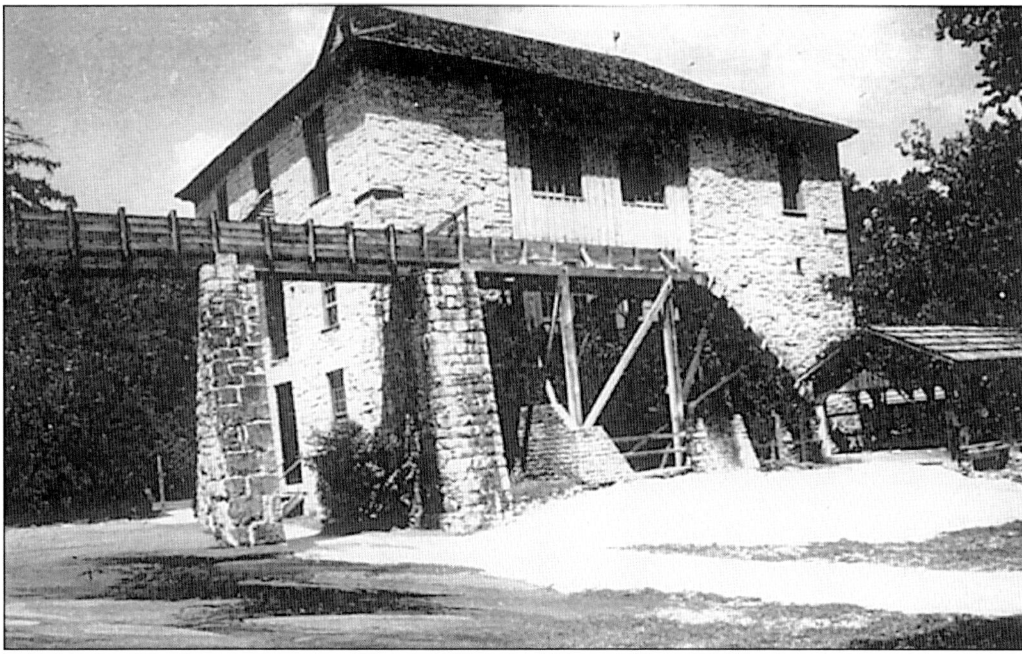

Hamer's Mill is located in Spring Mill State Park and is still in use. The working mill produces ground corn meal that can be purchased. Surrounding the mill is an 18th century village.

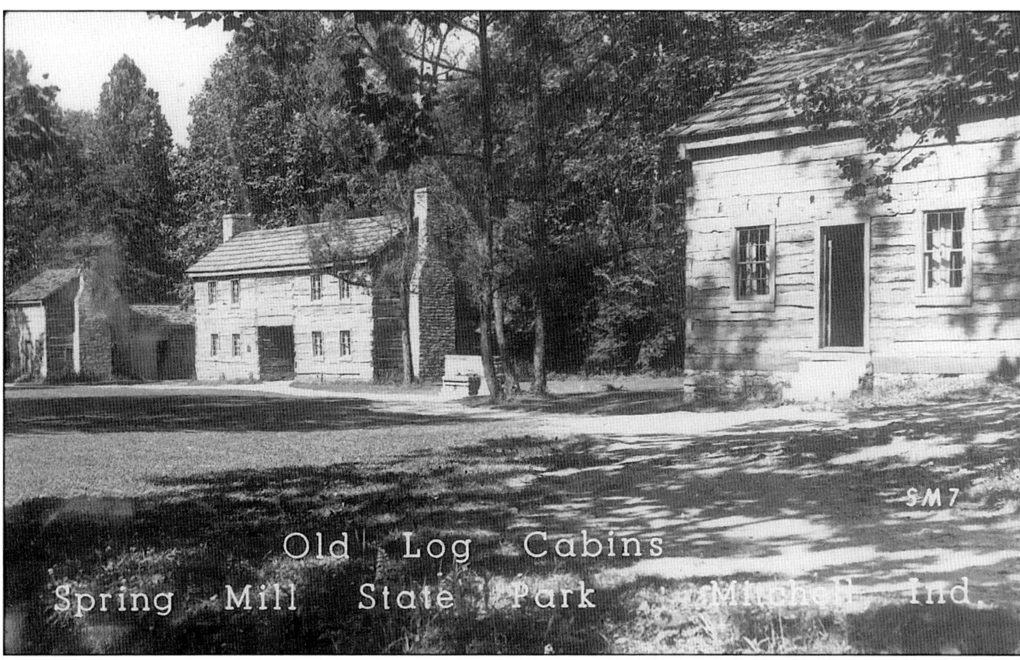

This is a view of the log houses in Spring Mill State Park, one of which is the "Granny White House," which originally stood in Leesville, Indiana.

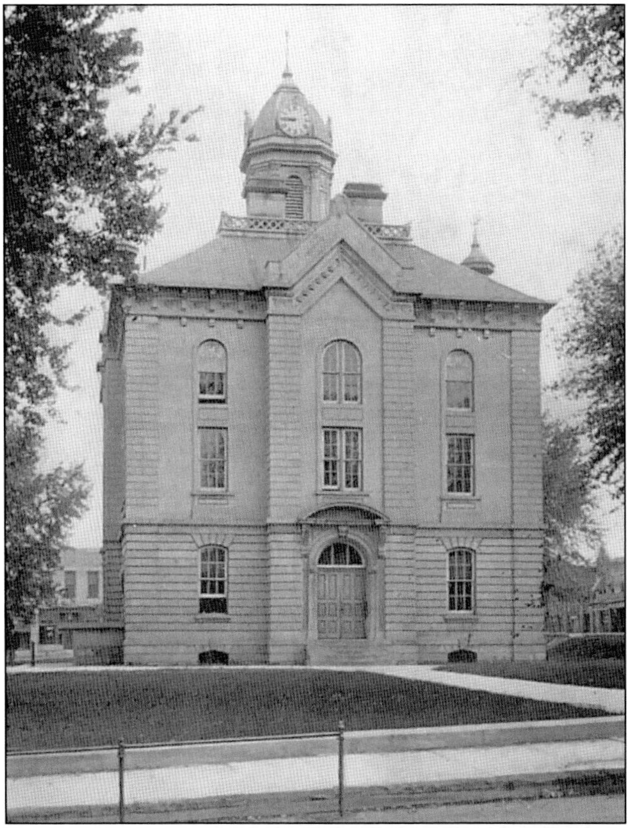

This is a picture of the original part of the courthouse in Bedford. This photo was taken in 1912 before two more wings were added.

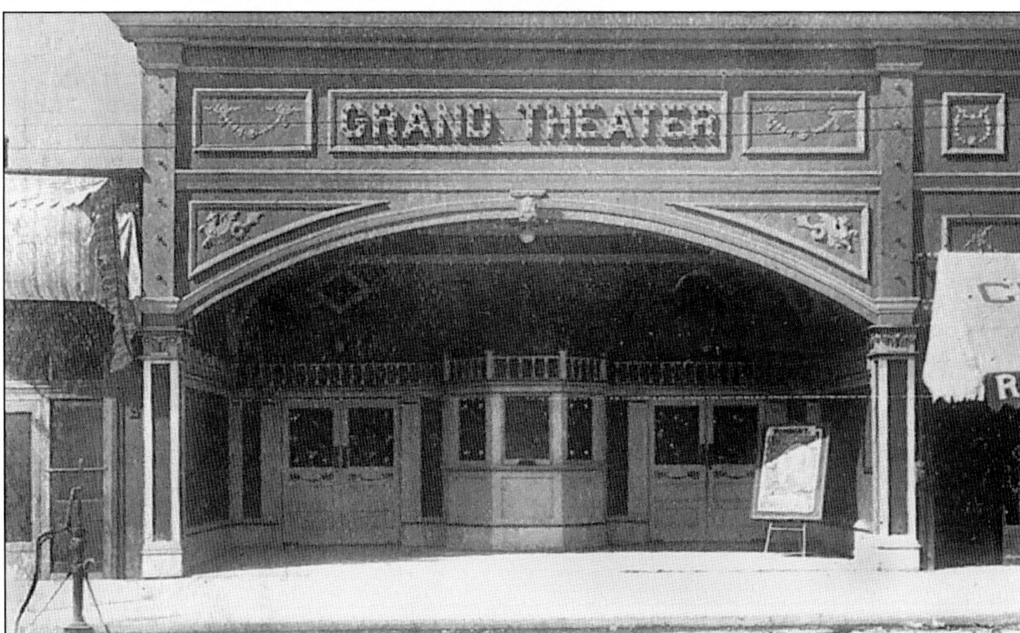

The old Grand Theater was a popular place in the early part of the 1920s. Notice the town pump in the foreground.

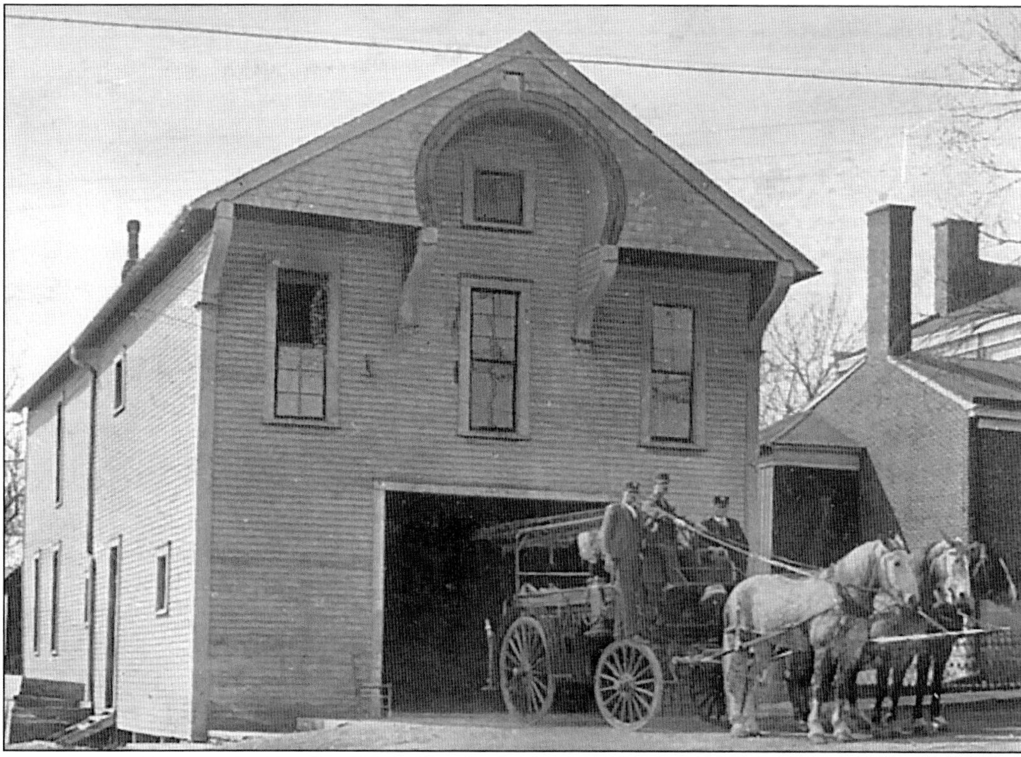

This postcard shows the Bedford Fire Station as it looked in 1911.

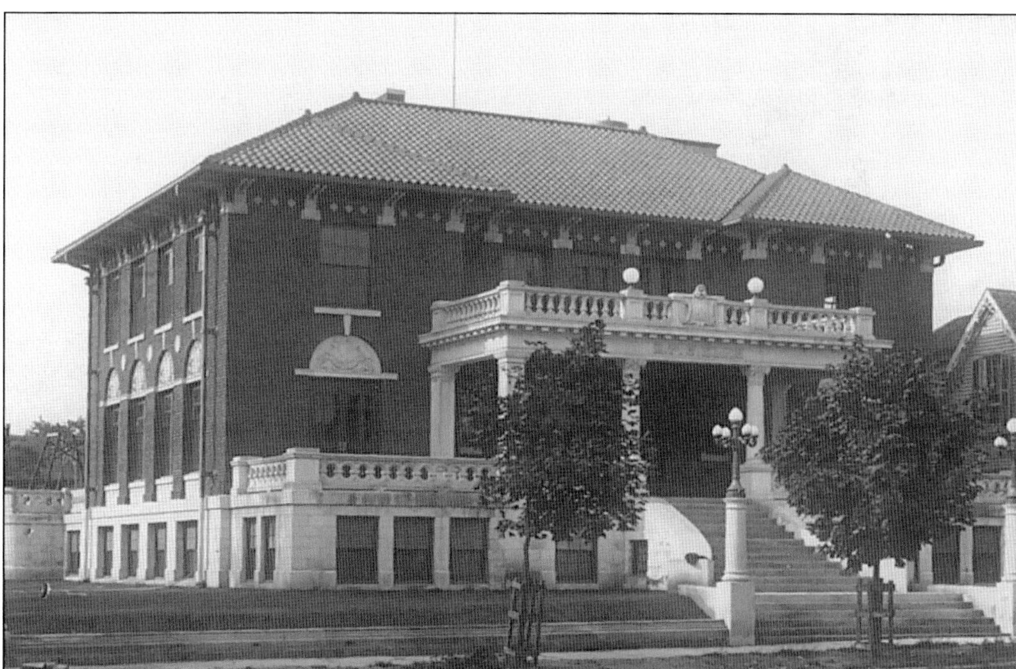

The Elk's Club in Bedford is located in this beautiful brick and stone building, which was once a residence. There are beautiful carvings over the windows.

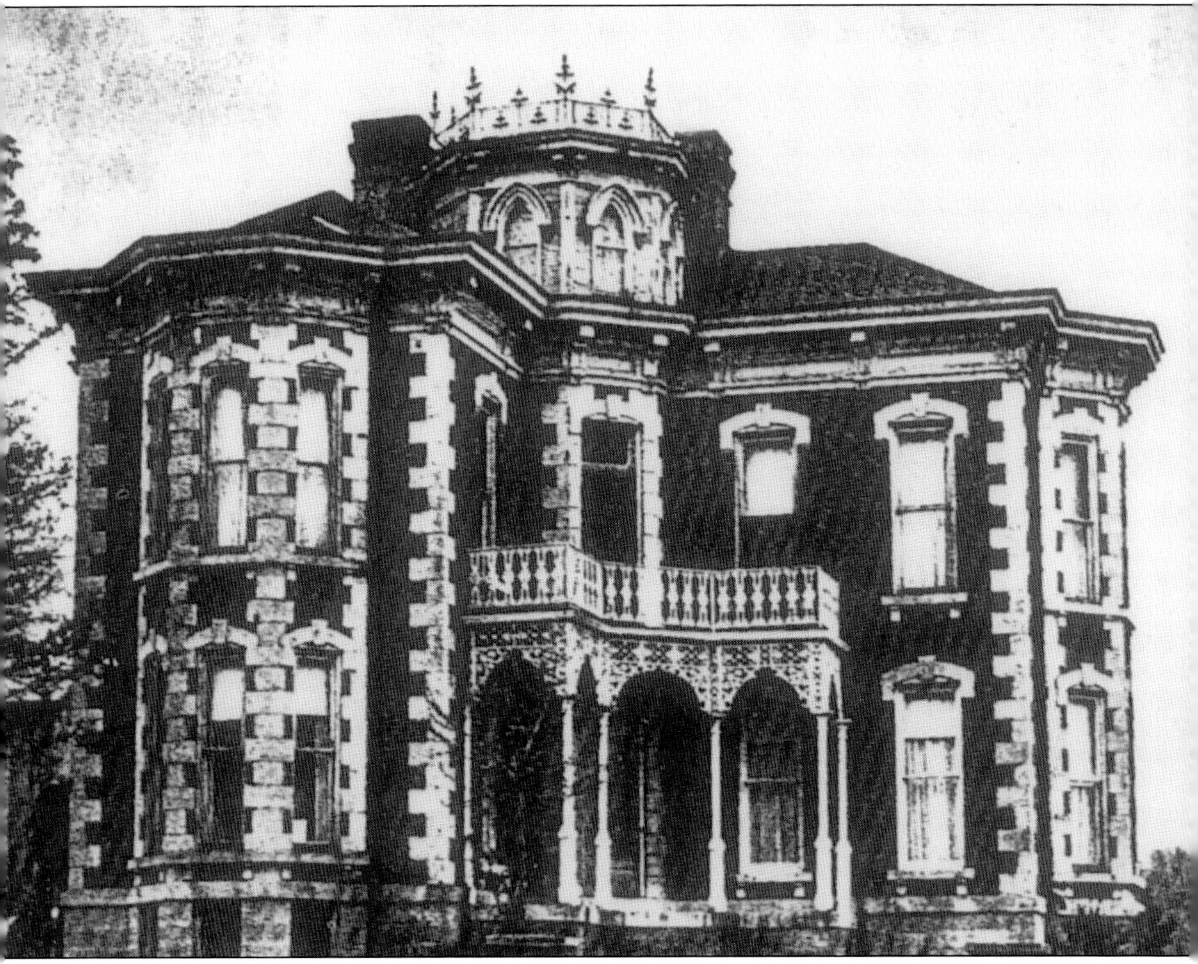

The Alfred Guthrie Mansion was built in 1878, and is located in Tunnelton, Indiana. The brick was fired on the property. It is an Italian style home with a limestone trim.

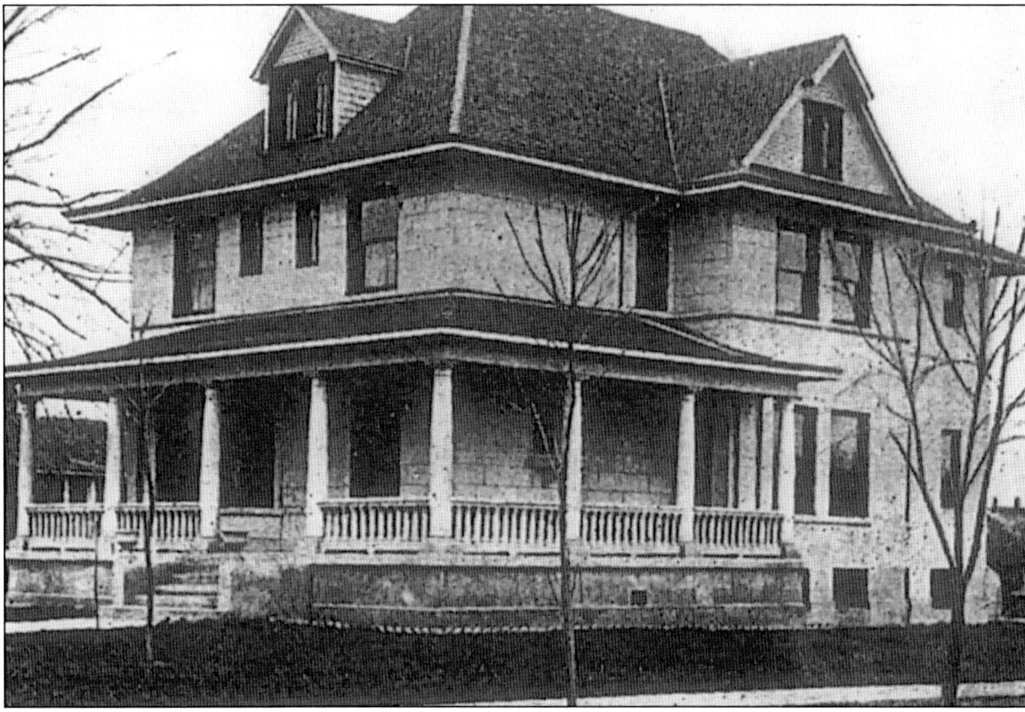

This solid stone house was built in the 1920s, and its first owner was Carl Furst who owned the Furst Stone Company in Bedford.

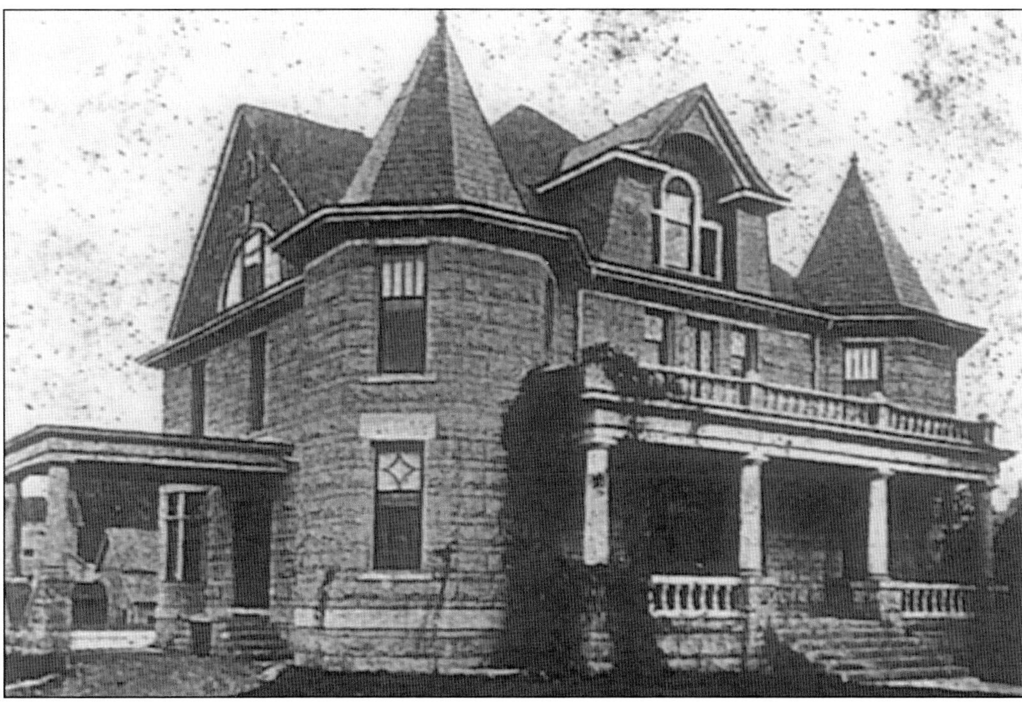

This beautiful old solid stone house is no longer standing. It was the Robert Reed home, which was torn down and replaced by a Goodyear Store.

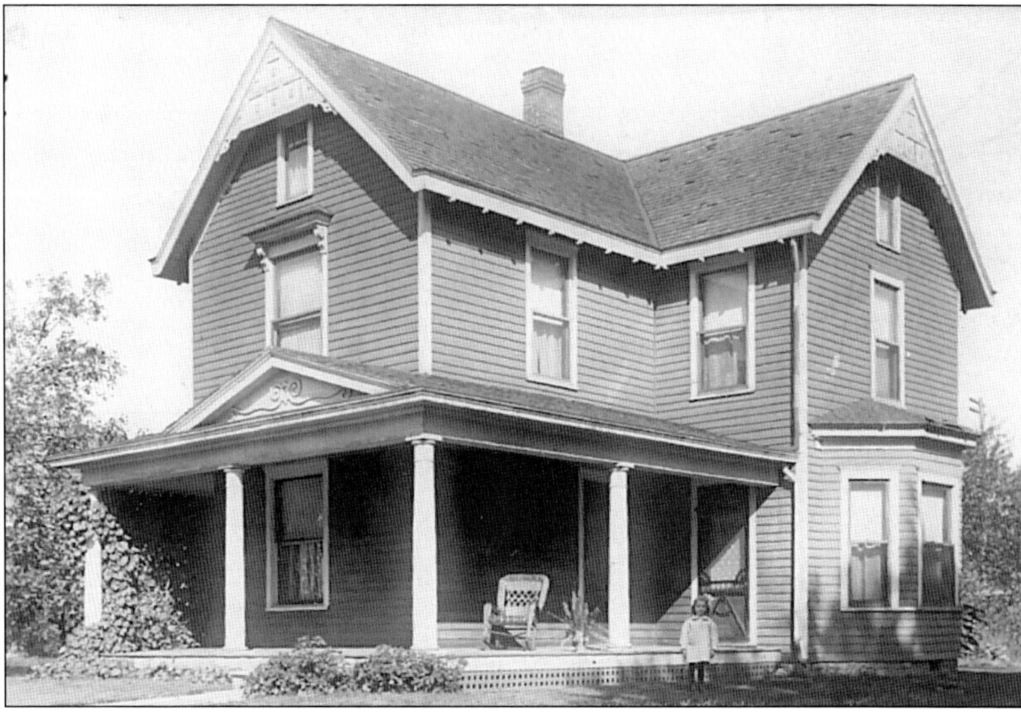

Charles M. Dodd, a master stone carver, lived in this house on West 13th Street in Bedford. Charles Dodd was the man who carved the War Memorial in the courthouse yard.

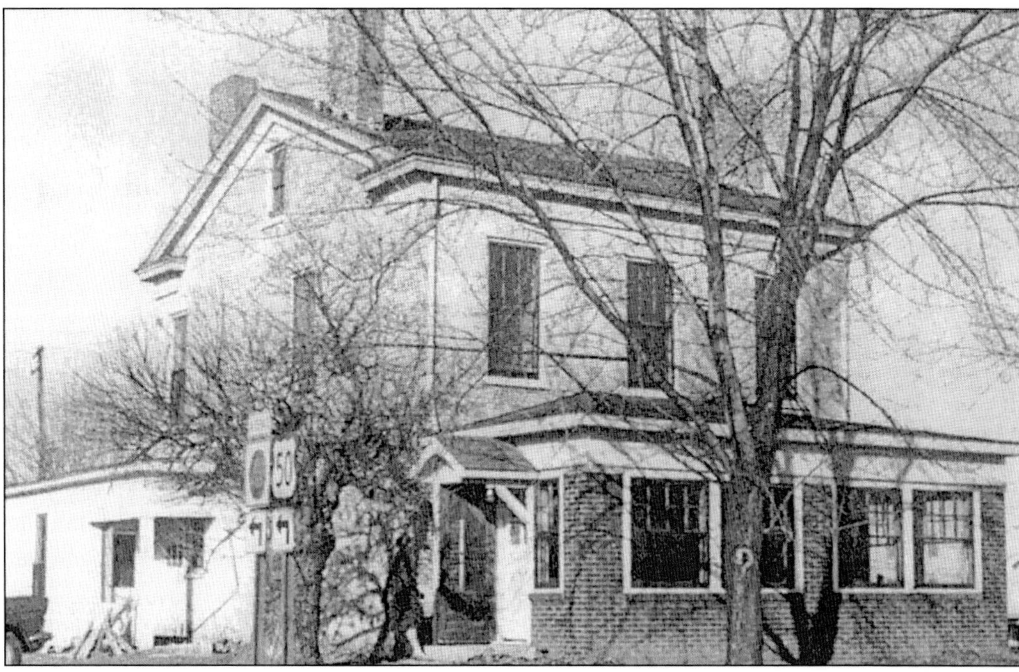

The George Rariden home was said to have a secret hideout by the fireplace, which was used to hide runaway slaves during the days of the Underground Railroad. This house is no longer standing.

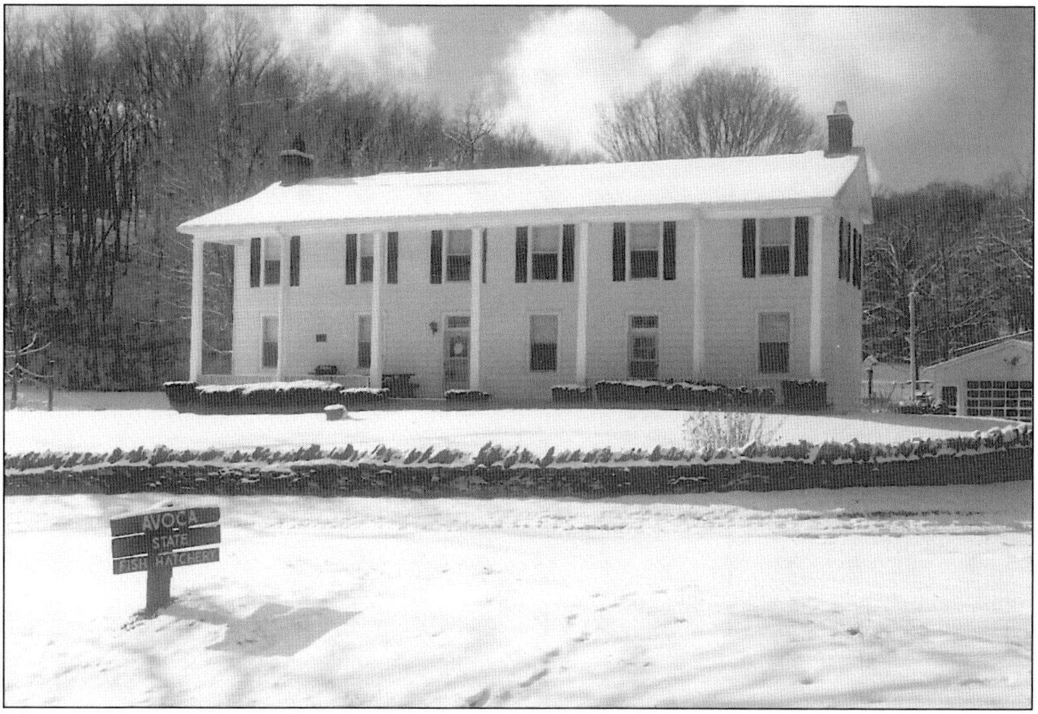

The caretaker's house at the Avoca Fish Hatchery was once a stagecoach inn. It was built in 1828, and there was a gristmill nearby. It is still in use, and looks much as it did then.

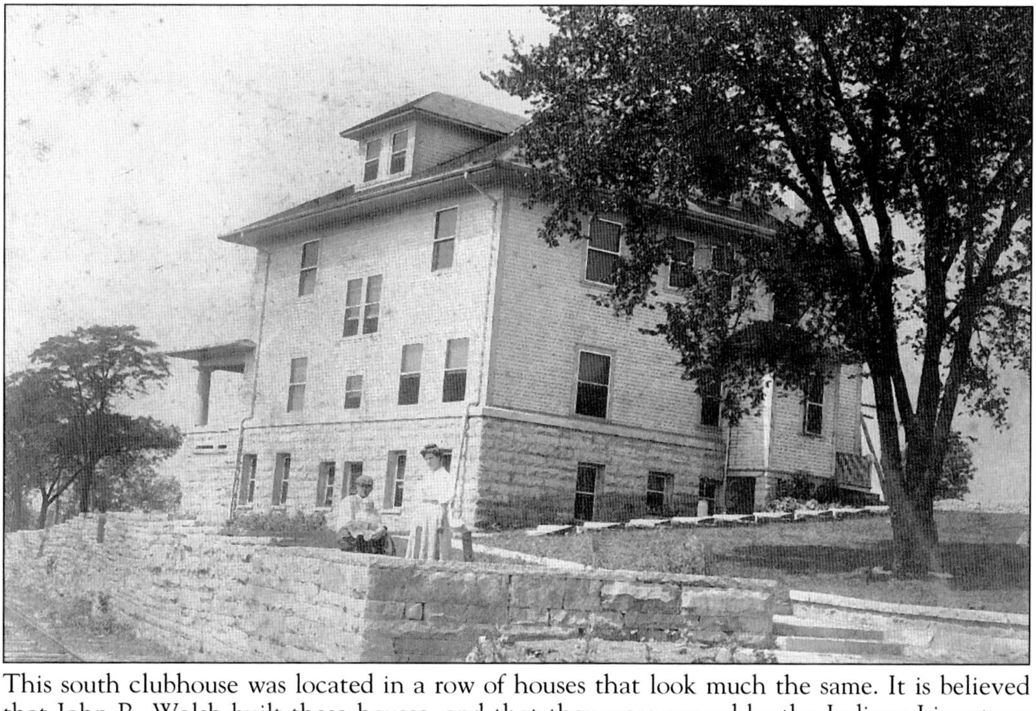

This south clubhouse was located in a row of houses that look much the same. It is believed that John R. Walsh built these houses, and that they were owned by the Indiana Limestone Company which built them for their employees.

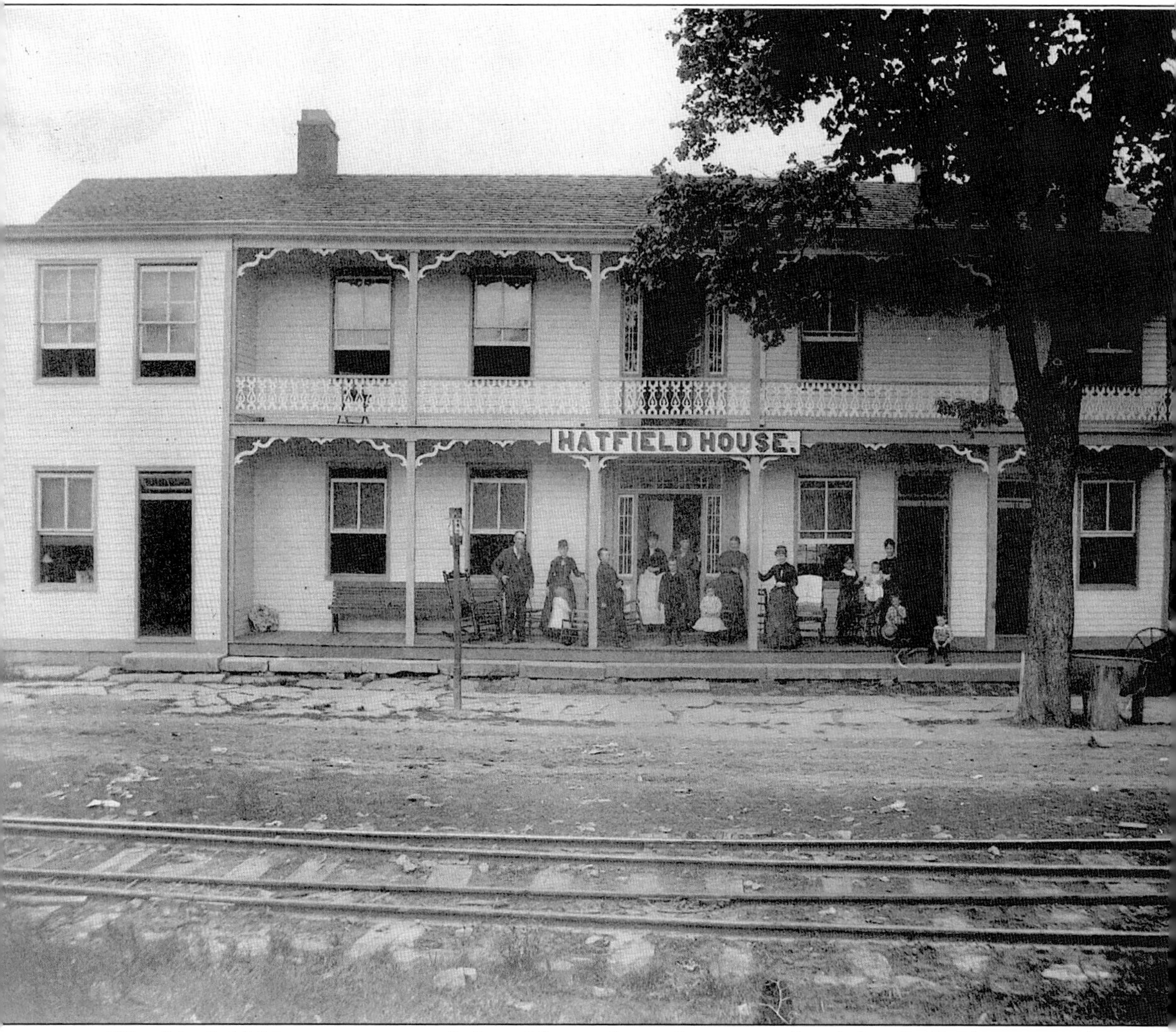

The Hatfield House was an early hotel located on the west side of the Bedford square. This photo was taken c. 1885

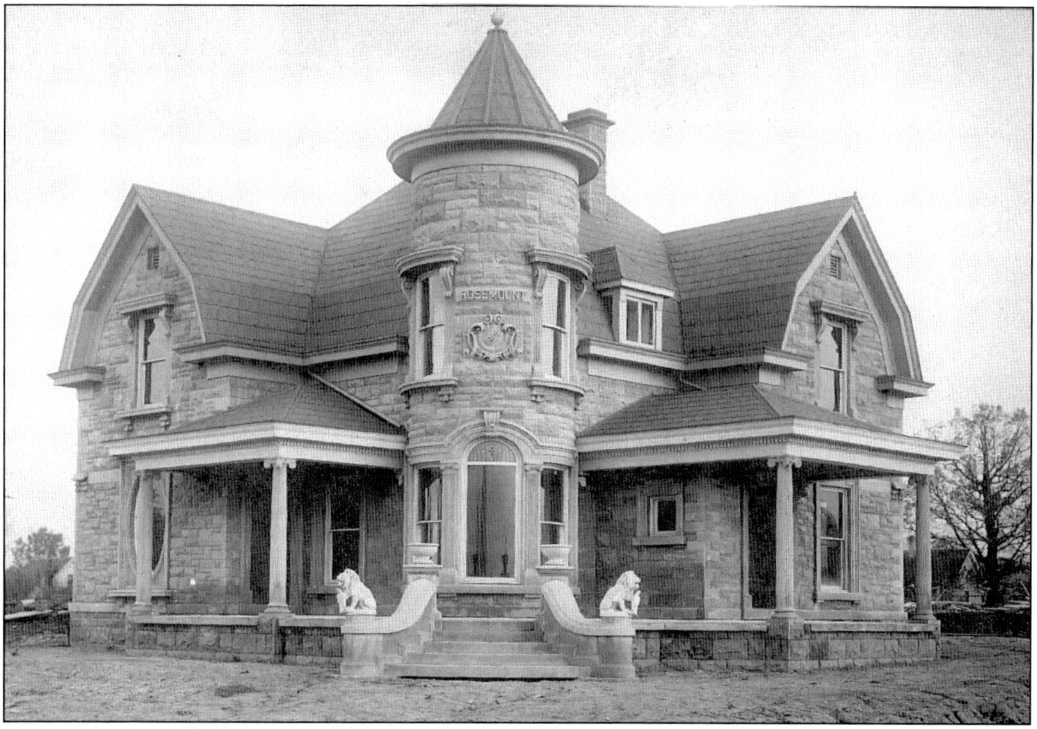

This solid stone house with its ornate carved lions in front was built in 1906. It has been renovated and made into a motel called Rosemount.

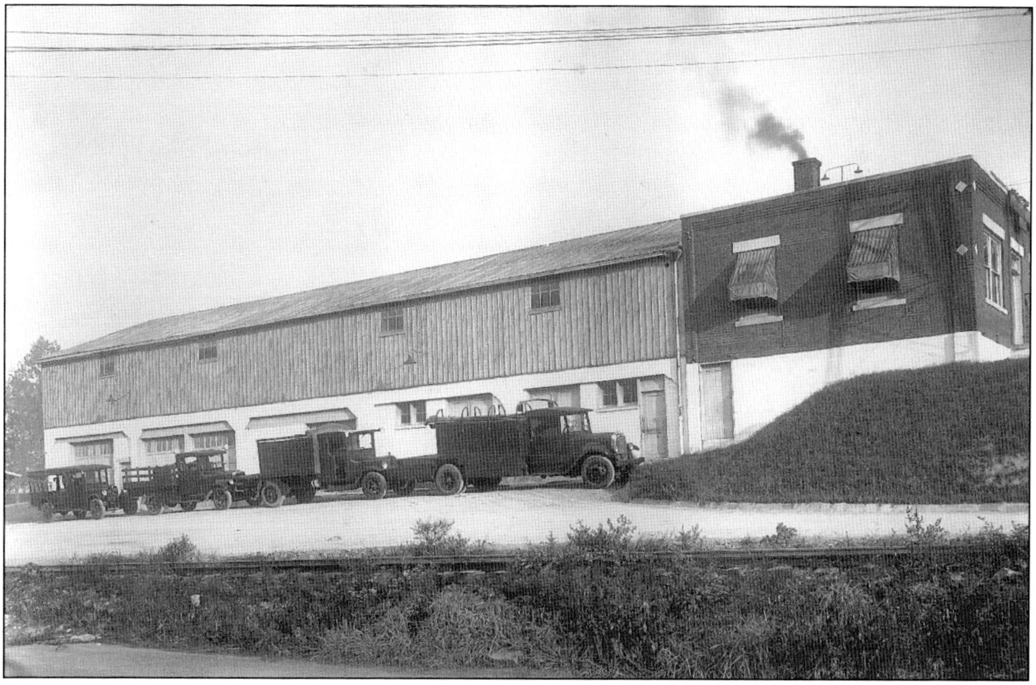

The old public service office was located between 8th and 11th on R Street in Bedford. This photo was taken in the 1920s.

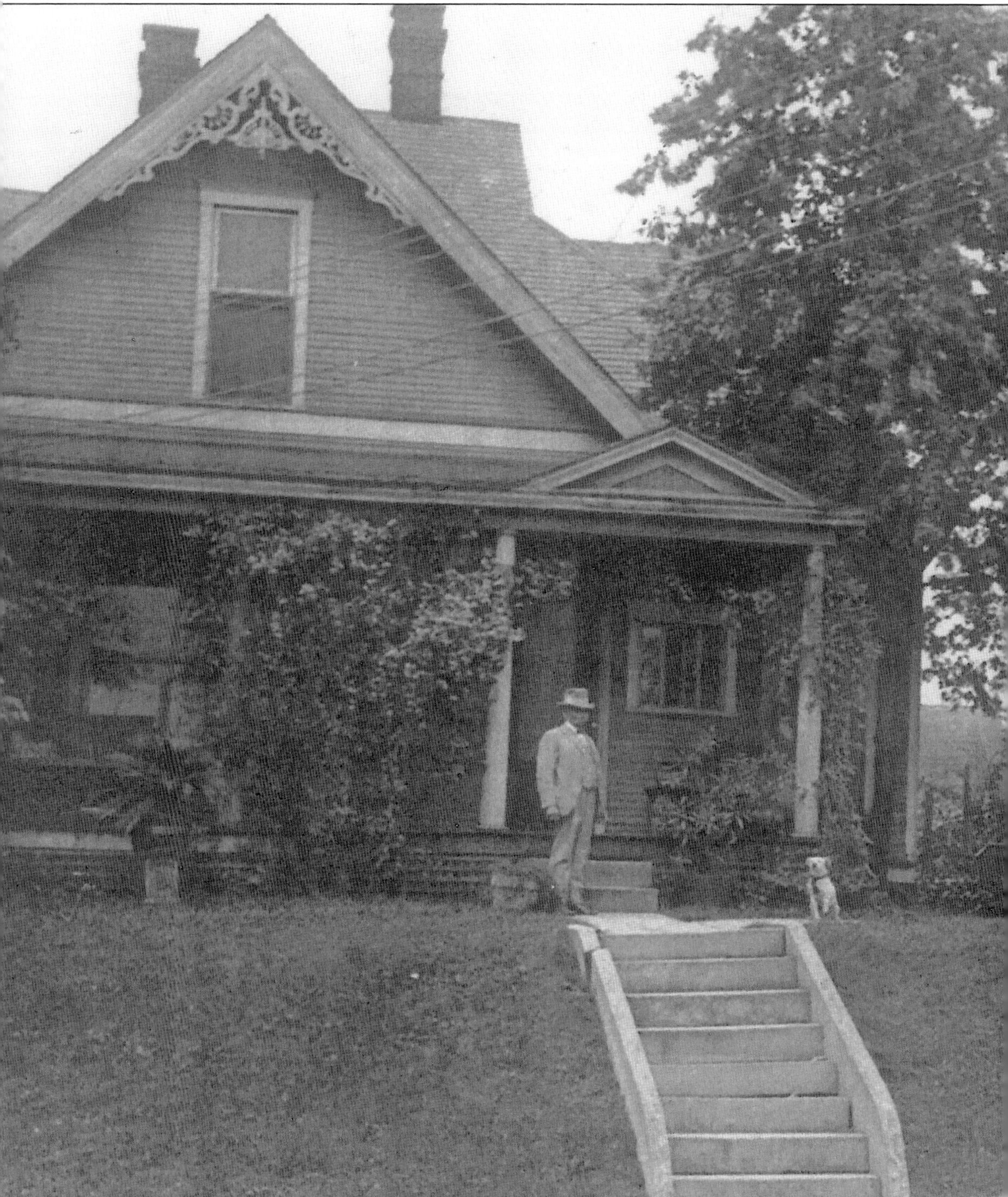

This house was built in the 1890s by William Jordan, who is pictured here by the porch. It is located at 1010 in Bedford and was owned by Mr. Jordan. John W. Quayle and his wife later owned it. Mr. Quayle was a master stone carver, and worked in the limestone industry.

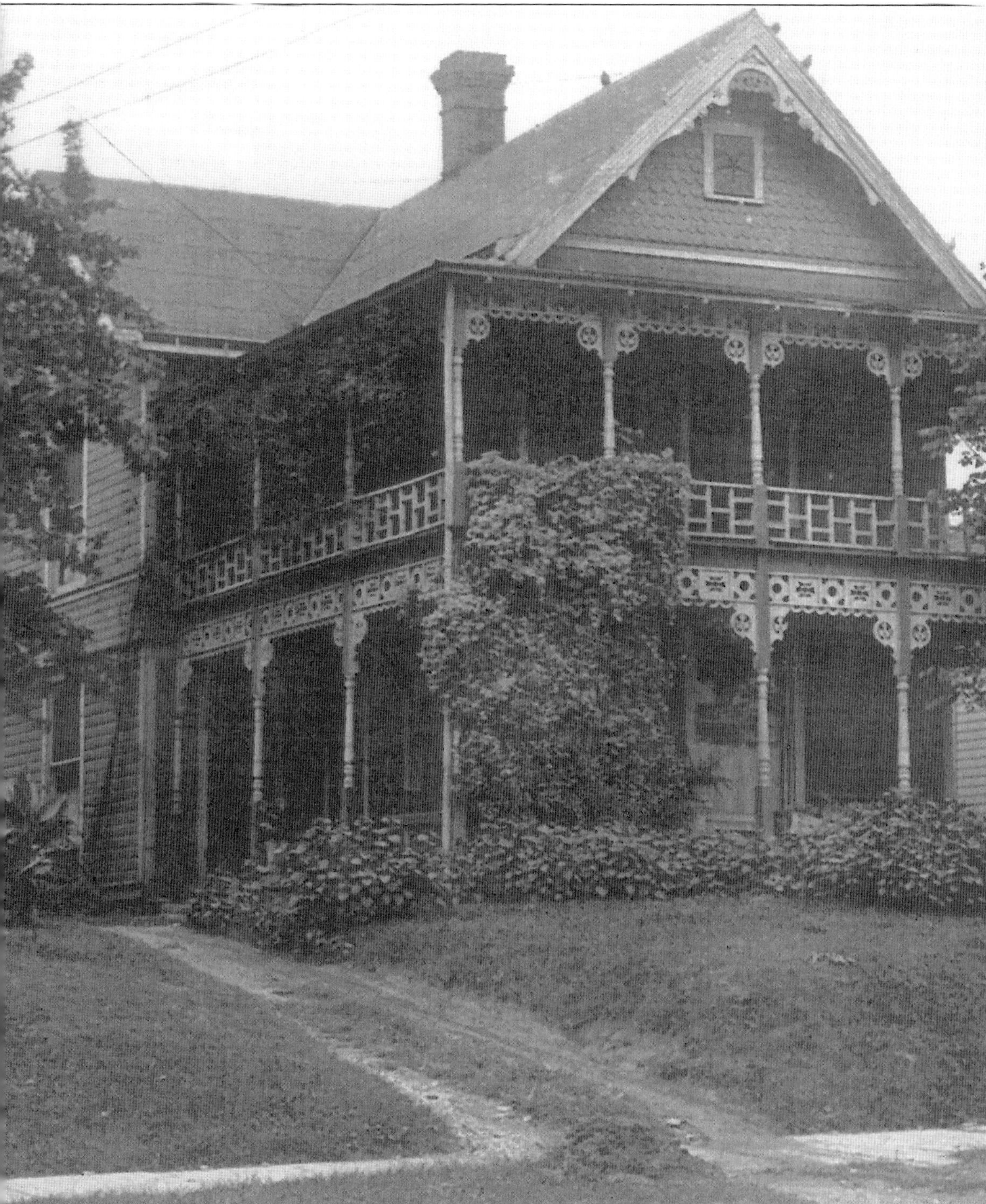

This Queen Ann Victorian home is also located on 13th Street. The owner is unknown. The house has since been renovated and does not look as it did in the early 1920s. During this period many Victorian homes were renovated, losing much of the ginger bread trim.

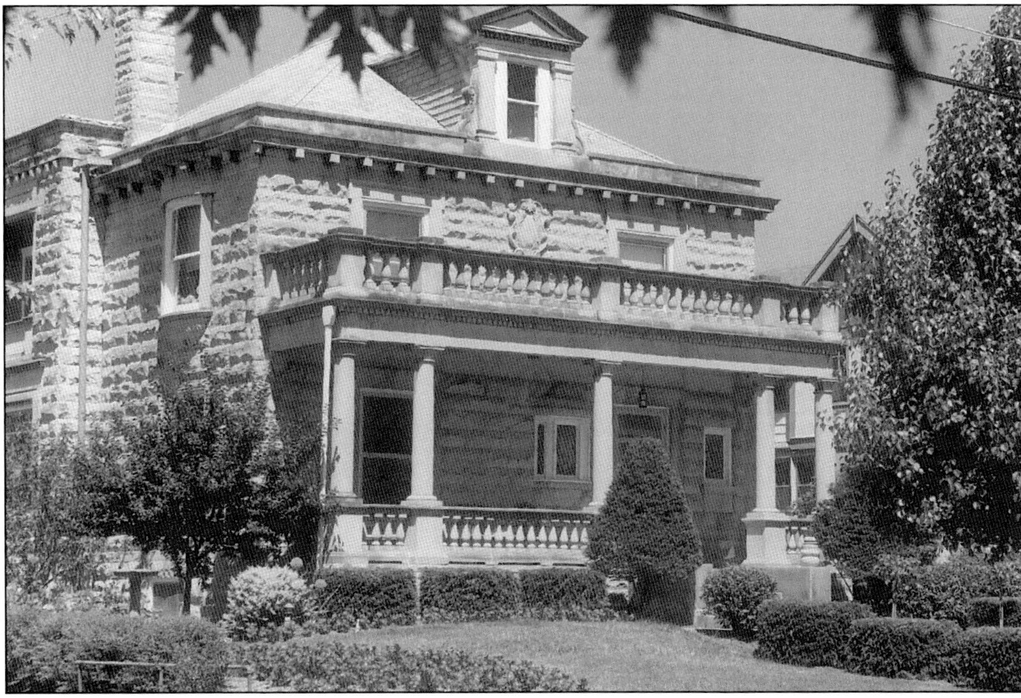

This house was built in the 1920s, and was owned by one of the presidents of a limestone company. It is quite ornate with its carving. The current owner takes pride in dressing the home in colorful lights during the Christmas season.

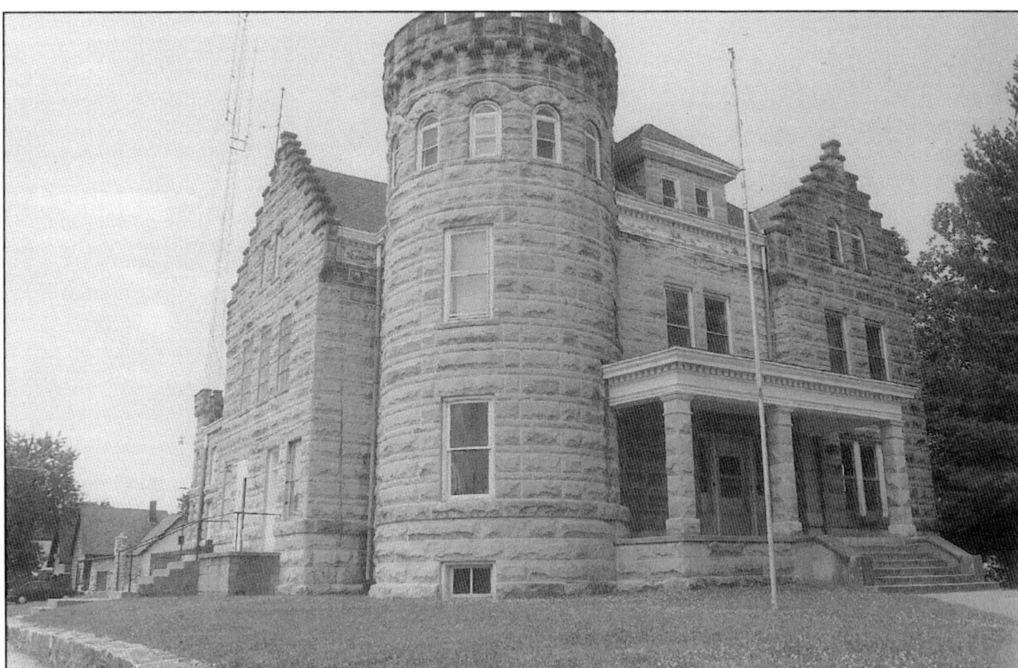

This old jail is now a residence. It was built on the foundation of an earlier jail. In the 1890s, there was a hanging by vigilantes of one of the inmates who had been held for murder.

Eight

LEGENDS

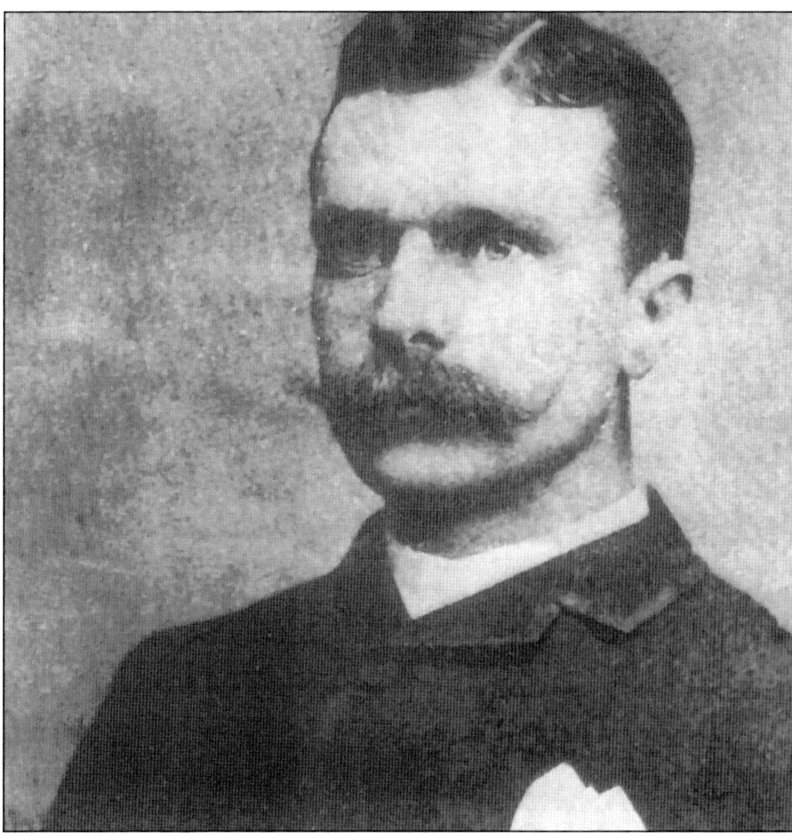

The outlaw Sam Bass was born in Lawrence County July 21, 1851. He was raised by his uncle, David Sheeks. At the age of 17, he left home, robbed trains in the west, and died in a shoot-out at Round Rock, Texas.

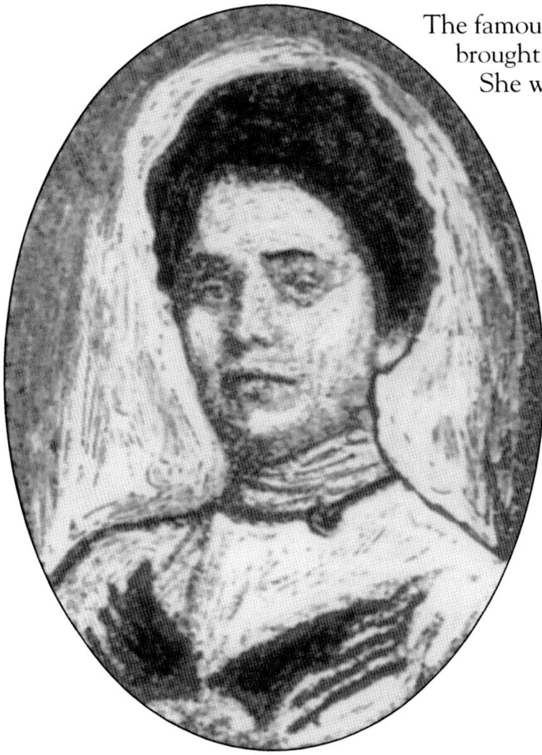

The famous unsolved murder of Sarah Schafer in 1904 brought the famous Pinkerton detectives to Bedford. She was a popular high school teacher.

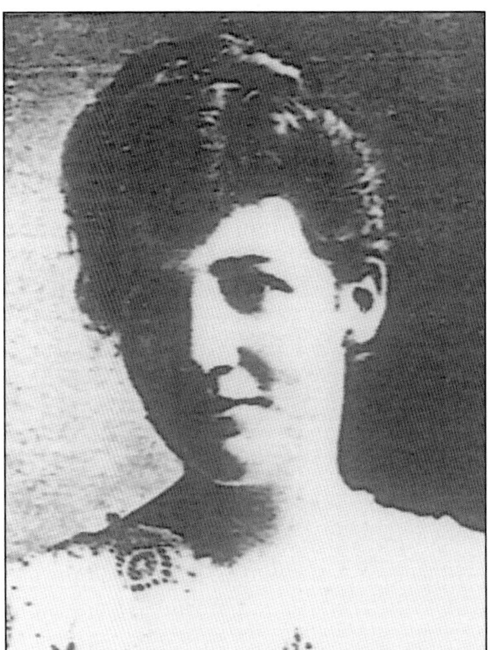

Eva Love, a roommate and friend of Sarah Schafer, was involved in a love triangle, and was allegedly the girl friend of the prosecutor.

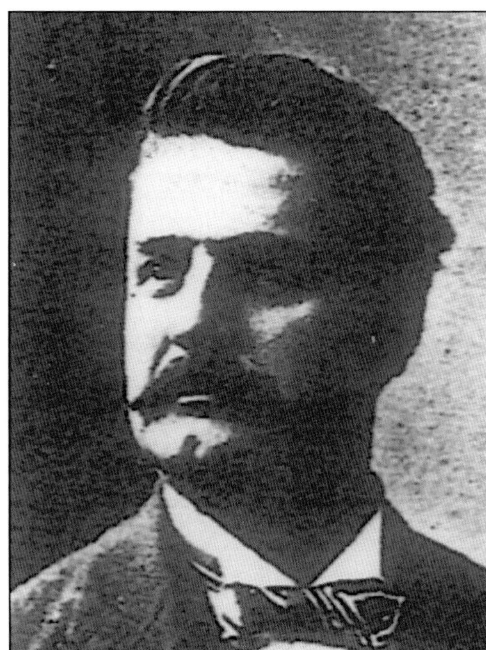

S. B. Lowe, a former teacher and prosecutor at the time of the murder, was suspected of hiring the killer, but was never brought to trial.

Joe Palooka, "champion of democracy," was carved in limestone in 1948, during the Limestone Centennial. A cartoon character by creator Ham Fisher now stands in front of the Oolitic Town Hall.

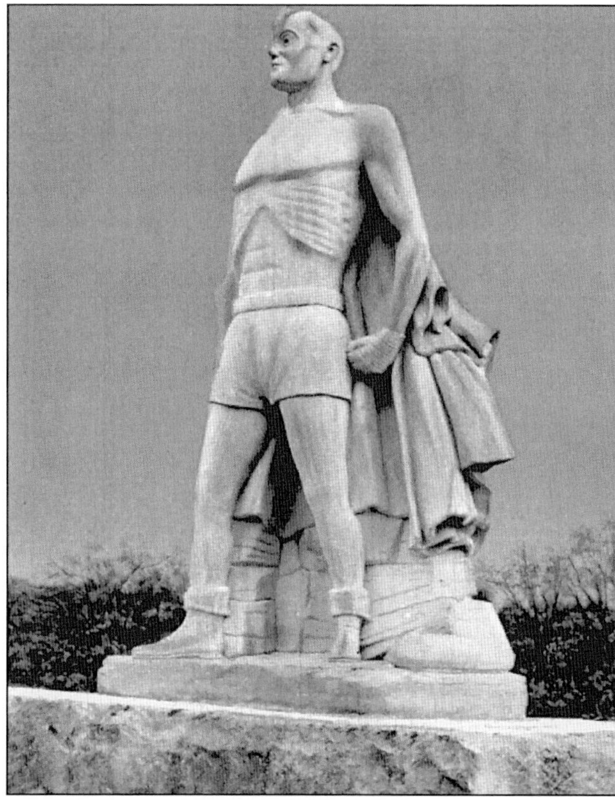

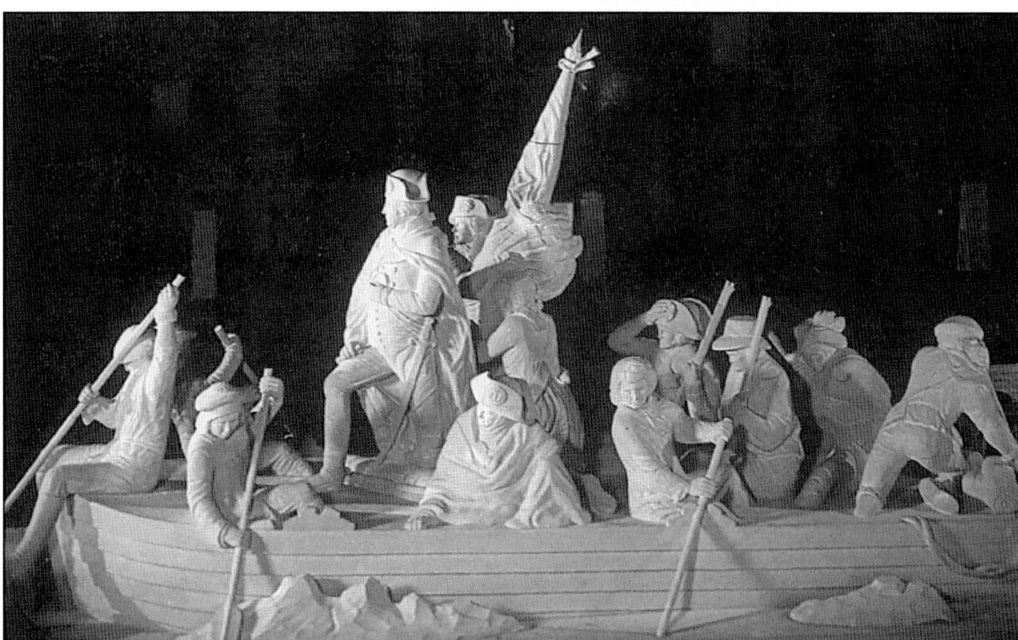

In 1976, the carving of "Washington Crossing the Delaware" was Lawrence County's gift to the nation. Master carver Frank Arena made the model. It currently stands at Washington Crossing, Pennsylvania.

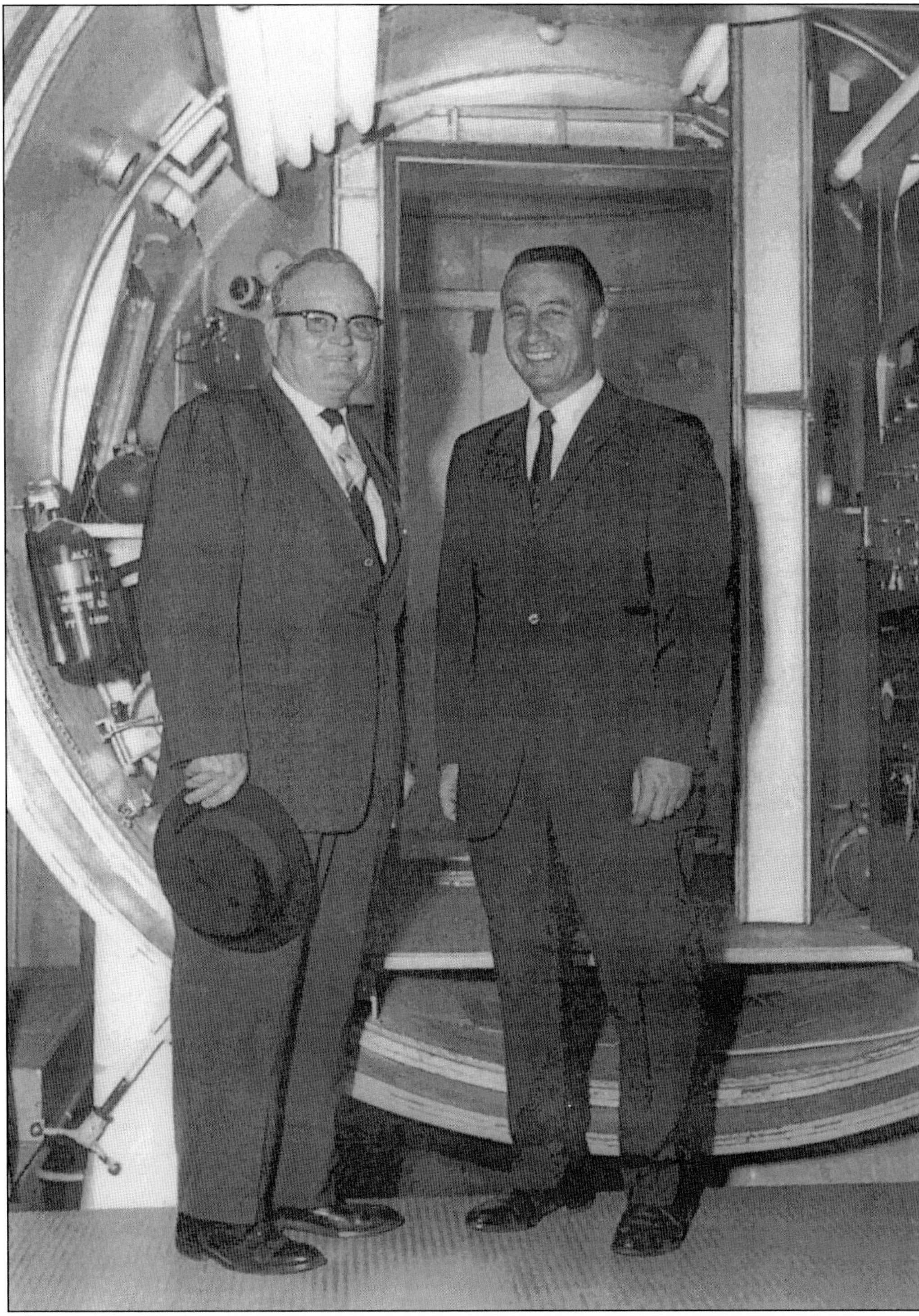

Indiana Congressman Earl Wilson and Astronaut "Gus" Grissom were photographed here on May 2, 1961. Lawrence County is the only county to have produced three astronauts: Gus Grissom, Charlie Walker, and Ken Bowersox. Congressman Wilson served the country many years.